Praise for *A Pocketful of Seeds*

"I love my friend, Debbie Johnson. I love her for *lots* of reasons. She's smart. She's talented. She cares. But most of all, she *acts*. Debbie doesn't just think about making a difference in her world—she *does* stuff. All kinds of stuff. Big stuff. Little stuff. *A Pocketful of Seeds* is her latest effort to make a dent for good in our world. Like Debbie, with one small seed at a time deposited in the dirt of the days of those we live alongside, we can change everything."

—**ELISA MORGAN,** speaker and author of
The Beauty of Broken and *She Did What She Could*

"Whether flying across the world or walking across the street, everyday we have countless opportunities to love, serve, and uplift our neighbors, *all* who are the LORD's beloved. We are walking answers to future prayers, and seeds of hope just waiting to be planted, so dig in and may this book help lead the way!"

—**BRAD CORRIGAN,** member of the indie band Dispatch;
founder and president of Love Light & Melody

"A book that is pointed, practical, applicable, biblical, life-giving, and in bite-sized pieces: that is my description of *A Pocketful of Seeds*. I appreciate the opportunity, day after day, to read and ponder and pray and see what God has for me that day. This book is going to be used by God to change lives."

—**BARB ROBERTS,** director of Caring Ministry at Cherry Creek
Presbyterian Church; author of *Helping Those Who Hurt*

"Debbie Johnson has been a cherished friend both personally and professionally for over three decades. I have watched our Master Gardener cultivate seeds of godly character in the soil of her heart that have continued to blossom and bless the lives of myriads of men and women around the world. Now she's sharing inspirational seeds through her thought-provoking daily devotional, *A Pocketful of Seeds,* that will lead you on an adventurous year-long journey that reveals profound principles for living and our ultimate purpose in life."

—**GREGG BETTIS,** assistant to the president, Kanakuk Ministries;
president emeritus, Kids Across America Kamps

"So many devotional books have been written, it's hard to find one that is unique, that rises above the norm. *A Pocketful of Seeds* is one of those rare achievements: a valuable collection of rich insights from an expert whose life has been touched and impacted by uncommon heartache and rich rewarding joy of her own and many with whom she has lived life."

—KEN ROBERTS, former moderator of the Evangelical Presbyterian Church

"This devotional is not just incredibly beautiful but so inspiring. What a beacon of light for everyone who reads its pages and sees the truth."

—MARCUS WEAVER, director of New Genesis; author and national speaker; Aurora Theater shooting survivor

WHEN WE SOW, LIFE HAPPENS

A Pocketful of Seeds

debbie johnson

Deep River
B O O K S

ISBN-13: 9781940269993
Library of Congress: 2016950370
Published in the United States of America.
Cover design by Connie Gabbert

Dedicated to my children,
Coy Austin and Morgan Elizabeth

Contents

Preface

✱
✱ ✱ It was a Saturday. I had stopped by my favorite coffee shop for that perfect cappuccino. Those moments are a touch of heaven, but wouldn't
you know it, I sat down in the middle of a hornets' nest. A couple was arguing
nearby. A guy at the next table was spewing out some pretty foul words. An
older man was staring out the window through tears.

So I gave up the peaceful cappuccino dream, took in the scene . . . and
had the craziest notion. I envisioned Jesus walking through, touching each
of those folks on the arm, and the fighting, cussing, and sadness just melting
away. Wouldn't that be the most amazing power to have? To touch people and
sow peace? That beats a peaceful cappuccino any day.

And then I wondered if maybe we *do* have that power. Maybe that's what
it means to walk in the Spirit. *Maybe that's what it means to reach into our
pocketful of seeds.*

Our pocketful of seeds? Here's the way I see it. After Jesus died and rose
again, He told His disciples to wait in Jerusalem for what the Father had
promised. Then He ascended into heaven and later, the Spirit came. Power arrived. And if we're Christ-followers, we have that same power. I think of that
power as my pocketful of seeds.

And seeds are big deals. None are insignificant, even when you or I think
we have nothing to offer. The Kingdom of God *"is like a mustard seed, which
is the smallest of all seeds on earth. Yet when planted, it grows and becomes the
largest of all garden plants, with such big branches that the birds can perch in its
shade"* (Mark 4:31–32, NIV).

Jesus said this about mustard-seed faith: *"Truly I tell you, if you have faith as
small as a mustard seed, you can say to this mountain, 'Move from here to there,' and
it will move. Nothing will be impossible for you"* (Matthew 17:20, NIV).

See what I mean? The smallest seed is a big deal.

A seed might be a word, an action, a note, a trip, a prayer, a touch on the
arm, a donation, an outcry. It might be an exchange between two people or
something more global. Such seeds can bring forth peace for a troubled soul

. . . or electricity for Africa . . . or literacy training for refugees . . . or the cure for a deadly disease . . . or non-violent answers for young Islamist men . . . or something simple like, you know, making someone's day. Remember, these are *power seeds* that can reach to the remotest parts of the earth.

My friend, Julie, invested $50 into a micro-loan program a few years ago. That one loan has enabled eight people to take the leap out of poverty (by starting a small business, for example). It's been paid back eight times. This could go on forever!

My friends at the Dalit Freedom Network petitioned Congress relentlessly, which resulted in the passing of HCR139 in 2007. This resolution expressed the sense that the United States should address the practice of untouchability with the government of India. A congressional resolution? On behalf of people considered to be of less value than insects? Groundbreaking.

The point is, whether we're in a restaurant or pressing the "donate" button on our computers or advocating for an oppressed people group, we can make a profound difference daily. We can sow a pocketful of seeds into the soil of the world. You might say we can become "seedy," not in the disreputable sense, but in the sowing sense.

Seeds were God's idea.

He embedded the spark of life into them.

He brings the increase.

So this is a practical idea book about what to do with that pocketful of life-giving seeds. Some of us stand around wringing our hands with indecision. Others think the problems are too great and that small steps don't matter. Still others say, "Yeah, but corrupt governments still exist, wrong ideology still exists, evil still exists."

Even so, despite the naysayers (including the ones in my head!), I've decided to push through my this-is-a-stupid-idea and people-will-think-I'm-naïve thoughts and put into writing this collection of 365 action steps/daily seeds.

What seediness does God have in mind for you?

Ghanian Israelmore Ayivor said this: "God calls big trees out of small seeds, so He prepares great monuments out of small minds. He will definitely call those wonderful things He put in you out of you. When He begins, do not resist."

Introduction

* I was raised in Little Rock, Arkansas in the thick of the civil rights movement. In college I completed a master's in Music Education, but my heart was in missions and social work. I first worked with a low-income housing program, then started a jobs ministry called DenverWorks, which I directed for ten years. Later, I went into international work focusing on India. And still later, I returned to DenverWorks. Quite a journey.

DenverWorks helps people who have barriers to employment with job training, mentoring, professional clothing, and job connections. We believe each person has a God-given design. We use a Petoskey stone as the symbol. A Petoskey stone looks like an ordinary rock on the shores of waterways in Michigan, but if polished, an intricate design comes out.

Petoskey stones are a lot like seeds. You can't see their inner beauty at first. The stone must be polished. The seed must be planted. *Then* the good stuff happens.

With the India ministries, the focus was on the Dalits, the 250 million people at the bottom of the caste system. Actually, they aren't even part of the caste system. They're outcasts and were formerly called Untouchables. Caste determines job tasks. The Dalits were relegated to the most menial, back-breaking, filthy jobs in society—like manual scavenging (cleaning feces from toilet-less bathroom floors). They're often denied education, medical care and more, but most sadly, they're denied respect. The Good News, the message of Jesus, is sweeping India. The message that they are made in God's image, equal, and loved is *exploding* among the Dalits.

So in both cases, among struggling U.S. jobseekers and the Dalits of India, the Jesus message is life-changing. Once people see who they are in Christ, they start thriving. It's much easier to rise up after that seed has been planted.

Now, I want to tell you a story. It contains the best message in the world . . . seriously.

Years ago on a Sunday morning, I was feeling unloved. I wrote a message to God. "God, it's OK if I don't feel loved." It was just a scribbled line on a yellow pad. It felt like an offering.

So I went to church and wouldn't you know it, we sang "Jesus, Lover of My Soul." And I felt God speaking to my spirit. "Debbie, don't *ever* say that again because I'll love you forever." For some reason, that day, *I got it!* I wanted to jump up and down on the pew. What an epiphany.

The best-message-in-the-world part is that God loves you too. So if neither you nor I ever planted a single positive seed of change, God would still love us, and would want a relationship with us.

That being said, this seed-sowing journey is joyful and important—not to be missed! Use this book as a reference for new ideas or daily inspiration. (And by the way, I'm a fellow learner, not a "seediness" expert.) So what if we *all* took a Seed Challenge and sowed seeds of positive change into the soil of the world every day for a year?

I wonder how we might be changed. I wonder how the world might be changed.

I dare us to try.

JANUARY

ACCENTUATE THE POSITIVE

A few nights ago I was working on this book and half-listening to a TV talk show from the next room. The guy being interviewed was so *positive*. I actually got up and went around the corner to see who it was. He was talking about the near-eradication of polio in our lifetime due to the work of the foundation he directs with his wife and the work of other like-minded folks. It was gripping. He was humble but contagious.

The speaker was Bill Gates. Obviously, he has a pocketful of dollars, but *he also has a pocketful of seeds.* He doesn't *have* to plant seeds with those dollars, but he's chosen to, and the world has been changed.

From time to time, I take day trips deep into the Rocky Mountains. For me, "looking unto the hills from whence cometh my help" from Psalm 121 is a literal thing. I can get stuck in negativity, frustration, weariness. Taking forays into the mountains helps me recalibrate my brain back to the positive, to possibilities, to right thinking, to faith. What helps you accentuate the positive?

Let's choose to start this day (and year) on a positive note. After all, seeds are positive things. They hold the essence of life. Planting seeds of positive change *will* bear fruit.

. . . But first we have to sow them.

DAILY SEED: Reach into your pocket. Sow a seed. Accentuate the positive.

"Finally, brothers and sisters, whatever is true, whatever is noble, whatever is right, whatever is pure, whatever is lovely, whatever is admirable—if anything is excellent or praiseworthy—think about such things" (Philippians 4:8).

JANUARY 2

ACT

* The fifth book of the New Testament is called the Acts of the Apostles.
* * Not the *thoughts* of the apostles or the *intentions* of the apostles. The acts. As Academy-Award-winning screenwriter Sonya Levien said, "Good intentions are not enough. They've never put an onion in the soup yet."

We can have good thoughts or intentions about being seedy, but unless we act, we're not really seedy.

The Book of Acts is full of things that the early church folks *did*. They wrote the book on it, literally. They didn't have any protocol; they just stepped out and performed miracles and shared their possessions with each other and stuff like that, all with the power of their recently-deceased-and-resurrected friend Jesus.

Jesus told them (and us) to go and *do*.

DAILY SEED: Act on something you've been intending to do.

"But one who looks intently at the perfect law, the law of liberty, and abides by it, not having become a forgetful hearer but an effectual doer, this man will be blessed in what he does." (James 1:25)

JANUARY 3

ACT LIKE A COLLEGE STUDENT

* College students! They think they can change the world. They string
* * up a sheet between two trees and show the *Invisible Children* film. They have barefoot days to stand in solidarity with those who have no shoes. They put tape on the sidewalk and invite students to attach dollars for hunger relief. Crazy kids.

I wonder how many lives they've saved.

DAILY SEED: Whether you're 19 or 91, draw on your youthful enthusiasm and do something to change the world.

"Let no one look down on your youthfulness, but rather in speech, conduct, love, faith and purity, show yourself an example of those who believe." (1 Timothy 4:12)

JANUARY 4

ACT LIKE THE FIRST LADY

When I was a child, everyone just threw trash out the window of the car. Can you believe that? The United States was covered with litter.

Then along came Lady Bird Johnson, wife of President Lyndon B. Johnson. She declared war on litter. Now we don't even leave an orange peel on a hiking trail.

First Ladies have a mission—literacy, advocacy for women, obesity elimination. They start social movements.

DAILY SEED: If you were one of the most influential people in the world (like the First Lady), what movement would you start?

"Don't ever underestimate the importance you can have because history has shown that courage is contagious and hope can take on a life of its own." (Michelle Obama, in a 2011 speech in Soweto, South Africa)

JANUARY 5

ACT WITH COMPASSION

I just read a blog post about Pope Francis' blessing of a disabled woman. The pope had hopped out of the car to do so, almost before it came to a stop. The blogger wrote that he was an atheist but could sort of understand the God-thing by watching the pope.

Why do we not act like the pope (with compassion) all the time? It doesn't take supernatural skill or intellect. The pope just makes the hurting in this world a priority. He kisses people on their foreheads, which makes news and changes the world.

A friend of mine is a "blesser." Once we were saying goodbye after we had lunch together and she prayed a blessing over me. It was short and sort of non-eventful, well, except that I've never forgotten it. She was really asking God to *bless* me, to bestow divine favor upon me.

Blessings. Kisses from the pope. Compassion.

DAILY SEED: Show compassion to someone today.

"Seeing the people, He felt compassion for them, because they were distressed and dispirited like sheep without a shepherd." (Matthew 9:36)

JANUARY 6

ADOPT A GRANDPARENT

Miss Stella was about eighty and lived in a cardboard house by the river. Well, maybe not cardboard but it was a dilapidated old place and really cold in the winter. A bunch of us from college decided to help with the city's weatherization program. We found out where the impoverished elderly lived. We knocked on doors and installed weather strips. Miss Stella lived in one of those houses.

Then we decided to keep those relationships going if the older folks were willing. We needed them and maybe we brought a little joy into their lives too.

So I just hung out with Miss Stella. She showed me her roses and I read the Bible to her. I treasured my own grandparents, but Miss Stella was my bonus grandma and she lived nearby.

There's something very tender and sacred about stepping out of our comfort zones to spend time with a Miss Stella.

DAILY SEED: Make an elderly person's day today.

"A gray head is a crown of glory; It is found in the way of righteousness." (Proverbs 16:31)

JANUARY 7

ADVOCATE

I'm guessing most Americans feel protected by our government. (Not all, but most.)

If our house is on fire, we call 911 and firefighters show up. Our children are actually required by law to receive an education. Our Coast Guard protects our shores from aggression. Most of us feel our infrastructure "has our back."

Not so, however, in a lot of countries. Governments and armies are the perpetrators of violence and torture *against their own people.* Sometimes things get skewed in our country too. We can speak up on behalf of those who are wronged. We really can be a voice for the voiceless. We really must. We must not let our comfort lull us into inaction. To paraphrase Luke 12:48, "To whom much is given, *must* is required."

To advocate, know the facts, create your clear and concise message—as brief as fifteen seconds—band with other advocates, and communicate your message as often as possible.

Can you imagine the comfort a tortured soul would get from knowing someone was fighting for him/her?

DAILY SEED: What person or people group comes to mind that needs your advocacy?

"We must always take sides. Neutrality helps the oppressor, never the victim. Silence encourages the tormentor, never the tormented." (Elie Wiesel, from his acceptance speech of the Nobel Peace Prize in Oslo, 1986)

JANUARY 8

AS A BUSINESS, PLANT SEEDS OF POSITIVE CHANGE

✳ Healthy businesses have multiple bottom lines, moving beyond profit ✳ ✳ and power to include care for the world.

For Christian corporate folk, businesses can integrate business goals with the call to the Church. Check out Business as Mission.[1] What a beautiful example of being "in the world but not *of* the world."

Businesses can be hands-on in their giving back. Swipe Away Poverty donates 10 percent of profit on participating accounts to Compassion International. Restaurants sponsor Give Back nights, donating a percentage of proceeds to a charity. Stores make a way for customers to round-up-to-the-nearest-dollar for donation to a cause. Employees can dress down on Fridays in exchange for a donation to that week's chosen charity.

Businesses can help nonprofits. Nonprofits have the same business needs as for-profits, like printing, marketing, website development, computers, and office furniture. Yet, for-profits sell goods and services, i.e., make a profit. Nonprofits have to receive the majority of their income from charity dollars *by law*. Receiving discounted rates or in-kind gifts from businesses are godsends for a nonprofit.

Businesses can hire vets or the disabled. Hiring a percentage of these candidates can be a form of tithing. And they just might turn out to be some of your best employees.

Businesses can match employee donations.

Businesses can sponsor drives, like professional clothing drives for jobseekers with barriers to employment.

DAILY SEED: If you are employed, think about your workplace. Is it a place of blessing or does it suck the life out of people (including you)? Do you have influence there? What seeds of positive change can you sow among customers/clients and fellow employees?

"Leadership is not about a title or a designation. It's about impact, influence and inspiration." (Robin S. Sharma, bestselling author of books on leadership)

JANUARY 9

AS A CHURCH, PLANT SEEDS OF POSITIVE CHANGE

Isn't the Church to be the prime example of seediness? To *profoundly* impact the world?

To offer grace, truth, and meaning to fellow pilgrims on the life journey?

To offer people a chance to lay down their burdens for God to pick up?

To offer love to those who need love, i.e. *all of us*?

To promote world change, whether the world is five feet or five thousand miles from the front door?

A lot of churches *are* outreach-oriented. The Friends Church in Yorba Linda, California says this about itself. "We are becoming a community of authentic Christ-followers compelled to change our world." And in response, one of their goals is to build one hundred Dalit schools in India. That'll serve about 25,000 kids. That's profound change.

A lot of churches do Dare to Care projects. Recently, a thousand people showed up on one day for our church's project. 1000! That's *a lot* of care. Our church also hangs the flags of countries where parishioners have served. There are *a lot* of flags.

In contrast, however, I've visited too many inreach-oriented, self-serving churches. Don't get me wrong, we need the inward pieces of church—the teaching, the counseling, the care for our children, the discipleship—but the more we grow, the more we should flow.

DAILY SEED: Does your church flow into the world around it?

"Sow your seed in the morning and do not be idle in the evening, for you do not know whether morning or evening sowing will succeed, or whether both of them alike will be good." (Ecclesiastes 11:6)

JANUARY 10

___

AS A SCHOOL, PLANT SEEDS OF POSITIVE CHANGE

✳   St. John's Lutheran School of Denver partnered with the United Inter-
✳ ✳ national School of Bangalore (India). The schools are 8,790 miles apart.
Distance doesn't matter, however, when it comes to innovative ideas for mutual
learning. Innovative connections can be made in a "cyber" kind of way.

Students can become pen pals with students of the same grade in the
other school.

Teachers can exchange ideas. Instruction about the other country's geog-
raphy, culture, money, etc., can come to life. Real-time Skype exchanges can
be arranged.

Here's a sample math assignment for a U.S. school partnering with an Indian school: convert to ⊠3,25,84,729.25 (three crore, twenty-five lakh, eighty-
four thousand, seven hundred twenty-nine rupees and twenty-five paise) to
U.S. dollars.

Good luck on that one.

DAILY SEED: Might this be an option for your school/your children's school?

"Learning is acquired by reading books; but the much more necessary
learning, the knowledge of the world, is acquired by reading man, and studying all the various editions of them." (Lord Chesterfield, excerpted from a
letter to his son)

JANUARY 11

___

ASK GOD TO EXPAND YOUR HORIZONS

✳   Once an elderly friend told me she had lived out west. "Where out west?"
✳ ✳ I asked, thinking she meant the Wild West.

"West Pine Street," she replied.

It's a funny little story, but expanding one's horizons doesn't have to mean moving to the Wild West or even off the street on which you grew up. It just means opening our eyes to the world around us. It means looking beyond our own skin. And doing so might bring great joy . . . or great sadness . . . or both. It will certainly bring growth.

DAILY SEED: Does your heart break for those who hurt around the world? Ask God to expand your horizons so you can know where to plug in (beyond self).

"You must learn day by day, year by year to broaden your horizon. The more things you love, the more you are interested in, the more you enjoy, the more you are indignant about, the more you have left when anything happens." (Ethel Barrymore, American actress regarded as the "First Lady of American Theater")

JANUARY 12

ASK GOD TO NARROW YOU DOWN

In contrast to needing broader horizons, sometimes we need a narrowing. When I moved to Denver in my mid-twenties, I was a wide-eyed optimist with lots of energy. I knew I had a call to missions, but I didn't know what that meant. Everywhere I looked there was pressing need. I needed focus.

My husband didn't want to move overseas, so I knew God would supply the mission field here in the U.S. And I had a master's in Music, not missions. What to do?

For starters, I asked God to narrow me down . . . and he did. I met Ray and Marilyn at a conference and they were focused on local poverty. We sat around their dining table for months, praying and studying about justice and more specifically, affordable housing. They started Hope Communities, which helped change the face of poverty in Denver. And I got to help. Our mission field was in our own city.

Twenty-five years later, after working with Hope and later DenverWorks, I got fidgety. I wanted to work globally, so I resigned from my position at

DenverWorks and started working on behalf of oppressed people in India. (Ten years later I returned as executive director of DenverWorks, but I'll save that story for another day.)

Two mission fields . . . urban Denver and impoverished India. Those are the "narrowed down" pieces of the pie with which God let me work.

DAILY SEED: What's your piece of the pie?

"Pursue some path, however narrow and crooked, in which you can walk with love and reverence." (Henry David Thoreau, from his *Journal*)

JANUARY 13

ASK PEOPLE WHAT THEY NEED

A task force of twenty-somethings (think naïve) met with a group of residents at the first Hope Communities apartment building in the late 70s. The goal was to inform them that they could own their own homes! The model was spearheaded by The Enterprise Foundation in Washington D.C. It was cutting edge. It was new.

The apartment building, however, was old. It had ten pages of code violations against it. Residents were using their ovens for heat. Peeling wallpaper revealed decades-old newspaper plastered onto the walls. It was grim.

The residents were skeptical. They said, "What we *really* need is for you (management) to get rid of the @#%! roaches."

To which we replied, "No, you don't understand. You can actually *own* a home!"

To which they replied, "No, *you* don't understand. What we *really* need is for you to get rid of the @#%! roaches."

A few days later, management met and decided to get rid of the @#%! roaches. And later, many of the residents owned their own homes.

But they knew what they needed first. It was vital to listen.

DAILY SEED: Who needs your listening ear today? Not your words, but your ears?

"It is the province of knowledge to speak. And it is the privilege of wisdom to listen." (Oliver Wendell Holmes, *The Poet at the Breakfast Table*)

JANUARY 14

ASK THE RIGHT QUESTIONS

*   Could you survive in poverty? Now *that*'s a good question.

* *   Aha! Process, Inc. has published a workbook called *A Framework for Understanding Poverty: 10 Actions to Educate Students*. In it you can find a survival survey.

Three questions are asked: Could you survive in poverty? Could you survive in the middle class? And could you survive in wealth? You're supposed to check the items you know how to do.

For example, do you know how to get the best interest rate on a new car loan? Do you own at least two homes that are staffed and maintained? Do you know where the free medical clinics are?

Guess which question falls under which category.

I urge you to check out the survey.[2] To understand others, we need to walk a mile in their shoes. At DenverWorks, the staff and I tried to put ourselves in our clients' shoes. We tried to ask the right questions. Peek into a staff meeting . . .

"We can help her get a job *but* . . .

. . . what about transportation? (Oops, the buses don't go there.)

. . . what about child care? (Oops, it would cost over half of her take-home pay.)

. . . what about that needed high school diploma? (Oops, she had to drop out of high school.)

Asking the right questions helped us empathize and fashion practical solutions. The task was long, hard, and tedious but doable in many cases. Asking the right questions was task #1.

DAILY SEED: Ask yourself the right questions about poverty by putting yourself in the shoes of the impoverished.

When Jonas Salk, developer of the polio vaccine, was asked when he first had the vision of what he might accomplish, he replied, "You never have an idea of what you might accomplish. All that you do is you pursue a question and see where it leads." (from a 1991 interview entitled "The Calling to Find a Cure")

JANUARY 15

ASK YBH

YBH stands for "Yes, But How?" Yes, wrongs and disasters are all around us, but how can we help? What can we do? And how can we push through the anguish of it all? That's the point of this whole book—the how-tos.

I believe we feel and think . . . and then do. The action of *doing* is a solution to the paralysis of anguish.

I once saw a plaque on an executive's desk that read, "Bring Me Solutions." I borrowed that idea. An antidote to hand-wringing (or griping) is to become part of the solution. Ask YBH. *Ask yourself.* Think hard. You have a good brain. *And ask God.* You'll get the how-tos, the solutions.

DAILY SEED: What baffles and disturbs you? Ask God . . . YBH.

"Rarely do we find men who willingly engage in hard, solid thinking. There is an almost universal quest for easy answers and half-baked solutions. Nothing pains some people more than having to think." (Martin Luther King Jr.)

ASSESS YOUR COMMUNITY'S NEEDS AND WORK TO MEET THEM

My church in Little Rock was one of the first in the nation to integrate and take a stand on racial equality. Now *that* was an assessed need in Little Rock, Arkansas, a few blocks from Central High School, in the late 50s and 60s.

And then the church noticed that the elderly needed some non-nursing home housing. So a beautiful old hotel next to the church was purchased for them.

Then the church noticed that since so many moms were entering the workforce, too many kids were left home alone. So Lake Nixon Day Camp was acquired.

And then the saga continued, for decades. What a privilege God has given us—to be His hands and feet in our own communities.

DAILY SEED: What are your community's needs?

*"Here is a simple rule of thumb for behavior: Ask yourself what you want people to do for you; then grab the initiative and do it for **them**!"* (Luke 6:31, MSG)

ATTEND CLASSES AND CONFERENCES

In the early 90s I went to a conference in Washington D.C. Apart from eating ethnic food in Adams-Morgan and walking the Mall and flat-out loving that city, the conference itself was great. I heard about ClevelandWorks and the innovative programs of Washington's Church of the Savior. I couldn't take notes fast enough. As a result, I put the DenverWorks model together in my head long before I implemented it.

Later, on a different "classes and conferences" note, I audited a class on democratization at a local university. It contributed hugely to my worldview, but didn't cost me a cent.

DAILY SEED: Avail yourself of classes and conferences.

"A year from now you'll wish you had started today." (Karen Lamb)

"Be diligent to present yourself approved to God as a workman who does not need to be ashamed, accurately handling the word of truth." (2 Timothy 2:15, NIV)

JANUARY 18

BE A CHAMPION

Tennis champ Billie Jean King said, "Champions keep playing until they get it right."

Every cause/event/project needs a champion, the go-to person, the one who will advocate for it, fight for it, make it happen, the one who will keep at it until it's right, the one who will see it to completion.

Let's say a church wanted to hold a Child Sponsorship Sunday, but nobody stepped up to champion it, to run it. Would it happen? Sadly, no.

DAILY SEED: Are you to be the champion for a cause dear to your heart?

"Just do it." (Nike)

JANUARY 19

BE A FAITH-IN-ACTION PERSON

I can say I believe a certain chair will hold me up, but I'm not putting my faith into action until I *sit* on the chair. Some among us envision a future where Christians put their faith into action. Take Sojourners for example. They push for *engagement* in public policy and focus on racial and social justice, life and peace, and the environment.[3]

We can *believe* that God loves justice until we're blue in the face, but unless we act, we're not putting our faith into action.

DAILY SEED: Put your faith into action today.

"But someone may well say, 'You have faith, and I have works; show me your faith without the works, and I will show you my faith by my works.'" (James 2:18)

JANUARY 20

BE A GOOD NEIGHBOR

Neighbors were really important during my growing-up years in Little Rock. We neighborhood kids played until dark-thirty, skinning our knees, riding our bikes, catching fireflies, building forts. One kid jumped off his roof with an open umbrella to see if Mary Poppins was on to something. She wasn't. He broke his arm.

But I digress.

About being neighborly, I was taught from an early age to love my citywide neighbors, my African-American peers, when all around me there was insane prejudice against them.

Since then, I've rubbed elbows with all kinds of neighbors—urban neighbors, suburban neighbors, gay neighbors, straight neighbors, happy neighbors, struggling neighbors, neighbors like us and neighbors very different from us. And recently, a neighbor came into my life whose only child passed away when he was a young adult. Words were inadequate, but I could *be* with her.

DAILY SEED: What neighbor is on your mind? Love that person.

"You shall love your neighbor as yourself; I am the Lord." (Leviticus 19:18b)

BE A GOOD SAMARITAN

There's the story about the seminary professor who had a strict deadline for his students' Good Samaritan essay. Unbeknownst to them, he staged an accident in front of the building. As the students bounded up the stairs to turn in their papers, each one sidestepped the accident . . . and failed the essay.

I'm one of those people pretty focused on deadlines and timelines. I'm more of a "Martha" than "Mary." (Read Luke 10:38–42.) How many times have I sidestepped needs in order to get that "A" on the test . . . and missed the whole point?

We can *grow* toward keen awareness of others. We can *grow* toward dropping what we are doing to help. We can *grow* toward the fullness of love instead of loathing interruptions.

DAILY SEED: Be cognizant of today's interruptions. They just might be the whole point.

"But a Samaritan, who was on a journey, came upon him; and when he saw him, he felt compassion . . . " (Luke 10:33)

BE A HUMANITARIAN RESPONDER

We've all seen the people in orange vests on TV, picking through debris after a disaster.

We've all visualized their grim task. And we've all been touched by the discovery of life under the rubble.

The Center for International Disaster Information website has information for volunteering after a disaster. You can register in their volunteer database. Candidates with the best chance of being selected have language fluency,

5–10 years of disaster relief experience, expertise in a relevant technical field, experience with a relief agency working in-country, an up-to-date immunization record and passport, and several weeks to several months of availability.[4]

DAILY SEED: Although not for everyone, are *you* drawn toward emergency care and humanitarian response?

"Nobody is born a warrior. You choose to be one when you refuse to stay seated." (from blog, "Being Caballero"[5])

JANUARY 23

BE A JOY GERM

My friend, Tiffany, has the coolest license plate. It says "Joy Germ," and she is that.

Just being around her is a blessing. Tiffany *sows* blessings.

A definition of "germ" is bud, offshoot, or *seed*—an initial stage for subsequent development. Germination means a period of dormancy followed by the seed coat rupturing when the conditions are right.

Let the seed within you germinate and "bust out" with joy. Isn't that a great visual?

DAILY SEED: Who needs your "joy germ" touch today?

"I used to visit and revisit it a dozen times a day, and stand in deep contemplation over my vegetable progeny with a love that nobody could share or conceive of who had never taken part in the process of creation. It was one of the most bewitching sights in the world to observe a hill of beans thrusting aside the soil, or a rose of early peas just peeping forth sufficiently to trace a line of delicate green." (Nathaniel Hawthorne, American novelist)

JANUARY 24

BE A POMEGRANATE

From my in-depth scholarly research (a quick Google search), it seems the seediest fruit is the pomegranate, which can contain up to 1400 seeds.

A pocketful of seeds is like a very seedy piece of fruit. In other words, our metaphor is a pocket *overflowing* with seeds or a piece of fruit *abounding* with seeds.

Keep a tally of your opportunities to plant seeds of change today. How many people can you touch on the arm and bless? How many times can you speak up in support of an oppressed people group? How many words of advocacy? How many actions of support?

The opportunities to plant seeds of change are endless. Like pomegranate seeds.

DAILY SEED: Be *really* seedy today.

"For the Lord your God is bringing you into a good land, a land of brooks of water, of fountains and springs, flowing forth in valleys and hills; a land of wheat and barley, of vines and fig trees and pomegranates, a land of olive oil and honey." (Deuteronomy 8:7–8)

JANUARY 25

BE A WORLD CITIZEN

In the past, a person in a different hemisphere wasn't necessarily a neighbor. Very few people crossed an ocean in a whole lifetime. Not so any more. I can be in India by tomorrow night.

I believe our generation is to do *both*—to love our (literal) neighbors as ourselves, but also to love our global neighbors. We can learn about everyday life in South Korea. We can learn how to help Palestinian Christian churches. We can learn perseverance from moms in Nigeria.

I'm not saying "do it all." I'm suggesting that we ask God how to love our global neighbors . . . and he *will* show the way if we are willing.

DAILY SEED: What remote part of the world is on your mind?

"But you will receive power when the Holy Spirit has come upon you; and you shall be My witnesses both in Jerusalem, and in all Judea and Samaria, and even to the remotest part of the earth." (Acts 1:8)

JANUARY 26

BE AN ACTIVIST

She sometimes wears trendy clothes, has a cute Lab for a pet, and loves beach vacations.

He participates in anti-war marches, writes scathing editorials, and is a vegan. Which is the activist?

Um, both. (The "she" is me.)

That's the point. Let's shed our stereotypes. If you live in an upscale neighborhood, *you* be the activist. Start a "Great Decisions" group or a scholarship fund. If you are part of the "working poor," *you* be the activist. Volunteer or weigh in on issues on a free-use computer at the library. And let's not let our emotional baggage get in the way. Some are confused and inactive because they feel guilty about their good fortune. Others are confused and inactive because they are angry over their bad fortune. We could *all* have some reason for inaction, but let's choose to dig into those reasons and get past them. They can become *motivational seeds*.

There's no shortage of activists in the world, it's just that so many are murderous activists. They wield weapons of hatred that wound. We must wield weapons of love that heal. Even if our activism is on a divisive issue like race relations or gay marriage, we must be so profoundly loving that we are heard. I recently took a risk on Facebook and asked a provocative question on a divisive issue. I had to. I couldn't rest until I did. I needed to choose activism over inaction.

Jesus was an activist. There's nothing passive about the way he drove the moneychangers out of the temple. (See Mark 11:15–18.) He was not popular for it but he did it out of love. Our activism may not be popular but it must be built on love and truth.

And God equips us for activism. Ephesians 6:10–18 (NIV) is full of equipment:

Finally, be strong in the Lord and in his mighty power. Put on the full armor of God, so that you can take your stand against the devil's schemes. For our struggle is not against flesh and blood, but against the rulers, against the authorities, against the powers of this dark world and against the spiritual forces of evil in the heavenly realms. Therefore put on the full armor of God, so that when the day of evil comes, you may be able to stand your ground, and after you have done everything, to stand. Stand firm then, with the belt of truth buckled around your waist, with the breastplate of righteousness in place, and with your feet fitted with the readiness that comes from the gospel of peace. In addition to all this, take up the shield of faith, with which you can extinguish all the flaming arrows of the evil one. Take the helmet of salvation and the sword of the Spirit, which is the word of God. And pray in the Spirit on all occasions with all kinds of prayers and requests. With this in mind, be alert and always keep on praying for all the Lord's people.

DAILY SEED: How is God drawing you to activism?

"Every Christian can be an activist, whether full- or part-time. Subversively, we act out our beliefs as they go against the grain of surrounding culture. When parents discard unwanted children, Christians make a home for them. When scientists seek ways to purify the gene pool, Christians look for special-needs babies to adopt. When politicians cut funding for the poor, Christians open shelters and feeding stations."

"Through volunteer work, prayer, and financial contributions, all of us can be activists." (Philip Yancey, *Vanishing Grace: What Ever Happened to the Good News*)

BE AN AMBASSADOR FOR A CAUSE

Tami's an ambassador for oppressed children. Once she was in Aspen, Colorado with friends. As they strolled through the upscale boutiques, they saw a famous movie star shopping as well, trying to be incognito behind sunglasses. Tami went right up to her and struck up a conversation. (This movie star happened to be an ambassador for children also.) However, at the moment, she was trying to ditch Tami. But Tami persisted. "No, no, no, I don't want your autograph! I want to talk about a children's project you and I are both involved with."

Then, the movie star pulled her aside, took off her sunglasses, gave her that big Goldie Hawn smile, and they had quite a conversation. She gave Tami her e-mail address and a beautiful connection was made.

Both Tami *and* the lady-in-sunglasses are stars in my opinion.

DAILY SEED: As you go about your daily life, beat the drum for your cause.

"Therefore, we are ambassadors for Christ, as though God were making an appeal through us . . . " (2 Corinthians 5:20a)

BE AN EXAMPLE

Randy is an advocate for the disabled. He's in a wheelchair with severe cerebral palsy. It takes him an hour to put on his socks. He tells me about the races he plans to run in heaven. He participates in local actions. Sometimes he wears a T-shirt that says "No Whining."

When I'm tempted to complain about my life, I think of Randy and his T-shirt. He's an example of an overcoming life.

DAILY SEED: Who serves as an example for you? Thank him/her. To whom are you an example?

"Example is leadership." (Albert Schweitzer, physician and 1952 Nobel Peace Prize winner)

JANUARY 29

BE BLESSED

Jesus said in Luke 6:38, *"Give, and it will be given to you. They will pour into your lap a good measure—pressed down, shaken together, **and** running over. For by your standard of measure it will be measured to you in return."*

God blesses us with joy in giving to people. Doing good shouldn't be motivated by the reward, but isn't the joy it brings a lovely reflection of God's heart? It reminds me of catching our children in the act of doing good and letting them know it was a very cool thing to do. And how many times do you hear volunteers say that they get more out of it than the people they're helping?

Loving people is a lovely thing, a blessed thing.

DAILY SEED: Help someone today and enjoy the blessing.

"Self-improvement comes mainly from trying to help others." (Sir John Templeton, philanthropist and mutual fund pioneer)

JANUARY 30

BE CREATIVE

Did you know that Mickey Mouse was "born" in 1928? With Mickey, a gazillion-dollar industry of creativity was unleashed. The Walt Disney Company says this . . . "Around here, we don't look backwards for very long. We keep moving forward, opening up new doors and doing new things, because we're curious . . . and curiosity keeps leading us down new paths."

Are you creative? Do you love making something out of nothing? Does your curiosity keep leading you down new paths? Does it excite you beyond words?

Some sew fabric panels together to make a memorial quilt . . . or write music . . . or dance . . . or debate . . . or invent . . . or decorate cakes . . . or act . . . or dream up smarter phones.

DAILY SEED: How can *your* creativity make the world a better place?

"Great is the human who has not lost his childlike heart." (Mencius [Meng-Tse], fourth century BC)

JANUARY 31

BE FILLED FIRST

It's impossible to drink from an empty cup. But metaphorically-speaking, we often try. We run on empty. We try to draw from a place of exhaustion or discouragement or dryness, but the well must have water. Then we can drink.

Even the airlines get this. Put *your* oxygen mask on first, then assist others.

So today, my plea for you is to get filled up with God's love and instruction. Absorb it. Arm yourself with it. Don't leave home without it. Then help someone else out of your abundance, not out of your lack.

DAILY SEED: Be filled. Take a big gulp.

"Jesus answered, 'Everyone who drinks this water will be thirsty again, but whoever drinks the water I give them will never thirst. Indeed, the water I give them will become in them a spring of water welling up to eternal life.' The woman said to him, 'Sir, give me this water so that I won't get thirsty and have to keep coming here to draw water.'" (John 4:13–15, NIV)

FEBRUARY

BE GREAT

✳ One day in mid-May, 2004, I was giving a lady a ride home from one
✳ ✳ of our workshops at DenverWorks. (She had brought a young neighbor
to the workshop and needed a lift afterward.) We had a nice conversation and
I asked her where she was from. "Topeka," she replied. I said, "Wow, Topeka's
really been in the news this week!" (It was the fiftieth anniversary of Brown
vs. the Board of Education).

To which she calmly started telling me the amazing story that she and her best
friend, Linda Brown, were the first two black students to go to that white school.

What?!?!! I practically screeched on my brakes and turned to her as if Rosa
Parks herself sat in my car!

She then calmly went on about not understanding what the big deal was.
The little white kids had been nice to them. (Aren't kids the best?) She had no
desire for celebrity status. She lived quietly and happily.

It's amazing what she accomplished. She was great. And she didn't care
who got the credit.

DAILY SEED: As we go about our days, let's be motivated by "God's hugs"
not people's applause.

"It is amazing what you can accomplish if you do not care who gets the
credit." (Harry S. Truman)

BE INFECTIOUS

✳ When my husband had knee-replacement surgery, I hung out with
✳ ✳ him in the hospital, noticing hospital culture. The infection-prevent-
ing measures are *drastic!* I started thinking about that word "infectious"

including its non-technical meaning, which is "the pleasantly irresistible quality of something," like infectious laughter. Wouldn't you love to be thought of as *pleasantly irresistible?*

I want to be *drastic* in the good sense of infectious—drastically happy, for example. George Müller, noted evangelist, said, "The first great and primary business to which I ought to attend every day is to have my soul happy in the Lord." What a fresh insight. That kind of happiness is contagious.

I also want to be drastically seedy, so here's my prayer. "Lord, today, at home, at the stores where I'll run my errands, among friends and family and strangers, may people get a glimpse of you through me. You are our Father, we are the clay." (See Isaiah 64:8.)

May the seeds that you and I sow today make a difference in the world. May they infect (influence) others. Yeah, that's what I'm talking about!

DAILY SEED: Watch for opportunities today to be infectious with actions that make a difference.

"In the same way, let your light shine before others, that they may see your good deeds and glorify your Father in heaven." (Matthew 5:16, NIV)

FEBRUARY 3

BE INSPIRED

This morning I crept downstairs before the household woke up. Twenty deer were grazing in our yard in the pinkish half-light before dawn. It took my breath away. I was inspired by beauty and peace.

An archaic sense of the word "inspire" is *to breathe life into.* God inspired Adam. He breathed life into him. *"Then the Lord God formed man of dust from the ground, and breathed into his nostrils the breath of life; and man became a living being"* (Genesis 2:7).

So it's one thing to be inspired by beauty and peace, but what if we could stand on holy ground every morning and ask *God* to inspire us, i.e., to breathe life into us? New vigor, new awareness, new sense of purpose, and new power for the deeds of that day? *We can.*

Living the seedy life isn't all sweetness and flowers. A lot of days I'm not motivated. I need God's inspiration. I need His viewpoint. This work is much too important to go it alone.

When the poor of India hear of God's love for them, they are never the same. Inspiration takes on a whole new meaning. They laugh and clap their hands. They *get it.*

Today, I want to be inspired by God at every turn.

DAILY SEED: Today breathe deeply of God . . . and let God breathe life into you.

"Make a place to sit down. Sit down. Be quiet. You must depend upon affection, reading, knowledge, skill—more of each than you have—inspiration, work, growing older, patience, for patience joins time to eternity . . . " (from "How to be a Poet" by Wendell Berry, in *Given*)

FEBRUARY 4

BE LIKE JESUS

Jesus was so practical. And he was always giving object lessons. He preached sometimes (like the Sermon on the Mount), but often he healed, cast out demons, walked on water, saved someone from being stoned to death . . . you know, real hands-on practical stuff.

DAILY SEED: As you go about your life today, be like Jesus. Meet practical needs and plant a Jesus seed in the process.

"As you go about, as you go,/Take the name of Him who loves you so./By His power and command/Go disciple every man/As you go about, as you go." (Bill and Linda Cates)

BE PRESENT

My church has a big heart for its neighbors. It's in a shopping center, right by the liquor store and Mexican restaurant. Around the corner is the church's MORE Life Center where people can get food, legal aid, and jobs assistance. Nearby is East Colfax, Denver's notoriously "seedy" street. The church has a presence on Colfax, where a lot of people barely eke out an existence.

A few months ago, the church voted against building a mega-building near two major highways. The church wants to be present, by the liquor store, near Colfax, where the people are.

It's one reason I go to Colorado Community Church.

DAILY SEED: Is your church (mega or not) *present* in its immediate community?

How can you (and I) be *present* in our community today?

"Wherever you are, be all there! Live to the hilt every situation you believe to be the will of God." (Jim Elliot, Christian missionary martyred for his faith in Ecuador)

BE RADICAL

A radical is a person subscribing to massive, unmeasured, and rapid change. We're not all flaming radicals. However, at some point, we must step out of our comfort zones. Eleanor Roosevelt said, "You gain strength, courage and confidence by every experience in which you really stop to look fear in the face. You are able to say to yourself, 'I have lived through this horror. I can take the next thing that comes along.' You must do the thing you think you cannot do."[6]

That's being radical.

DAILY SEED: What radical thing is on your mind?

"When you are right, you cannot be too radical." (Martin Luther King, Jr.)

FEBRUARY 7

BE RESULTS-ORIENTED

One of a grant writer's main tasks is to document results (projected or achieved). Frankly, foundations don't care about how *nice* the people requesting support are. They want to see results.

We need to think about this as we go about planting seeds of change. Are we contributing to solutions? Could we tweak our programs to be stronger? If your program serves a hundred people per year, could it serve two hundred equally well? Or should it serve fifty, but better? Being results-oriented doesn't necessarily mean bigger-is-better, it just means that the outcomes should be measureable and meaningful.

"Hanging out with at-risk kids" is a means, not a result. Funders want to know the *results* of the hanging out, even though in their hearts they may think hanging out is a cool thing to do. Remember, this is about planting seeds of change, so we need to be clear on the change we wish to see. (And believe me, hanging out is one of my favorite things to do!)

DAILY SEED: Envision the results of your project or passion, not just the process.

"Begin with the end in mind." (Stephen Covey, *The 7 Habits of Highly Effective People*)

FEBRUARY 8

BE THE CHANGE

Apparently Gandhi didn't really say, "Be the change you wish to see in the world" as the bumper stickers suggest. His quote was, "If we could change ourselves, the tendencies in the world would also change. As a man changes his own nature, so does the attitude of the world change towards him. . . . We need not wait to see what others do."

So, as you'll see, this book is about starting within and being willing to be the one to start the change, even though . . . it doesn't seem fair that *we* have to fix problems that we didn't create.

It doesn't seem fair that *we* have to be the change.

Yet, it doesn't seem fair that our children have to fix problems *we* created. Hmmm.

Someone has to start.

DAILY SEED: What does "be the change" look like in your life?

"You have heard that it was said, 'An eye for an eye, and a tooth for a tooth.' But I say to you, do not resist an evil person; but whoever slaps you on your right cheek, turn the other to him also. If anyone wants to sue you and take your shirt, let him have your coat also." (Matthew 5:38–40)

FEBRUARY 9

BE THE CHURCH

According to a 2013 Barna study, only 20 percent of people born between 1984 and 2002 believe going to church is important. However, one of the top three reasons they *do* cite for attending is that "the Church is God's hands and feet in the world."

What does it mean to *be the Church* when most Millennials don't put much value on *going to church?* The Church is the bride of Christ. Christ *loves* us. So now, more than ever, we must *be* the beloved. We must be his hands and feet in the world. We must be the Church. Only God knows what the Church will look like in twenty years, but let us never forsake assembling together . . . as the Church.

DAILY SEED: All of us, whether male or female, have a need to be treasured (like a bride). And once treasured, we can pay it forward to the world around us. That is the Church.

"For no one ever hated his own flesh, but nourishes and cherishes it, just as Christ also does the church." (Ephesians 5:29)

FEBRUARY 10

BE THE ONE

The Church Unleashed by Frank Tillapaugh is a book about being the ministers at church rather than leaving ministry to the paid professionals. For example, let's say someone brought an idea before a church committee. "I think someone should start a skateboarding ministry!" says that someone. The committee might reply, "Great idea. Are you the one to start it?"

Being "the one" sounds so singular, so alone. In my experience, however, the oneness is temporary. If the idea has merit, others will come alongside.

DAILY SEED: Is God calling you to be *the one* for some cause?

"I am only one, but I am one. I cannot do everything, but I can do something. And I will not let what I cannot do interfere with what I can do. And by the grace of God, I will." (Edward Everett Hale, author of *The Man without a Country*)

FEBRUARY 11

BE A QUILT

At the end of my life, if I'm standing on a mountaintop looking back at my path, it will look zig-zaggy. I've made some mistakes. I've committed some flat-out sins. I have regrets. And yes, some of life has been tough but not my fault. And yes, I've done some things well and made some good decisions and stayed the course. So . . . I feel like a quilt. Scraps that God has sewn together. And you know what? Quilts are beautiful and full of meaning. In fact, I'd rather be a quilt than a perfect, flawless, untouchable coverlet.

My favorite people in the world are quilts too. I believe God uses us *because of* our quilt-ness, not in spite of it.

You are the only person in the world with your unique design. Only you can plant certain seeds of positive change into the soil of the world. God will use *you,* warts and all. As Dr. Mark Brewer[7] says, God just wants us to give all we know of ourselves to all we know of him.

DAILY SEED: Be quilt-y. Be seedy. Be you . . . and let God bring the increase.

"God doesn't call the qualified. He qualifies the called." (Elisabeth Elliot, *Keep a Quiet Heart*)

FEBRUARY 12

BEAR EACH OTHER'S BURDENS

There's a difference between bearing another's burdens and doing for them what they can do for themselves. The former is godliness. The latter is codependency.

Galatians 6:2 says *"Bear one another's burdens, and thereby fulfill the law of Christ."* But Galatians 6:5 (three verses later) says, *"For each one will bear his own load."*

OK, which is it?

Well, try this on. Let's say I'm struggling with someone. My friends shouldn't yell at that person *for* me. They should help *me* figure out how to deal with the person. And they might contact me within a few days to see how it's going. And when I feel their support, even though the situation has nothing to do with them, I'd know they are sharing my load, i.e., bearing my burden with me. But let's say I'm just utterly spent. At that time I might need more hands-on burden-bearing. And I would be so thankful . . .

DAILY SEED: Who needs you? How can you bear his/her burden as God intends?

"No one is useless in this world who lightens the burden of it for anyone else." (Charles Dickens)

FEBRUARY 13

BEAR FRUIT

"I am the true vine, and My Father is the vinedresser. Every branch in Me that does not bear fruit, He takes away; and every branch that bears fruit, He prunes it, so that it may bear more fruit. . . . I am the vine, you are the branches; he who abides in Me, and I in him, he bears much fruit, for apart from Me you can do nothing." (John 15:1-2, 5)

We need to stay hooked up to the Vine (Jesus) and then bear fruit. Staying connected doesn't require exhaustion. We don't have to *strain* to bear fruit. It just seems to flow from a life connected. It does have its painful side though . . . pruning. Pruning is like discipline—short-term pain for long-term gain.

But who among us wants to bear skinny, tasteless fruit? Let's bear fruit with *zest*, pruning and all, by staying connected to the Vine.

DAILY SEED: Is your life bearing fruit?

"No seedling is ever useful if it doesn't produce fruit." (Israelmore Ayivor)

FEBRUARY 14

BEAR FRUIT—LOVE

*"But the fruit of the Spirit is **love,** joy, peace, patience, kindness, goodness, faithfulness, gentleness, self-control; against such things there is no law"* (Galatians 5:22–23).

Mother Teresa said, "The greatest disease in the West today is not TB or leprosy; it is being unwanted, unloved, and uncared for. We can cure physical diseases with medicine, but the only cure for loneliness, despair, and hopelessness is love. There are many in the world who are dying for a piece of bread but there are many more dying for a little love. The poverty in the West is a different kind of poverty—it is not only a poverty of loneliness but also of spirituality. There's a hunger for love, as there is a hunger for God."[8]

If we bear spiritual fruit, we love. If we really, *really* got that, this book could end right here. If everybody loved, there would be so much seed-planting going on that it might look like the Garden of Eden, or at least how the Garden was intended to be. Love does a lot. It covers a multitude of sins. It doesn't take into account a wrong suffered. It never fails. It's the greatest. "And now these three remain: faith, hope and love. But the greatest of these is love" (1 Corinthians 13:13, NIV).

"God is love" (1 John 4:8). Isn't that remarkable? God *is* love.

If we forget everything else, we can remember to love.

DAILY SEED: Find love in your journey today . . . and pass it on to someone else.

"Darkness cannot drive out darkness: only light can do that. Hate cannot drive out hate: only love can do that." (Martin Luther King, *A Testament of Hope: The Essential Writings and Speeches*)

FEBRUARY 15

BEAR FRUIT—JOY

✳
✳ ✳ *"But the fruit of the Spirit is love, **joy**, peace, patience, kindness, goodness, faithfulness, gentleness, self-control; against such things there is no law"* (Galatians 5:22–23).

What is joy anyway? Overwhelming happiness? A sense of calm and meaning?

Do you ever have moments when all seems right with the world, like a peaceful Norman Rockwell painting? Those moments usually last about 1.8 seconds for me . . . but they're glimpses.

Real joy, however, is something different. Or so they say. I have to admit that abiding joy eludes me sometimes. I'm too aware of the downside of life.

I wouldn't say I'm morose. I just see life from the serious side. Aristotle said "to perceive is to suffer."

Maybe you're like that too.

But that being said, the older I get, the more I experience real gut-level joy. It's when I'm living out my mission. Or when I give my burdens to God and refuse to pick them up again. Or when my grandkids run into my arms. In other words, all doesn't have to be right with the world before we can experience joy. As Christians, we know that even though we're in the heat of battle, the war has ultimately been won.

So we can drop joy seeds all around regardless of today's *feelings*. We can smile, give a compliment, pay attention to someone, whistle, *belly laugh*.

DAILY SEED: Find joy in your journey today . . . and pass it on to someone else.

"A merry heart does good, like medicine, but a broken spirit dries the bones." (Proverbs 17:22, NKJV)

BEAR FRUIT—PEACE

*"But the fruit of the Spirit is love, joy, **peace**, patience, kindness, goodness, faithfulness, gentleness, self-control; against such things there is no law"* (Galatians 5:22–23).

Before Solomon was born, his parents were given this information: *"Behold, a son will be born to you, who shall be a man of rest; and I will give him rest from all his enemies on every side; for his name shall be Solomon, and I will give peace and quiet to Israel in his days"* (1 Chronicles 22:9).

Now wouldn't *that* be exciting news for prospective parents? But how do *we* receive and give peace?

Jesus came to the disciples after His resurrection and the first thing out of His mouth was, "Peace be with you" (John 20:19). We receive peace from *him.* Then, like a handshake or fist bump or high five or hug, we pass it on to others. In some churches, it's called the Passing of the Peace. One person turns to another and says, "The peace of the Lord be with you" and the recipient answers, "And also with you."

Maybe we should take that more literally.

DAILY SEED: Find peace in your journey today . . . and pass it on to someone else.

"We look forward to the time when the Power of Love will replace the Love of Power. Then will our world know the blessings of peace." (William Gladstone, four-time British prime minister)

BEAR FRUIT—PATIENCE

*"But the fruit of the Spirit is love, joy, peace, **patience**, kindness, goodness, faithfulness, gentleness, self-control; against such things there is no law"* (Galatians 5:22–23).

One morning, I woke up looking forward to a breakfast outing with my sister. But my husband needed my help with a project and the help couldn't wait. *Oh,* I was peeved. In my mind, I let him have it about the unfairness of it all. *I had to delay my breakfast by thirty minutes!*

But then a patience seed found its way into my heart. "Debbie, the Dalits have been waiting for freedom for 3000 years. You're driving to your break-fast, albeit a little late. The Dalits don't have a car . . . or breakfast. Be patient. . . . And grow up."

Gulp.

DAILY SEED: Find patience in your journey today . . . and pass it on to someone else.

"As our self-will floats to the top under the heat of pain, patience is formed." (Charles R. Swindoll)

BEAR FRUIT—KINDNESS

*"But the fruit of the Spirit is love, joy, peace, patience, **kindness**, goodness, faithfulness, gentleness, self-control; against such things there is no law."* (Galatians 5:22–23).

Here's a tale of three Lindas.

Linda E. was a high school friend who was always asking me questions about *me.*

Linda M. is a high school counselor who loves kids with hard-knock lives. Linda S. is a friend of means who has time for the underprivileged.

All three have taught me the art of being other-oriented. In a word, kind.

DAILY SEED: Find kindness in your journey today . . . and pass it on to someone else.

*"He has told you, O man, what is good; and what does the Lord require of you but to do justice, to love **kindness**, and to walk humbly with your God?"* (Micah 6:8)

"Always be kind, for everyone is fighting a hard battle." (Scotsman Ian MacLaren, pen name of Rev. John Watson)

FEBRUARY 19

BEAR FRUIT—GOODNESS

*"But the fruit of the Spirit is love, joy, peace, patience, kindness, **goodness**, faithfulness, gentleness, self-control; against such things there is no law"* (Galatians 5:22–23).

An American Indian proverb speaks of an old Cherokee teaching his grandson about life. He told the boy that a fight between two wolves was going on inside of him, and inside all of us. One wolf was evil—full of anger, regret, greed, arrogance, lies. The other was good—full of joy, peace, love, generosity, truth, compassion. The boy asked his grandfather, "Which wolf will win?" The old Cherokee simply replied, "The one you feed."

We have choice. We can shun evil and feed the good.

DAILY SEED: Find goodness in your journey today . . . and pass it on to someone else.

"Do your little bit of good where you are; it's those little bits of good put together that overwhelm the world." (Desmond Tutu)

FEBRUARY 20

BEAR FRUIT—FAITHFULNESS

"But the fruit of the Spirit is love, joy, peace, patience, kindness, goodness, faithfulness, gentleness, self-control; against such things there is no law" (Galatians 5:22–23).

"For whatever is born of God overcomes the world; and this is the victory that has overcome the world—our faith. And who is the one who overcomes the world, but he who believes that Jesus is the Son of God?" (1 John 5:4–5). What a remarkable Scripture.

How can we be faithful in everyday life? By keeping our word. By honoring our promises. By believing God against all odds, which interestingly, is called *taking a leap of faith.*

In *The Fellowship of the Ring*, Frodo's friends told him he could trust them to stick with him to the bitter end and keep his secrets, but that he couldn't trust them to let him face trouble alone.

That's faithfulness.

DAILY SEED: Find faithfulness in your journey today . . . and pass it on to someone else.

"His master said to him, 'Well done, good and faithful slave. You were faithful with a few things, I will put you in charge of many things; enter into the joy of your master.'" (Matthew 25:21)

FEBRUARY 21

BEAR FRUIT—GENTLENESS

"But the fruit of the Spirit is love, joy, peace, patience, kindness, goodness, faithfulness, gentleness, self-control; against such things there is no law" (Galatians 5:22–23).

I was born in America in an era of violence. Well, so were my ancestors. And so were you.

When I was a child, we would see Vietnam atrocities, race riots, and assassinations on TV. For my ancestors, there were wars—world wars. For you? You get the picture.

So why the emphasis on gentleness? How can we stand up for our rights, resist evil, protect the oppressed, and still be gentle? Would gentleness have won the war against slavery in our country?

Let's spin this backward. What if the Southern slave owners had chosen the gentle path? To cut their profits and convert their slaves to paid employees? To treat them with fairness and dignity?

I always have the feeling that God is on to something. If we would just trust His notions, the world would become a better place, but greed and self always seem to win the day.

It's the way of this world.

We are called to something higher. As the saying goes, "You catch more flies with honey than you do with vinegar." As Romans 12:18 goes, *"If possible, so far as it depends on you, be at peace with all men."* The onus is on us. We start the gentle path. Scripture speaks of growing gentle fruit, not violent fruit. We just can't know the burdens others are bearing, so being gentle with them is God's wisdom.

DAILY SEED: Find gentleness in your journey today . . . and pass it on to someone else.

"Nothing is so strong as gentleness. Nothing is so gentle as real strength." (Ralph W. Sockman, pastor, author, featured speaker on the *National Radio Pulpit*)

BEAR FRUIT—SELF-CONTROL

* *"But the fruit of the Spirit is love, joy, peace, patience, kindness, goodness,
* * faithfulness, gentleness, **self-control**; against such things there is no law"*
(Galatians 5:22–23).

Genghis Khan's view of leadership started with self-control. He believed self-control to be two-fold—the mastery of pride (which was harder to subdue than a wild lion) and the mastery of anger (which was harder to defeat than the greatest wrestler).[9]

I believe we should practice self-control in small things as practice for the biggies in life.

We can exercise self-control over our tongues when we're tempted to gossip.

We can exercise self-control over our bodies when we're tempted to indulge.

We can exercise self-control over our thoughts when we're tempted to let them stray.

Then, if we are faced with something really hard, our practice, discipline, and self-control will kick in and enable us to do the right thing.

DAILY SEED: Find self-control in your journey today.

"If anyone thinks himself to be religious, and yet does not bridle his tongue but deceives his own heart, this man's religion is worthless." (James 1:26)

BECOME A SOCIAL ENTREPRENEUR

* I'm privileged to know some *serious* social entrepreneurs in India. They're
* * driven. They challenge the status quo. They fight for the rights of millions of Dalits by creatively combining church-planting with social programs. They're not afraid of risk. They go to the "pipe village" where people literally

live in drainage pipes as bonded slaves. They fight the establishment that does the enslaving.

Despite the risk of persecution for their brave acts, they and people like them are increasingly stepping in to solve problems where governments and bureaucracies have failed.

DAILY SEED: An entrepreneur is a person who organizes and manages an enterprise, usually with considerable initiative and risk. Are you an entrepreneur?

"With determination and innovation, even a single person can make a surprising difference." (David Bornstein, *How to Change the World: Social Entrepreneurs and the Power of New Ideas*)

FEBRUARY 24

BEFRIEND AN INTERNATIONAL STUDENT

If you live near a university, chances are there are students from all parts of the world there—Muslim students, Hindu students, Christians, Buddhists. Chances are they don't understand our culture. Chances are their spouses are lonely. Chances are they would love an American friend. The whole wide world may be just a few blocks away.

My friend Karen loves international students. She's also an avid hiker. OK, that's an understatement. I believe the word is *gonzo.* She's climbed all of Colorado "fourteeners," including the feared knife edge on Capitol Peak.

Karen takes her international student friends hiking (but fortunately, not to the knife edge). She invites them over for cooking frenzies in her kitchen. She teaches them English. She takes them to church. She opens her front door and the world comes in.

DAILY SEED: Check out International Students Inc.[10] or other international student ministries for volunteer opportunities.

"Simple exchanges can break down walls between us, for when people come together and speak to one another and share a common experience, then their common humanity is revealed. We are reminded that we're joined together by our pursuit of a life that's productive and purposeful, and when that happens mistrust begins to fade and our smaller differences no longer overshadow the things that we share. And that's where progress begins." (Barack Obama)

FEBRUARY 25

BEFRIEND THE LONELY

A February 2014 article in *The Guardian* entitled "Loneliness Is Killing Us" reports that "doctors have now quantified the effects of the loneliness disease, warning that lonely people are nearly twice as likely to die prematurely as those who do not suffer feelings of isolation. Being lonely, it seems, is a lot more worrying for your health than obesity." Yikes!

Are you lonely? Do you know anyone who is? Have you ever spent a holiday by yourself? *That's lonely.*

Try to include a single adult or college student or widow/widower or *anyone* who is lonely in your holiday plans. And don't worry if the kids are chasing each other through the kitchen or the dog eats the turkey. Shared experiences with a good dose of laughter equals . . . belonging.

DAILY SEED: Think of a lonely acquaintance and give him/her a call today.

"Loneliness and the feeling of being unwanted is the most terrible poverty." (Mother Teresa)

BELIEVE

✻
✻ ✻ *"Do not be overcome by evil, but overcome evil with good."* (Romans 12:21)
Do you believe that we can overcome evil with good? What a remarkable belief to carry around with us every day. It's dashboard-worthy! Watch for opportunities to do so.

The New Testament uses the word "believe" 221 times. Romans 10:9–11 says *"that if you confess with your mouth Jesus as Lord, and believe in your heart that God raised Him from the dead, you will be saved; for with the heart a person believes, resulting in righteousness, and with the mouth he confesses, resulting in salvation. For the Scripture says, 'Whoever believes in Him will not be disappointed.'"*

Sometimes it seems evil is like a water bed; if you push it down on one side, it pops up somewhere else. Terrorism and oppression seem to be getting worse, not better, but God said to overcome evil with good, so it IS possible. Just read the book of Revelation to see the end of the story, that our good God ultimately defeats evil. My overarching goal is to point us all in this direction, because love wins.

Part of God's call to believers is to do good works. What if we didn't? I can't even imagine the chaos that would ensue. Planting seeds of change into the soil of the world matters. It's part of the equation for a meaningful life. It *saves* lives.

So today, you and I will have ample opportunities to practice Romans 12:21. We will hear about evil in the news. We might even witness it ourselves. And we've been given a solution.

DAILY SEED: Believe the Gospel. Believe Romans 12:21.

"Sir, my concern is not whether God is on our side; my greatest concern is to be on God's side, for God is always right." (Abraham Lincoln, when asked if he believed God was on the Union side in the American Civil War)

BLESS PEOPLE SECRETLY OR ABUNDANTLY

Percy Ross lived a tough life but finally scored big when he bought a plastic bag company. He went into the business of giving, first by donating more than a thousand bikes to children and later by passing out nearly $20,000 to people at a parade.

In 1983, he started a newspaper column called "Thanks a Million." It ran in eight hundred newspapers for sixteen years. Thousands of people wrote in, asking Ross for money. Often, he happily gave them money, but he turned down those he felt could secure money for themselves.

He did his last column in 1999, having given out $30 million—all of his money.

DAILY SEED: Sneak a blessing to someone today.
"Freely you received, freely give." (Matthew 10:8b)

BORROW THE BEST FUNDRAISING TIP EVER

My friend, Gregg, is the best fundraiser I know—and he almost never asks for money. He hangs out with people of means (and those without). He tells them about Kids Across America. He introduces them to gang-members-turned-Christian-community-leaders. He takes them water skiing at their Missouri camp.

And he asks them, "Who do you know, who if properly informed, might be interested in this work?" Often they say *"Me!"* and pull out the checkbook. Occasionally they can't give but can provide him with the names of others. It's a win/win . . . and painless to all.

DAILY SEED: Do you need to raise funds for your cause? Try Gregg's approach.

"Fundraisers are the catalysts of change." (Unknown)

"We don't work in the nonprofit sector. We work in the for-change sector!" (Unknown)

.

MARCH

BOYCOTT

✳
✳ ✳ Years ago, a boycott was organized against a major food company. (It's a brand you would recognize.) The brand was producing infant formula used in under-developed countries and the formula was causing problems. Long story short, the boycott worked. The bottom line of profit was affected. The company no longer produces that product, but to its credit, it's still in business.

The bottom line is usually economic. We can speak by not buying certain products, not going to certain movies, not condoning certain things. If it affects the bottom line, our actions *scream* without having to say a word.

The Montgomery bus boycott of 1955–56 resulted in the U.S. Supreme Court deciding that segregation on buses was unconstitutional. Blacks were three-fourths of the Montgomery bus clientele. They had people-power to wield.

DAILY SEED: If something ticks you off, boycott it!

"In South Africa, we could not have achieved our freedom and just peace without the help of people around the world, who through the use of non-violent means, such as boycotts and divestment, encouraged their governments and other corporate actors to reverse decades-long support for the Apartheid regime." (Desmond Tutu)

BRING ANOTHER PERSON ALONG

✳
✳ ✳ Asking another person to join you in a seed-planting endeavor means 100 percent replication. Sue is always bringing people along with her— to charity events, on mission trips, to church. She's so contagious about her faith she just can't help herself.

Philip, one of Jesus' disciples, brought people to Jesus. "Come and see!" he said to Nathanael, who also became a disciple.

As you go about planting seeds, invite someone else to plant with you. Invite someone to help on that Habitat house or in that food pantry or with that fundraising event. The garden gets planted twice as fast that way.

DAILY SEED: Who comes to mind that could join you on your journey?

"For where two or three have gathered together in My name, I am there in their midst." (Matthew 18:20)

MARCH 3

BUILD SERVICE INTO THE FABRIC OF SOCIETY

* * * Jeff Pryor, CEO of Pathfinder Solutions, believes virtually *everyone* should be involved in community service. He co-wrote a book with Alex Mitchell called *Compassionate Careers: Making a Living by Making a Difference.* In the book's foreword, Archbishop Desmond invites us to a life of goodness and concludes that "It will change your life and wipe the tears from God's eyes."[11]

Wow.

AmeriCorps, the Peace Corps, and City Vision Internships (Christian counterpart to AmeriCorps/Peace Corps) are programs that *do* build service into the fabric of society. Corporations are increasingly building service into their business models. Millions of people volunteer weekly.

The stronger the fabric of society, the better the country. Service is a vital strand.

DAILY SEED: Think of ways to engage in and encourage service in your community.

"As each one has received a special gift, employ it in serving one another as good stewards of the manifold grace of God." (1 Peter 4:10)

MARCH 4

BUY HEALTHY PRODUCTS

* * * We're encouraged to buy green, organic, fair trade, cruelty-free, locally-sourced, bio-based, environmentally-preferred, recycled, and energy and water efficient. Whah? How do we know what those terms mean? Even Smart Planet[12] says labeling is confusing.

The point is "garbage in, garbage out." Obesity and pollutants damage us. It behooves us to be wise in our eating and use of products. And it behooves us to support good agriculture and environmental soundness in developing countries.

The U.S. General Services Administration reports that 95 percent of new federal agency contracts are required to contain recycled content and sustainable materials.[13] That's a good start.

DAILY SEED: How can you buy better?

"Consumers have not been told effectively enough that they have huge power and that purchasing and shopping involve a moral choice." (Anita Roddick, environment activist best known as the founder of The Body Shop)

MARCH 5

BUY SOMETHING FOR A GLOBAL NEIGHBOR

* * * The One Laptop Per Child program has been a game changer. These children don't lack capability, they lack access. Over two million have received a laptop. Access to technology is sometimes out of reach for the masses. A laptop gives those kids a fighting chance. A bus gets them to school. A sewing machine provides a career for their moms. A flock of chickens or a vegetable cart or a phone kiosk or a bicycle purchased through a micro-loan might mean self-sufficiency for their families.

A little ding to our budgets equals a world of difference to others.

DAILY SEED: Consider a purchase or a loan to a global neighbor.[14]

"Go out into the world and do good until there is too much good in the world." (Larry H. Miller, businessman and philanthropist)

MARCH 6

CARE FOR CAREGIVERS

We all know to care for people who suffer—the disabled, the desperately poor, the sick, but what about the caregivers? One of the "bibles" for caregivers of Alzheimer's patients is called *The 36-Hour Day*. That kinda nails it.

Often caregivers are family members who get paid $0. And paid ones don't exactly get rich. They work long hours, lift heavy objects, clean up messes, and are expected to have a good attitude. Right.

Let's be aware . . . and care.

DAILY SEED: What caregiver(s) do you know? Send that person an encouraging word today.

If you *are* a caregiver, try to give yourself permission to rest and replenish today.

"There are four kinds of people in the world: those who have been caregivers, those who currently are caregivers, those who will be caregivers, and those who will need caregivers." (Rosalynn Carter, former First Lady)

MARCH 7

CARE FOR CREATION (THE ENVIRONMENT)

Some think of environmentalists as ultra left-wing, anti-fracking tree-huggers. (And I'm guessing they'd say "thank you" to that description.)

But creation care is so much more than landing on a certain side of the political fence. Caring for the environment means respecting what God created, which He called "good." That's in the first couple of pages of the whole Bible! When we trash the air, land, or water, we're disrespecting creation.

"So," I ask myself, "what does that mean for me? I don't dump my garbage into the river."

Well, I can boycott those who do. I can drive a little less and bike a little more. I can support businesses who subscribe to the soul of the next economy—which includes taking environmental responsibility seriously.

DAILY SEED: Do something good for the environment today.
"God saw all that He had made, and behold, it was very good." (Genesis 1:31a)

MARCH 8

CARE FOR THE BROKENHEARTED

✳
✳ ✳ "A Poem by Laurallee," Resident/Staff at Street's Hope (for women escaping sex trafficking):
It all started with grandfather's hands over me,
The cycle continued, and then picked up by others.
The threats began telling me to tell no other.
Eventually I found drugs to cover up the pain,
Everyday feeling like I was going insane.
I ended up being homeless, and having no hope.
Wandering the streets, smoking more dope . . .
I got to the point of total defeat.
Then I heard of this place called Street's Hope . . .
So I showed up realizing this was just no ordinary place.
They welcomed me there with a big embrace . . .
So I decided to give it a real try,
Do you know I had to be taught to cry? . . .

With case management, trauma therapy, and so many classes to do
I finally learned to work on . . . well "you know who."
I even found the Lord, and was baptized too . . .
I eventually graduated, having a new outlook on life,
Becoming a Peer Mentor, and then Overnight Staff . . .
The role I play is not only hope for their future, but mine as well.
Street's Hope pulled me from a life of pure hell.

DAILY SEED: Who needs your care today?

"The most beautiful people we have known are those who have known defeat, known suffering, known struggle, known loss, and have found their way out of the depths. These persons have an appreciation, a sensitivity, and an understanding of life that fills them with compassion, gentleness, and a deep loving concern. Beautiful people do not just happen." (Elisabeth Kübler-Ross, author of *On Death and Dying*)

MARCH 9

CARRY THE CRUSHED

A few days ago as I am writing this, the so-called Islamic State beheaded children from a Christian minority group.

There are no words. For some things, we just have to drop everything and drop to our knees.

We carry the little crushed bodies in our hearts. We carry the crushed parents. We weep with those who weep.

Ragan Courtney wrote these words in the musical drama *Celebrate Life*. Mary, mother of Jesus, was singing about her son as they disengaged his hands and feet from the nails and carried him to the tomb. "Carry him gently, my child. Carry him far from suffering. Let him rest for a while. . . . His work, his work is done."

Oh God, carry the crushed.

My friend, Sunny, wrote this. "Last night I found it hard to sleep; I was so enraged at the atrocities happening in Iraq and Syria. *Then* the still small voice came. 'Paul also brutally murdered Christians.' I knew what He was telling me. God alone can change the hearts of these men and women. They may be like animals now but His purpose is not for them to perish. *Pray* for their salvation, that Jesus (Yeshua) will touch their hearts, bring conviction to them. Pray that they will have a road to Damascus experience just as Paul had. Let the conviction of the Holy Spirit fall on them. Change their hearts of stone to hearts of flesh. *Change them, Father!* This does not have to be won by strategies of man. It can be won from the heavenlies!"

There are no words . . . except . . . there *are* words. We can utter them to God. And we can carry the crushed in our hearts. May God transform our feeble carryings into miracles. He is able.

DAILY SEED: How can you carry someone you know (or know of) who has been crushed in life?

"The Lord is near to the brokenhearted and saves those who are crushed in spirit." (Psalm 34:18)

MARCH 10

CHOOSE TO LIVE MADLY

Carol has a sign on her desk that says, "Are you MAD?"

First I need to tell you about Carol. Spend ten seconds with her and you'll be laughing hysterically. She loves life, which is terribly contagious. You'll also be motivated to make a difference in the world. Believe me, Carol certainly does. So when Carol asks if you're MAD, she's inviting you to **M**ake **A D**ifference.

Why choose a MAD worldview?

Because a lot of things in this world are a mess.

Because we can.

Because MAD matters.

Because it's good for our own souls.

DAILY SEED: Are you MAD?

"My faith demands that I do whatever I can, wherever I am, whenever I can, for as long as I can with whatever I have to try to make a difference." (former President Jimmy Carter)

MARCH 11

COLLECT AND DONATE LOOSE CHANGE

✱
✱ ✱ Find a piggy bank. Feed it with your change. Send the kids on scavenger hunts around the house for coins—in pockets, at the bottom of the purse, under couch cushions. Then once a month, deposit the coins and write a check for that amount to a charity. Each family member can weigh in on charity choices. At the end of the year, twelve causes have been helped with money you barely miss.

DAILY SEED: Start a piggy bank today. *Every penny of help matters.*

"And He sat down opposite the treasury, and began observing how the people were putting money into the treasury; and many rich people were putting in large sums. And a poor widow came and put in two small copper coins, which amount to a cent. Calling His disciples to Him, He said to them, *"Truly I say to you, this poor widow put in more than all the contributors to the treasury; for they all put in out of their surplus, but she, out of her poverty, put in all she owned, all she had to live on." (Mark 12:41–44)*

COMMIT

On life's journey, don't necessarily jump ship when something doesn't go your way, because something *won't* go your way—guaranteed. That being said, however, sometimes we should make a change for reasons like corrupt management, abuse, or mission drift. But if we're just bored . . . nah. We need to hang in there and commit to the tedious process of seed-planting, watering, weeding, waiting . . .

DAILY SEED: If you're wavering on a commitment, check your motives. Then re-commit or let it go for the right reasons, with confidence.

"Trust in the Lord and do good; dwell in the land and cultivate faithfulness./ Delight yourself in the Lord; and He will give you the desires of your heart./Commit your way to the Lord, trust also in Him, and He will do it./He will bring forth your righteousness as the light and your judgment as the noonday." (Psalm 37:3–6)

COMPETE

Leading up to Super Bowl XLVIII, the Women of Vision of Seattle and the Women of Vision of Denver decided to get in on the action. (Women of Vision is a volunteer ministry of World Vision.) The Seattle and Denver ladies put out a request. Give to your local Women of Vision chapter. Winner-takes-all. So to my chagrin as a Broncos fan, all of the money raised went to those pesky Seahawks fans. But *actually*, all of the money went to support women and children around the world. How cool is that?!

The Apostle Paul said this about competition in 1 Corinthians 9:24–25. *"Do you not know that those who run in a race all run, but only one receives the prize? Run in such a way that you may win. Everyone who competes in the games exercises self-control in all things. They then do it to receive a perishable wreath, but we an imperishable."*

God doesn't want us to sit on our laurels and let the world drift by. He said to run is such a way that we may win. We're supposed to get busy—competitive, even!

DAILY SEED: How can some healthy competition benefit the needy in your world?

"If you aren't going all the way, why go at all?" (Joe Namath, famed NFL quarterback)

MARCH 14

CONSIDER A GAP YEAR OR SABBATICAL

More and more people are thinking about multiple bottom lines—not just profit bottom lines, but *life* bottom lines. That kind of thinking can lead to restructuring one's whole worldview. Sabbaticals are needed, either for rest and reflection . . . or for giving back.

"Sabbatical" is derived from the word "Sabbath," meaning a period of rest. In training for a half marathon, I've become aware of the physiological need for rest. It seems one can't run as well apart from resting the muscles. So it's not just a bonus, it's necessary for peak performance.

Taking a gap year between high school graduation and college works for some. Others take sabbaticals later in life. They are willing to risk the "make-the-most-money-you-can" bottom line in favor of the "make-the-most-difference-you-can" bottom line.

The Global Ideas Bank published a book called *500 Ways to Change the World.*[15] It proposes taking a sabbatical to another culture three times in life—first, after high school. Secondly, at mid-life. Thirdly, just after retirement. It recommends a year as the minimum amount of time, to move from "they do it all wrong here" to "they do it all wrong back home" to an understanding that we all do it right (and wrong).

The age component is important. When we're young, we have the desire but not the skills. At middle age, we need the perspective of others. As elders, we have wisdom to share.

The book also proposes taking a sabbatical every seventh year—radical but interesting.

I've never met a person who didn't benefit from their sabbatical, although I've met a lot of people who decided to take one much too late.

DAILY SEED: What does a sabbatical look like in your life?

"Remember the Sabbath day, to keep it holy." (Exodus 20:8)

"Come to Me, all who are weary and heavy-laden, and I will give you rest. Take My yoke upon you, and learn from Me, for I am gentle and humble in heart; and you will find rest for your souls. For My yoke is easy and My burden is light." (Matthew 11:28–30)

MARCH 15

CONSIDER AN ENCORE CAREER

※
※ ※ Encore careers are second half of life (often post-retirement) careers. "Encore" (the organization) calls them second acts for the greater good. Not freedom from work but the freedom *to* work. Encore careers combine personal fulfillment, social impact and continued income, enabling people to put their passion to work for the greater good.[16]

I've been fortunate to do work I love during my first act of life, but as I go into the encore phase *(woo-hoo!)* I'm excited! I see things differently now. I don't get as hung up when I run into different viewpoints. I don't work 24/7. (I've been known to wake up exhausted because I was working on a spreadsheet in my dreams—good grief!) I value people over projects more.

In generations past, retirement was the beginning of the end. No longer! Retirement now marks the end of the beginning. There is much more to do, with greater wisdom, greater patience, greater enjoyment, and even potentially greater effectiveness. Look forward to it!

DAILY SEED: What legacy do you want to leave? Will it be accomplished during the first half of life or second half . . . or both?

"If more people take on encore careers . . . the boomers who arrived on the scene by igniting a sexual revolution could leave by staging a give-back revolution. Boomers may just be remembered more for what they did in their 60s than for what they did in the Sixties." (Nicholas Kristof, Pulitzer Prize-winning author, in a 2008 *New York Times* article, "Geezers Doing Good")

MARCH 16

CONSIDER AN URBAN OR GLOBAL IMMERSION

✳   Here are a few examples or immersions lasting a semester or longer.
✳ ✳   *Denver Urban Semester:* DUS is a Christian ministry that connects college students to a training experience among under-served urban populations.[17]

City Year: City Year AmeriCorps members spend eleven months working with a small group of students to help change their educational outcomes.[18]

USAID: USAID offers a semester of webchats and lectures for those interested in improving the lives of people around the world. Participants explore poverty, hunger, violence, injustice and environmental degradation. USAID also provides student internships, eInternships, fellowships, jobs, farmer-to-farmer programs, and international corporate volunteerism opportunities.[19]

DAILY SEED: If you could immerse yourself in learning something deeply for a period of time, what would it be?

"Make better happen." (City Year)

CONSIDER ONE LOCAL + ONE GLOBAL

✳ Acts 1:8 says, *"But you will receive power when the Holy Spirit has come*
✳ ✳ *upon you; and you shall be My witnesses both in Jerusalem, and in all Judea and Samaria, and even to the remotest part of the earth."* In other words, start locally and expand to the remotest part of the earth. I believe these are words to Christians *as a whole.* We've been commissioned to make disciples of all the nations. Disciples of Love.

But as individuals, desiring to make a difference in the world can be overwhelming. Simply choosing one local endeavor and one global one worked for me. Maybe it would work for you too.

DAILY SEED: If you had to choose one local and one global project in the next fifteen seconds, what would you choose?

"Any intelligent fool can make things bigger, more complex, and more violent. It takes a touch of genius—and a lot of courage—to move in the opposite direction." (from essay, "Small Is Beautiful," by E.F. Schumacher, British economist)

CONSIDER RELOCATION, RECONCILIATION, AND REDISTRIBUTION

✳ The three pillars of the Christian Community Development Associa-
✳ ✳ tion (CCDA[20]), started by John Perkins, are Relocation, Reconciliation, and Redistribution (the 3 Rs). I had friends who opted for this radical lifestyle, and I decided to as well. My children and I dove right in. It's unusual for some but the only way to go for others. I'll unpack it over the next few days.

DAILY SEED: Consider the word "shalom"—a condition where nothing is missing and nothing is broken.

"Many of us have a deep sense that the world is not as it should be. Broken relationships. Divided communities. Poverty and violence in our neighborhoods. The good news is that God longs to work through us to help restore things to the way they were intended to be. In the language of the Old Testament, this wholeness is called shalom." (from CCDA website)

MARCH 19

RELOCATION

How did Jesus love?

"The Word became flesh and dwelt among us, and we beheld His glory as of the only begotten from the Father, full of grace and truth" (John 1:14). Jesus relocated. He became one of us. He didn't commute back and forth to heaven. Similarly, the most effective messenger of the gospel to the poor will also live among the poor that God has called the person to. A key phrase to understand relocation is incarnational ministry."[21]

We relocated from the suburbs to a mixed urban neighborhood. There was a mansion on one corner, apartments two doors down (usually blaring mariachi music), a married same-sex couple across the street (long before that was legal), a high-level professional businessman next door . . . and us. There was never a dull moment. We loved the diversity. The burden was light. In fact, it wasn't a burden at all. Beautiful downtown Denver, parks, bike paths, and some of the country's best cultural venues were within walking distance.

DAILY SEED: I'm not suggesting that everyone relocate. You may be living in the "sweet spot" God has prepared for you. What a blessing! Others may long for something different. If you long to relocate, explore your options.

"Go to the people

Live among them

Learn from them
Love them
Start with what they know
Build on what they have:
But of the best leaders,
When their task is done
The people will remark, 'We have done it ourselves.'" (Ancient Chinese proverb)

MARCH 20

RECONCILIATION

※
※ ※ The question is this: Can a gospel that reconciles people to God without reconciling people to people be the true gospel of Jesus Christ?

"A person's love for Christ should break down every racial, ethnic and economic barrier. As Christians come together to solve the problems of their community, the great challenge is to partner and witness together across these barriers in order to demonstrate our oneness in Christ."[22]

Reconciliation doesn't require relocation, of course. We can just choose to make relational reconciliation and racial reconciliation a big priority. *I believe this "R" is for everyone.*

One of my African-American friends used to have big struggles with me. I reminded her of a white lady who had been mean to her when she was a child. This broke my heart, but also made me mad. (I wasn't that mean lady!) However, slowly, it dawned on me to buck up and show grace. Sometimes the reconciliation we need to offer isn't over our own issues. There are just hurts that are miles deep and generations long.

DAILY SEED: What might reconciliation look like in your community or within your network?

"Therefore if anyone is in Christ, he is a new creature; the old things passed away, behold, new things have come. Now all these things are from God, who

reconciled us to Himself through Christ and gave us the ministry of reconciliation." (2 Corinthians 5:17–18)

MARCH 21

REDISTRIBUTION

✳ "When God's people with resources (regardless of their race or cul-
✳ ✳ ture) commit to living in underserved communities seeking to be good neighbors, being examples of what it means to be a follower of Christ, working for justice for the entire community, and utilizing their skills and resources to address the problems of that community alongside their neighbors, then redistribution is being practiced."[23]

Redistribution is radical, but Mr. Perkins called himself an "ordinary radical."

My kids and I relocated, but we didn't live communally or practice radical redistribution. We just did life with our neighbors and they did life with us.

DAILY SEED: What might redistribution look like in your community or within your network?

"They devoted themselves to the apostles' teaching and to fellowship, to the breaking of bread and to prayer. Everyone was filled with awe at the many wonders and signs performed by the apostles. All the believers were together and had everything in common. They sold property and possessions to give to anyone who had need. Every day they continued to meet together in the temple courts. They broke bread in their homes and ate together with glad and sincere hearts, praising God and enjoying the favor of all the people. And the Lord added to their number daily those who were being saved." (Acts 2:42–47, NIV)

CONSTRUCT A HOME OR SCHOOL

*** A church in Denver started a homebuilding project just across the Mexican border. Border towns are notorious for poverty, and this was serious poverty. The houses were pieces of tin and boards lashed together and covered with plastic bags.

This reconstruction project poured concrete slabs, erected wooden homes, and supplied a simple heater. People incompetent with tools (like me) could help. The family to live in the home helped. My daughter went along and, after returning, didn't really want those expensive shoes after all.

Many churches/nonprofits provide opportunities to construct a home or school—either in the "hands-on" way or by providing funds.

DAILY SEED: Interested? Explore your options. It makes an amazing family project.

"For every house is built by someone, but the builder of all things is God." (Hebrews 3:4)

CONTINUE TO PAY ATTENTION
TO UNFINISHED BUSINESS

*** The spate of white officers killing unarmed black youth starting 2015-ish showed us that racial tension is unfinished business in the United States. The Free the Dalit movement is unfinished business. The gendercide of baby girls in China and India is unfinished business. A little Indian girl dies from gender discrimination every four minutes.[24]

We must pay attention, stay the course, and speak up on these issues every chance we get.

DAILY SEED: What unfinished business still exists in the world around you?

"Do stuff. Be clenched, curious. Not waiting for inspiration's shove or society's kiss on your forehead. Pay attention." (Susan Sontag, American author)

MARCH 24

COUNT ON SETBACKS

I had my share of setbacks at DenverWorks. The board said no to some of my ideas. They used to tease me by making a little "reeling in" motion, like I was a fish on a hook, to rein in my enthusiasm . . . sigh.

Foundations sometimes said no to grant applications. Receiving funds from 1 out of 3 was *good*.

Not all of our clients got jobs, even the most promising among them.

Giving up over setbacks is, well, not a good idea. Usually, it's two steps forward, one step back. Look for net gain.

In attempting to be a world-changer, you might find that the world doesn't want what you/we have to offer, there's not enough money to fund it, or the premise is good but the method needs tweaking.

Christopher Columbus, upon realizing he had missed the East Indies, thought his 1492 voyage was a setback.

Sometimes the setbacks are the whole point.

DAILY SEED: Keep your eye on the prize, but count on setbacks.

"Jesus praised faith and trust—even more than love. It takes a foundational trust to fall, or to fail, and not to fall apart." (Richard Rohr, *Falling Upward: A Spirituality for the Two Halves of Life*)

COUNT THE COST

* * * I know of a young pastor who went to a Christian rally in 2006. He was killed there by Hindu radicals. He paid the ultimate price.

Dean Hill in *Cover to Cover: A Journey through the Scriptures* said this: "We [live in a culture] that says the ultimate goal of this life is to *never* be taken advantage of, treated unjustly, or wounded by another. Yet Paul, in 1 Corinthians 5–8, says that at times it may be better to be offended and never get justice, or to be wounded and endure it quietly instead of seeking recourse. Are you willing to lose for Christ? To what extent?"

Hard but true words.

DAILY SEED: What are the costs to pay on your journey?

"For, I think, God has exhibited us apostles last of all, as men condemned to death . . . fools for Christ's sake . . . hungry and thirsty . . . the dregs of all things." (excerpted from 1 Corinthians 4:9–13)

But also . . .

"Blessed is a man who perseveres under trial; for once he has been approved, he will receive the crown of life which the Lord has promised to those who love Him." (James 1:12)

COUNTER TERRORISM

* * * The CELL is located in downtown Denver. CELL stands for Counterterrorism Education Learning Lab. I visited recently and left feeling as I had walking out of the Holocaust Museum in Washington, D.C. . . . wordless and tearful.

Did you know that there were over 20,000 acts of terrorism worldwide 1998–2014?

The CELL defines terrorism as "the pre-meditated use of violence or the threat of violence targeting civilians or their property for political, religious or ideological gain. It is a tactic used to create an environment of fear, chaos and intimidation in order to further the terrorists' objectives."

I also left thinking of the gains made by the *non*-violent—Martin Luther King, Nelson Mandela, Gandhi. *What have the violent accomplished that is in any way good?*

The exhibit includes practical ways ordinary citizens can be involved, including recognizing the eight signs of terrorism. Terrorism is something we must understand, but as one speaker said, "to understand" is not the same as "to be understanding." Inflicting horror is not a legitimate way to further one's political or religious agenda. In fact, it is evil to do so . . . yet we are not to return evil in kind. May we, as a nation, never be accused of "the pre-meditated use of violence or the threat of violence targeting civilians or their property for political, religious or ideological gain, a tactic used to create an environment of fear, chaos and intimidation in order to further the terrorists' objectives."

DAILY SEED: If you have the opportunity, visit The CELL in Denver or their website.[25]

Be educated, engaged, and empowered.

"The Lord tests the righteous and the wicked, and the one who loves violence His soul hate." (Psalm 11:5)

Yet the Bible goes on to say,

"Never take your own revenge, beloved, but leave room for the wrath of God, for it is written, 'Vengeance is Mine, I will repay,' says the Lord" (Romans 12:19) and

"See that no one repays another with evil for evil, but always seek after that which is good for one another and for all people." (1 Thessalonians 5:15)

MARCH 27

CREATE A CAUSE CALENDAR

Churches have a liturgical calendar—Ash Wednesday, Lent, Easter, etc. One practical idea is to add a few issue-oriented earmarks into your *personal* calendar.

For example,

International Women's Day is March 8.

Compassion Sunday is the first Sunday in May.

International Children's Day is June 1.

International Day of the Girl Child is Oct. 11.

Orphan Sunday is the first Sunday in November.

International Day of Prayer for the Persecuted Church is the second Sunday in November.

Human Rights Day is Dec. 10.

There's probably a "day" for everything! Choosing one or a few can focus attention on what's important to you. They are days of remembrance.

DAILY SEED: Choose an issue that's important to you. Research whether or not a remembrance day has been designated for it. If so, add it to your calendar. If not, you might designate a day for it anyway!

"Remember the Sabbath day, to keep it holy." (Exodus 20:8, NKJV)

"Remember the poor." (Galatians 2:10)

"Do this in remembrance of me." (Luke 22:19)

MARCH 28

CREATE WIN/WINS

My sister attended a trade show where a vendor had a great win/win idea. If you visited their booth, you'd get a $10 voucher which could be dropped into one of several buckets—the "educate girls in Pakistan" bucket, the "provide vaccinations in Africa" bucket, and so on. The vendor would then send those funds to the selected NGOs.

The vendor won by getting more booth visitors. The booth visitor won by doing good.

And the people in Pakistan and Africa won with needed funds.

DAILY SEED: Don't shy away from philanthropic ideas that benefit you too.

"Nothing brings me more happiness than trying to help the most vulnerable people in society. It is a goal and an essential part of my life—a kind of destiny." (Diana, Princess of Wales)

"It is one of the most beautiful compensations of this life that no man can sincerely try to help another without helping himself . . . Serve and thou shall be served." (Ralph Waldo Emerson)

MARCH 29

CROSS BORDERS

Emily's the daughter of one of my best friends. She's a math and science whiz and goes to Cal Poly. The "problem" is that her heart is in the people-helping sector. I have no doubt that she'll be able to merge her head and her heart—to cross traditional disciplinary borders. She's already a young world-changer. Won't it be interesting to see how God uses her, merging her math "head" with her people "heart?"

Crossing disciplinary borders is a thing I believe their generation will master. And Emily's problem won't be a problem at all.

We can cross so many borders—racial, socio-economic, geographic. We can "cross the tracks" to different neighborhoods. God is borderless. *Here there is no Gentile or Jew, circumcised or uncircumcised, barbarian, Scythian, slave or free, but Christ is all, and is in all"* (Colossians 3:11, NIV).

The "Without Borders" organizations cross borders all the time. That's the point. Doctors Without Borders represents itself this way . . . "Doctors Without Borders is neutral. We do not take sides in armed conflicts, we provide care on the basis of need, and we push for independent access to victims of conflict as required under international humanitarian law."[26]

DAILY SEED: Get creative in crossing borders.

"Borders can't stop love." (Unknown)

MARCH 30

CRY

A friend, after returning from India, broke down in tears while sitting at an intersection in her car. There is a cost to seeing the gut-wrenching poverty in India. We pay the price in our comfort zones.

I deal with the tears by being around *solutions*, like visiting schools for Dalit children.

Operation Mobilization/India has a goal of reaching 25 million Dalits by 2025. That goal was formed from millions of Dalit tears . . . and millions of our tears. Tears are important. What if nothing broke our hearts? But the story doesn't need to end on a sad note. Those tears can become channels of blessings.

DAILY SEED: Weep with those who weep and rejoice with those who rejoice.

"Those who sow in tears shall reap with joyful shouting./ He who goes to and fro weeping, carrying his bag of seed,/ Shall indeed come again with a shout of joy, bringing his sheaves with him." (Psalm 126:5–6)

MARCH 31

CUT YOUR SALARY

＊ I know, you may be slamming the book at this point and saying I've
＊ ＊ gone too far, but hear me out. The doctors at the Inner City Health Center cut their salaries in half. They have a traditional medical practice half-time and donate the other half to uninsured patients, very poor and sick patients, who come into the health center. It's one idea. . . .

Warren Buffett has pledged to give away 99 percent of his fortune. Mr. Buffett and Bill Gates originated the Giving Pledge, which is a commitment to donate at least one-half of one's fortune before they die.[27]

At least one entry of these 365 needs to be directed toward those who can live on less. Today, there are 1,645 billionaires in the world with an aggregate wealth of $6.6 trillion, but I'm not *just* talking about them. Maybe a few others might consider the Inner City Health Center model . . . limiting one's money-making time to free up more volunteer time.

And maybe a few are wealthy enough to take the Giving Pledge.

DAILY SEED: What would it look like to live on less and give away more?

"She says she wants to give it all away; that she wants the last check she writes to bounce due to "insufficient funds." (Michael Zitz, author of *Giving It All Away: The Doris Buffett Story*)

APRIL

DECIDE AGAINST INACTION

We have a big vegetable garden. One year, we left part of it fallow. It didn't just sit there as nice, rich soil. It filled up with giant weeds.

That's what could happen if we don't act to change the world. Things wouldn't stay the same.

They would get worse. It's the principle of entropy, descent into chaos, social decline, degeneration.

For example, Hinduism advocates caste, meaning some people are born into a low caste because of sins committed in a previous life. Atrocities can happen to the low caste because they "deserve it." In other words, "we shouldn't mess with their fate." Therefore, the outcasts (Dalits) have been oppressed for 3000 years.

Should we just let that continue? I believe not. There is a line between accepting other religions and accepting the violations of human rights done in the name of religion. The point is that we must speak up. We must *decide against just letting things flow along when they are wreaking havoc, destruction, and death.*

DAILY SEED: Has God been tugging at your heart about something? Decide against inaction, because inaction breeds weeds.

"Iron rusts from disuse; stagnant water loses its purity and in cold weather becomes frozen; even so does inaction sap the vigor of the mind." (Leonardo da Vinci, *The Notebooks*)

DECLARE WAR ON EXTREME EVIL

The horror stories haunt me the most. The atrocities, torture, agony, evil. Yet Jesus is greater than these enemies in our world. Love incarnate can establish a foothold.

Amnesty International has campaigns to stop torture and ethnic cleansing. Although I don't agree with all of Amnesty's stances, I certainly support their actions in these areas of extreme evil. We can donate, earmarking programs like anti-torture campaigns.[28]

And we can pray prayers evoking God's greatness over extreme evil. When you hear the horror stories, claim 1 John 4:4 (see below). Pray for a miraculous victory.

DAILY SEED: Let us make a pact together, you and I, to claim 1 John 4:4 when we hear the horror stories in the news. Let's pray that God will be overcome the evil in that situation.

"Greater is He who is in you than he who is in the world." (1 John 4:4b)

APRIL 3

DEFEND AND VINDICATE

Have you ever been in a tough spot (like being bullied) and somebody spoke up in your defense? I have. I think being defended is one of the best feelings in the world.

When I was in junior high, I was mean to some classmates. I was insecure, so there were a couple of incidents when *I* was the bully. I'm mortified now. If there's a silver lining, it's that my embarrassment and remorse have caused me to stand on the other side, the defense, the freedom fighters' side. I stand against bullying.

We can sow seeds of support for others. We have some amazing tools in our toolbox, or more to the point, seeds in our "seedbox." Those seeds can be sown to defend the defenseless and vindicate those who have been wronged.

DAILY SEED: Who needs you to speak up for them?

"Open your mouth, judge righteously, and defend the rights of the afflicted and needy." (Proverbs 31:9)

DEFEND THE ORPHAN

✳
✳ ✳ "When I visit the orphans I actually feel like I am walking on Holy Ground. It's truly Jesus himself holding the orphans. And when I crawl into the big cribs, the workers are changed to see folks (me) loving the unlovable, but what they are really seeing is God himself. God has such a deep love for the orphans."

These are Tami's words about her trips overseas to visit and train caregivers of orphans. I remember Tami when she was "business-suit-and-heels" corporate. She was successful and comfortable, except for her longing to help the children. That trumped everything.

Long-story-short, she ended up adopting Tabi from Kyrgyzstan. Tabi was an orphan who needed facial reconstruction surgery. Tabi is now a thriving pre-teen with a calling of her own. And Tami continues to travel the world advocating for orphans, often with Tabi by her side.

DAILY SEED: Know any orphans or children in distress? Reach out to them.

"Pure and undefiled religion in the sight of our God and Father is this: to visit orphans and widows in their distress, and to keep oneself unstained by the world." (James 1:27)

DEVELOP A FUTURE LEADER

✳
✳ ✳ When my daughter was in high school, she took a part-time job as a receptionist for an international ministry. After she'd been there a week, people that had worked there for years started treating her like she was the nerve center of the organization. She didn't have answers to their questions, but she quickly found out the answers. She *led*. (I call her the Pied Piper.)

Later, I had occasion to meet with the lieutenant governor of our state. I told her about my daughter's first week on the job. She laughed and compared that to being lieutenant governor! The learning curve is short and steep . . . and one just needs to step out and lead.

We need to be aware of the young leaders around us, whether they're our own children or the future of developing countries. We must ensure that they develop their spiritual gift of leadership. We need to build their confidence. The Willow Creek Association has developed the *Global* Leadership Summit to do just that—develop Christian leaders internationally.

DAILY SEED: Who, in *your* world, do you identify as an emerging leader?

"A leadership development plan has to address these three phases: identifying emerging leaders, investing in the development of emerging leaders, [and] entrusting responsibility to emerging leaders." (Bill Hybels, in *Courageous Leadership)*

APRIL 6

DEVELOP YOUR PERSONAL MISSION STATEMENT

✱ A mission statement is the intentional, overarching "to do" in our lives.
✱ ✱ I believe that much of the despair in lives around us has to do with lack of purpose, i.e., mission. But *with* a clear mission, life starts coming together. It is more intentional. It's more meaningful. And for me, a lot more fun.

My mission statement is, "to live an abundant life in Christ (John 10:10) and to motivate my fellow Americans and fellow Christians to become more involved in the world, making a difference both spiritually and practically."

Hence, my work . . . and this book . . . and my happy place.

DAILY SEED: Fill in the blank. My mission in life is to _____.

If you've never voiced your mission statement, take your time. Find the words. Stay the course until it feels right.

"When you discover your mission, you will feel its demand. It will fill you with enthusiasm and a burning desire to get to work on it." (W. Clement Stone, businessman and philanthropist)

DEVELOP YOUR PERSONAL VISION STATEMENT

A vision statement, unlike a mission statement, should encompass what one would like to *see*. In 1982, urban developer Jim Rouse and his wife Patty founded The Enterprise Foundation,[29] with the vision of making sure every American lives in a decent, affordable home. That's what Jim and Patty wanted to *see*.

My vision is to see a slavery-free world, freedom from oppression, poverty, trafficking, addictions, or any of the other thieves of whole and happy life. My mission supports my vision.

What do you want to see? What is your vision?

Visualize a better world. When we visualize something larger than life, we have hope. We can move toward our vision. Jim and Patty Rouse's vision was a stretch of reality, but that didn't stop them from envisioning every American in a decent, affordable home.

DAILY SEED: Fill in the blank. My vision in life is to see _____
_____.

"Where there is no vision, the people are unrestrained." (Proverbs 29:18a) Or, in *The Message* version, *"If people can't see what God is doing, they stumble all over themselves; But when they attend to what he reveals, they are most blessed."*

APRIL 8

DISCOVER AND USE YOUR PLACE ON THE LEADERSHIP GRID

Whether we are leaders or followers, I think we all have a place on the leadership line.

It's interesting to think of followers as leaders, but we all have gifts. We all have a sphere of influence. If we live our lives with excellence and integrity, we are leading the way.

Are you a visionary, a *creator?*

Maybe you like to *develop* the vision, actually putting substance to it.

Some love to take the original idea and *refine* it, like polishing silver.

And, without the long-term *maintain*ers, the whole thing would fold anyway.

Are you most comfortable and invigorated by creating, developing/refining, or maintaining? All are essential.

DAILY SEED: Discover your "sweet spot" of leadership as you go about making a difference in the world. Are you a creator, developer, refiner, or maintainer?

"A true leader has the confidence to stand alone, the courage to make tough decisions, and the compassion to listen to the needs of others. He does not set out to be a leader, but becomes one by the equality of his actions and the integrity of his intent." (Douglas MacArthur, World War II five-star general)

APRIL 9

DISCOVER AND USE YOUR SPIRITUAL GIFT(S)

One of the most *freeing* things I've ever experienced was discovering my spiritual gifts.

It freed me from feeling I had to be great at *all* of them.

Here's a quiz . . .

If a friend is in the hospital, how do you help?

Do you sit by the bedside and hold the friend's hand? (Mercy)

Do you clean his/her house or babysit the kids? (Service)

Do you organize food delivery to the family? (Administration)

Do you prepare a talk on the biblical view of healing? (Preaching or Teaching)

Here's another quiz.

If you had the opportunity to spend a year in the poorest country in the world, how would you help?

Would you visit the sick and dying? (Mercy)

Would you help with a water project? (Service)

Would you organize the database for raising funds? (Administration)

Would you preach or teach? (Preaching or Teaching)

Your spiritual gift(s) inform how you can best help. If you don't know about your gifting, take a spiritual gifts inventory and study the source, the Bible.

DAILY SEED: Study 1 Corinthians 12–14. Let God show you how you are *gifted* to plant seeds of change.

"Now there are varieties of gifts, but the same Spirit. And there are varieties of ministries, and the same Lord. And there are varieties of effects, but the same God who works all things in all persons. But to each one is given the manifestation of the Spirit for the common good." (1 Corinthians 12:4–7)

APRIL 10

DO GOOD

Michael Norton of the Harvard Business School wrote in a Huffington Post blog (April 2014) that there had been little evidence that companies can make money by being nicer. So they gave cash to members of teams and asked them to spend it on each other. And they found that those teams tended to perform better, even better than teams that got the more typical bonus (money for themselves).

They also did a study at a call center raising scholarship funds. They brought in a scholarship recipient who talked for ten minutes. A month later, employees were still making more calls and raising more money (than before).

The results suggested a redefining of success to include impact-making . . . doing good. And the bottom line bore it out.

DAILY SEED: Consider how you (or your business) might "do good" in a fresh way today.

"Cling to what is good." (Romans 12:9)

"If you don't know what you're here to do, then just do some good." (Maya Angelou)

APRIL 11

DO RESEARCH

When I worked at Hope Communities, people from the neighborhood would come in and say, "What I *really* need is a good-paying job so I could afford the rent." After a few of those drop-ins, I went to our director and asked if we could start a jobs program. Wisely, he said no. "But," he continued, *"somebody* should."

So *I* did. I left Hope Communities with their blessings and started DenverWorks.

A lot of people asked if I had done research about the need for a jobs program. And I had.

(At that time, the only jobs services were the government unemployment office and "niche" programs. A program for *all* jobseekers with employment barriers from a Christian perspective was non-existent.) The need was great.

I could have kept researching it to death but at some point it was time to act. To take the leap. To assemble a board. To apply for 501c3 status. To hang out the shingle.

Eight people came to the first workshop. This year marks the twentieth anniversary and over 30,000 people have been helped.

Make sure the project is viable, then go for it. If it's not viable, God has something else in mind for you.

DAILY SEED: Have you researched the matters that tug on your heart? If not, dive into the research. If so, is it time to act?

"Research is formalized curiosity. It is poking and prying with a purpose." (Zora Neale Hurston, American folklorist of the Harlem Renaissance movement)

APRIL 12

—————

DO SOCIAL EXPERIMENTS

A friend of mine decided to live the homeless life for three days, sleeping on a sidewalk, penniless. He lasted two days. And I was impressed with that.

Others have tried to live on a welfare income for period of time. I think what such experiments have in common is the pain the experimenters feel as they are treated with disdain and regarded as unimportant or invisible.

The sixth-graders at our church recently spent a night on the sidewalk in cardboard boxes. The next morning they were given a meager meal to last the whole day. They found the homeless man, Terry, who lived his summers in the field near the church. The church had reached out to him, but he had never come in. He didn't look good. The kids gave him their food.

The next day, Terry was found lying next to the church wall. He had died. The kids had blessed him with his last meal. He hadn't come in, but they had taken Church to him.

DAILY SEED: Put yourself in someone else's shoes today, someone homeless or poor or unfairly treated. And watch the film *Brown Eyes, Blue Eyes* on YouTube. It's a social experiment on racism and it is unforgettable.

"Never criticize a man until you've walked a mile in his moccasins." (American Indian proverb)

APRIL 13

DO SOME MANUAL LABOR

* * * Project CURE is the largest provider of donated medical supplies and equipment to developing countries around the world. It all started in (where else?) a *garage* in 1987, and now thousands of volunteers nationwide send two to three cargo containers to needy countries *every week*. That's a lot of manual labor, meaning a lot of life-saving.

Some of the work we can do is just that—a lot of *work*! It might be repetitive or boring, but it gets the job done.

DAILY SEED: Extend a hand.

"She extends her hand to the poor; and she stretches out her hands to the needy." (Proverbs 31:20)

APRIL 14

DO THE MATH

* * * According to a 2011 Pew Research Center survey, there are 2.2 billion Christians around the world. There are 400 million deeply impoverished children in the world today.[30] What if 20 percent of the Christians (440 million) chose to sponsor an impoverished child? Yep, it would cover the bases. (No doubt many of the impoverished children are from Christian families, but the amount needed to sponsor a child is within reach of many *American* Christians.)

It took Compassion International, one of the largest child sponsorship programs in the world, fifty years to reach one million sponsorships. What if that number could escalate significantly? What if every Christian family you know chose to sponsor a child?

DAILY SEED: What would happen if responsible investment in impoverished children went up dramatically? What if *millions* of us sponsored a child?

"Why is it that a child's death amounts to a tragedy, but the death of millions is merely a statistic?" (Patrick McDonald, founder, Viva Network)

APRIL 15

DO THE NEXT THING

✳
✳ ✳ The best piece of advice I ever got was to "do the next thing." We can become paralyzed with fear or indecision or unwillingness, so doing the next thing is what we *can* do.

Elisabeth Elliot was overwhelmed after the death of her husband, Jim, on the mission field. She coped by going to a poem written about an old Saxon saying, "Do it immediately; do it with prayer;/ do it reliantly, casting all care;/ do it with reverence, tracing His hand/ Who placed it before thee with earnest command./ Stayed on Omnipotence, safe 'neath His wing,/ leave all resultings. *Do the next thing.*"

So she went back to her mission station with her baby and "tried to take each duty quietly as the will of God for the moment."[31]

For me, doing the next thing seemed all I could do on trips to India. The spiritual battles can be intense there, and I experienced times of confusion and depression. During those times, I reminded myself *to just do the next thing.* To trust our rock-solid leaders. To keep putting one foot in front of the other for the sake of the people. To trust God, plain and simple.

And as I did that, the darkness fled.

When you are out there working for change, you might feel alone. You might second-guess yourself. You might be afraid. When that happens, do the next thing.

DAILY SEED: Do you need to "do the next thing" in any situation today?

"I can do all things through Him who strengthens me." (Philippians 4:13)

APRIL 16

CAMEO (by Elisa Morgan)

What if—every day—I did what I could? Just that? Not *aallll* that I could but *what* I could? What if—every day—because I'm convinced that Jesus loves me and I love him—I did what I could?

In Mark 14:1–9 Jesus makes this exact point. Responding to Mary of Bethany as she anointed him with oil, Jesus said in verses 6–9, "She has done a beautiful thing to me . . . *She did what she could.* She poured perfume on my body beforehand to prepare for my burial . . . wherever the gospel is preached throughout the world, what she has done will also be told, in memory of her."

Five words have changed my life: *She did what she could.*

She: God chose a girl!

Did: . . . who acted . . .

What: . . . by investing what she had in a moment that would never be repeated . . .

She: . . . out of relationship with Jesus.

Could: She acted with what she had where she was.

Because a relationship with Jesus results in a response, Mary put feet on her faith. She lived *loved.*

What if I did what I could? What if I acted today? I'm a woman loved by God, shaped by everything he's allowed in my life. What if I acted—unapologetically giving out of who he has made me to be today?

What if we did what we could? You plus me equals we. What could we do together that we couldn't do by ourselves?

Go ahead! Get out there and DWYC![32]

DAILY SEED: Do what you can today.

"If you can't change the world, you can change one person's world." (multiple attributions)

DO YOUR PART

It seems every time I return from India, someone will ask, "How can you stand to go there? There's so much poverty. What can one person do? Don't you get discouraged?"

And I want to scream. Yes, I can stand going there. As a matter of fact, I love going there.

Yes, there's so much poverty, but doing the ostrich thing (putting your head in the sand, pretending it doesn't exist) *isn't* the answer. Yes, I'm just one person, but I'm one person who has told hundreds of others about the amazing things God is doing there. Yes, I get discouraged, but no more than I do here in the United States. I feel ineffective, and there's a lot of bad stuff out there, but I serve a great God who is all-powerful. Sometimes we just have to wait and see what He's doing . . . and offer ourselves as one six-billionth of the answer.

I can do my part. If I try to do more than my part, I get codependent and ineffective and crabby and eventually flame out. If I do less than my part, I under-achieve. It's about finding my sweet spot—the balanced life that includes time with family and friends, time for self-care, rest, and plenty of laughs.

And a lot of people, each living the "sweet spot" life, banding together, equals some pretty healthy world-changing.

DAILY SEED: Are you overachieving, underachieving, or operating in your sweet spot?

"Most people never truly find their sweet spot, the intersection of their greatest strength and their greatest passion. I am troubled by the epidemic of men and women who are good at their job but hate it. This is misery. Conversely, we all know people who love what they are doing but are not very good at it. This is frustration. The most successful among us find their sweet spot and stay there. This is fulfillment." (Ken Coleman, author of *One Question: Life- Changing Answers from Today's Leading Voices*)

APRIL 18

DONATE

✳   My son and his friend Nathan worked at a new, hip restaurant in town.
✳ ✳ They decided to donate every Tuesday night's tips to a charity. (Those new, hip places promote the giving mentality. They *get it.*)

Oseola McCarty washed and ironed for a living for seventy-five years, then donated $150,000 to the University of Southern Mississippi to endow a scholarship fund for African-American students.

A number of years ago, a disabled lady in low-income housing gave me $10 for cleaning her house. I hadn't asked her to pay me; I just cleaned for her because she had asked for help. But interestingly, I was living very close to the edge myself and the $10 helped.

The Apostle Paul says this in Acts 20:35—" In everything I showed you that by working hard in this manner you must help the weak and remember the words of the Lord Jesus, that He Himself said, 'It is more blessed to give than to receive.'"

Givers and donors are blessed. I hope Oseola and the disabled lady felt the blessing of giving.

DAILY SEED: Does someone (or some entity) in your world need your donation?

"Giving is the highest expression of potency. In the very act of giving, I experience my strength, my wealth, my power. This experience of heightened vitality and potency fills me with joy. I experience myself as overflowing, spending, alive, hence as joyous. Giving is more joyous than receiving, not because it is a deprivation, but because in the act of giving lies the expression of my aliveness." (Erich Fromm, author of *The Art of Loving*)

APRIL 19

DONATE AN ORGAN

Barry had been awaiting a kidney for years. Family members were tested—no matches. And then, his sister's *fiancé* was tested as a match—and was indeed a match. The surgery took place a few months ago and Barry, his sister's fiancé, and the kidney are all thriving.

100,000 people are awaiting a lifesaving organ. Others await blood or bone marrow. Consider giving the gift of life.

DAILY SEED: Check out www.bethematch.org, www.organdonor.gov and www.redcrossblood.org.

"The greatest hero I never knew was the organ donor who saved my life." (My2ndheartbeat.wordpress.com)

APRIL 20

DONATE SOMETHING ORDINARY

In 1910, a group of people in the poor state of Mizoram, India started giving a handful of rice to God every time they prepared a meal. They believed that "as long as we have something to eat every day, we have something to give to God every day." The Mizoram Presbyterian Church recently celebrated 100 Years of the Handful of Rice ministry by raising $1.5 million for God's work.

Rice. Ordinary rice.

DAILY SEED: What ordinary thing can you donate today?

"There is one who scatters, and yet increases all the more, and there is one who withholds what is justly due, and yet it results only in want. The generous man will be prosperous, and he who waters will himself be watered." (Proverbs 11:24–25)

APRIL 21

DONATE SOMETHING TANGIBLE

A vehicle, air miles, old stuff. "One man's trash is another man's treasure." We've donated a car and a boat. My son's old car had been around the block . . . a lot. And my husband's old sailboat had deteriorated . . . a lot. Vehicle donation really is painless. The biggest pain is finding that old title.

If your airline allows transferrable mileage credit, this is a way to bless a ministry/nonprofit. As we all know, travel can be costly.

And about that old *stuff,* you know the donation sites. You might consider buying from those sites too. Bud's Warehouse is "Denver's Home Improvement Thrift Store." Granite, doors, windows, etc., at up to 70 percent off retail. *And,* it's a faith-based job training program for people rebuilding their lives after prison or homelessness.

DAILY SEED: What tangible thing can you donate today? Check out organizations like www.vehiclesforcharity.org or your local rescue mission.

"As for the complex ways of living, I love them not, however much I practice them. In as many places as possible, I will get my feet down to the earth." (Henry David Thoreau, *Journal*)

EDUCATE YOURSELF ABOUT GIVING

Mary passed away recently. Talk about a giver! Four days before her accident, she tried to sneak up to the porch of the home of dear friends, but aha! They caught her and invited her in. She "didn't want to bother them . . . just wanted to leave some cookies on their doorstep."

That's *so* Mary. She had the gift of giving.

There are some great teachings on financial giving out there—Generous Giving, Women Doing Well, and the Faith & Money Network to name a few. They don't promote any particular church or charity, just the concept of giving and the joy it brings.

DAILY SEED: Re-visit the concept of joyful giving. Read books on the topic. Be inspired.

Be Mary-esque.

"As for the rich in this present age, charge them not to be haughty, nor to set their hopes on the uncertainty of riches, but on God, who richly provides us with everything to enjoy. They are to do good, to be rich in good works, to be generous and ready to share, thus storing up treasure for themselves as a good foundation for the future, so that they may take hold of that which is truly life." (1 Timothy 6:17–19, ESV)

ELEVATE ALL PEOPLE

Our church is *so* diverse. According to Pastor Robert Gelinas, on a Sunday morning, you might share a row with "a guy in a fine suit or a sweat suit." Or with a lady who arrived by BMW—or RTD (our bus system)."

Our church welcomes the poor and the rich. All ages, all shades, all abilities.

Our church preaches the Gospel, tells the truth, and doesn't show favoritism.

And our church embraces people with special needs. Once a year it holds a prom for people with disabilities (or diff-abilities, as I've heard them called). The families of special needs people often feel isolated, so this year, the prom will launch a whole series of events for them.

I really do believe all feel elevated at our church. It's not a perfect church . . . it's just a weekly glimpse into the heart of Jesus. And I believe it's changing the world. I hope your church is too.

DAILY SEED: Elevate someone today. Make their day!

"Do nothing from selfishness or empty conceit, but with humility of mind regard one another as more important than yourselves." (Philippians 2:3)

APRIL 24

EMPATHIZE

We can put ourselves in another person's shoes. We can imagine their needs . . . or we can ask them what they need. "What do you need?" can be a most lovely question.

I was a single mom. I didn't have much money. To be able to go to the grocery store by myself while somebody took care of my kids was a glorious gift. Some friends could see my weariness. They took care of my kids. They empathized.

I heard of a lady who has a ministry of taking someone to lunch once a week. Most of the recipients really need such a godsend. She empathizes.

Sometimes, empathy is just *being with* someone. It's the vicarious experiencing of another's thoughts or feelings. It takes intention and real care.

DAILY SEED: Think of the people in your sphere. Who among them has a need or two? Empathize.

"The friend who can be silent with us in a moment of despair or confusion . . . who can tolerate not knowing, not curing, not healing and face with us the reality of our powerlessness, that is a friend who cares." (Henri J.M. Nouwen, *Out of Solitude: Three Meditations on the Christian Life*)

EMPOWER NATIONALS AND INDIGENOUS CHURCHES

In the Church of the past, the missions model was to send U.S. missionaries to unreached countries. Now, those countries send missionaries to us. Plus, the model of sending the "haves to the have-nots" is less effective and efficient than supporting indigenous pastors.

The same concept is true of international aid. Is it better to throw money at a need or support the locals in dealing with the need?

Here's my story. I am more effective on this side of the ocean than on the other side. I was willing to go to the other side of the ocean, even excited to go, but let me be frank. When I'm in India, I'm just in the way. I marvel at the skill and passion of the local church workers. It's much better for me to raise funds for *them* to be equipped to do the work, than for me to do the work myself. (And they love me for doing the fundraising.)

DAILY SEED: Some are called to go. Some are called to stay. We can *all* support indigenous work.

"Solutions will not be found while indigenous people are treated as victims for whom someone else must find solutions." (Malcolm Fraser, former prime ministry of Australia)

"The problem with politicians getting to know the issues in indigenous townships is that we tend to suffer from what Aboriginal people call the 'seagull syndrome'—we fly in, scratch around and fly out." (Tony Abbott, former prime ministry of Australia)

APRIL 26

EMPOWER MEN

One day, when my children were small, my daughter and I were celebrating something and gave each other a high five and a "Girls Rule!" And my little son sat there in silence.

I quit using that "girls rule" line. Nobody *rules*.

Our generation has made great gains in elevating women and that's *good!* But we must be careful about collateral damage. In our zest to dismantle stereotypes, have we dismantled the healthy side of manliness (and womanliness)?

Craig Glass runs an organization called Peregrine Ministries and writes a blog called *Men Matter.* He cites a quote from a Kenyan who focuses on rites of passage work in his country: "The boys in the village must be initiated into healthy manhood, or they will burn down the village just to feel the heat." Craig says, "That still gives me chills; *so* true in our nation (also)."

Maybe it's coincidence, but I seem to know a lot of young men who are having a hard time finding their way, their vitality, their purpose . . . the heat. My prayer is that God will raise them up in an unprecedented way. I can't even imagine the positive power once that heat is refocused from self-destruction to leadership.

I look forward to the day when the language of empowerment is no longer needed, when the content of one's character is the measuring stick (per Martin Luther King). But in the meantime, we have a responsibility to elevate each other . . . blacks, whites, old, young, women, men.

DAILY SEED: Do you know a young man who could use encouragement?

"There is neither Jew nor Greek, there is neither slave nor free man, there is neither male nor female; for you are all one in Christ Jesus." (Galatians 3:28)

EMPOWER WOMEN

When I was in my mid-teens, three ladies without makeup (gasp!), wearing camo and undainty boots, came to our school and gave a passionate talk. We were alarmed, but fascinated. They were *women's libbers!* And it took that extreme to start turning the ship. Yet horrendous exploitation of women in the world still exists, with a vengeance.

Sheryl WuDunn and Nicholas Kristof in their book, *Half the Sky*, highlight the ongoing atrocities, but also illuminate the *power* of women. They say that "unleashing women's potential is the key to economic progress and is also the best strategy for fighting poverty."

Let's emphasize that. *Unleashing women's potential is the key to economic progress and is also the best strategy for fighting poverty.*

I look forward to the day when all people, regardless of gender, are treated well—when the men are treated with respect and the women are treasured, and the men are treasured and the women are treated with respect.

DAILY SEED: Do you know a young woman who could use encouragement? "Women hold up half the sky." (Chinese proverb)

ENDURE

"Consider it all joy, my brethren, when you encounter various trials, knowing that the testing of your faith produces endurance. And let endurance have its perfect result, so that you may be perfect and complete, lacking in nothing" (James 1:2–4).

Perfect and complete, lacking in nothing? All from endurance? *"But the one who endures to the end, he will be saved. This gospel of the kingdom shall be preached in the whole world as a testimony to all the nations, and then the end will come"* (Matthew 24:13–14).

So why is endurance the key to perfection and completion and saving anyway? Why is the word not "victory" or "success?" Let victory have its perfect result so we'll be perfect and complete. Victory sounds like a lot more fun than endurance. But no, the word is endurance.

So as we go about planting those seeds of change, we need to *endure*. Christ have mercy on us and give us strength.

DAILY SEED: Hang on. Hold out. Sustain without yielding. Bear with patience.

"Every calamity is to be overcome by endurance." (Virgil)

APRIL 29

ENVISION THE LIFE YOU WANT TO LIVE

Charles Handy, social scientist and management expert, came up with the idea of a portfolio life while trying to evolve a lifestyle for himself. He resigned a full-time professorship and allocated the days of his year like this: one hundred days a year for making money, one hundred days for writing, one hundred days for spending time with his wife, and fifty days for what he considered to be good works.[33]

Like Handy's fifty days for good works, we can build "seed-planting" into our portfolio life.

DAILY SEED: Design the life you want to live.

"Carpe diem quam minimum credula postero" (Horace) can be translated as, "Seize the day, put very little trust in tomorrow/the future." In other words, do all you can today to make your future better.

ERADICATE ABHORRENT PRACTICES

Foot-binding was dealt a serious blow from the pressure of world awareness, but the following practices still exist. Female genital mutilation. Bride-burnings. Acid attacks. Honor killings. Sex slavery. Child marriages. Torture.

How can we speak up regarding practices in countries/cultures other than our own? We can arm ourselves with universal bedrock, both from the Bible and from the UN Declaration of Human Rights.

DAILY SEED: What practice breaks your heart the most? Weigh in on it. Visit www.un.org or other humanitarian websites for how-tos.

"When you come into the land that the Lord your God is giving you, you must not learn to imitate the abhorrent practices of those nations. No one shall be found among you who makes a son or daughter pass through fire. . . . " (Deuteronomy 18:9–10, NRSV)

MAY

ESTEEM OTHERS AS HIGHER THAN YOURSELF

Jesus modeled this for us, *"who, although He existed in the form of God, did not regard equality with God a thing to be grasped, but emptied Himself,* **taking the form of a bond-servant,** *and being made in the likeness of men. Being found in appearance as a man, He humbled Himself by becoming obedient to the point of death, even death on a cross"* (Philippians 2:6–8).

The priest in "Les Miserables" esteemed Jean Valjean as higher than himself. So do the children in India who, when given a cookie, break it in half, eat half, and take the other half home to their siblings.

If the whole world practiced this esteeming, that would pretty much take care of our social ills.

DAILY SEED: Who can you esteem more highly than yourself today?

"Humility does not mean you think less of yourself. It means you think of yourself less." (Ken Blanchard, author of *The One Minute Manager*)

CAMEO (by Barb Roberts[34])

Do I have compassion—really? Giving thought to the subject of compassion, I ask myself, "Am I a compassionate person? Are you?" Recognizing that my compassion has limits, yet desirous of having the kind of compassion that includes kindness, mercy, and forgiveness, I often fall short of extending that compassion to *all* around me. There are many in my life for whom showing compassion is easy—others not so much! They are those "irregular people" in my life—difficult to care for; difficult to show compassion to.

If we accept the premise that we ALL have a need for compassion, how might that need be met? As you look in the mirror, would you describe the person looking back as a compassionate person? Even if the answer is yes, what might the limits of that compassion be? There are certain people in our lives or in the news who elicit compassion from us: the special needs child who runs his hardest and crosses the finish line with a smile on his face; the new mommy whose husband has just been deployed; the baby who has been abused; the friend who recently lost his job.

But—what about other examples: the husband who decides to leave his wife; the classroom bully; the "talker" in a meeting who has all the answers; the passive-aggressive person. Where is our compassion for these people?

Listen to this verse from Scripture: "Because of the Lord's great love we are not consumed, for His compassions never fail . . . " His compassion does not have limits—it is compassion beyond measure! Understanding that not only do we all *need* compassion, but that God's compassion never fails, perhaps our assignment from God is more about sharing His compassion with others; letting them know of His love for them.

God uses theory and practice, but God uses you and God uses me. It is having a view from another's eyes, seeing others as God does. I can do nothing on my own without Him; however, "I can do *all* things through Him who strengthens me."

DAILY SEED: Is there an "irregular person" in your life who needs God's compassion—through you?

"What is the [compassion] application for us? Perhaps it involves being in someone's pain with them and being all there." (Barb Roberts)

MAY 3

EXERCISE

My word for the year is "exercise." Sure, it means physical exercise because I plan to run a half marathon in a few weeks. But it means more than that.

When I'm cranky toward someone, I can exercise my mercy muscles. When I'm anxious, I can exercise my prayer muscles. When I'm frustrated at the state of the world, I can exercise my seed-planting muscles.

I don't know if practice makes *perfect*, but without practice, we can't accomplish much. We can steadily repeat those efforts that are focused on the change we wish to see in the world.

We can practice them daily, pushing the envelope a little more each day.

I can run farther now than I could a few weeks ago. The only variable has been exercise.

We can make a difference in the world if we exercise those make-a-difference muscles daily.

DAILY SEED: What, in your life, needs a daily exercise campaign? What change do you wish to see in a few weeks? A skinnier you? A more compassionate you? A better world?

"Therefore, since we have so great a cloud of witnesses surrounding us, let us also lay aside every encumbrance and the sin which so easily entangles us, and let us run with endurance the race that is set before us." (Hebrews 12:1)

MAY 4

FAST

"What's for dinner? For one in eight, it's probably nothing." World Vision has a program in which people can collectively do a 30-hour fast (famine) to raise funds for hunger relief.[35]

"Life isn't fair—and neither is this." At an Oxfam America Hunger Banquet*, the place where you sit and the meal you eat are determined by the luck of the draw—just as in real life some of us are born into relative prosperity and others into poverty.[36] Oxfam's hunger banquet highlights food disparities and can be used to raise awareness (and righteous anger). Some eat a lavish meal while their peers at the next table eat a bit of rice and water.

These activities forever change the way you view hunger. Anger, frustration, jealousy, and a growling stomach speak louder than words.

DAILY SEED: Have you ever fasted for spiritual reasons, discipline, or to better understand world hunger? If your health permits, try a 24-hour fast.

"I am convinced that when God's people fast with a proper Biblical motive with a broken, repentant, and contrite spirit, God will hear from heaven and heal our lives, our world." (Dr. Bill Bright, founder of Campus Crusade for Christ [Cru])

MAY 5

FEEL

Emotion comes more easily for some than it does for others. Some think their way to decisions; others feel their way. I cry during Olympics commercials, but I power my way through tough decisions without shedding a tear. We're all somewhere on the spectrum.

That being said, my defining moment about trying to do something to make a difference came decades ago. I *felt* agony when reading about child soldiers in Africa—kidnapped, drugged, forced to watch while their families were killed (or forced to kill them themselves), and if they resisted, their hands or feet were chopped off.

Feel. And then ask God for your next step . . . while you still have a hand or a foot. Some don't. They are begging for our help.

DAILY SEED: Let yourself feel someone's pain (or joy) today.

"The best and most beautiful things in the world cannot be seen or even touched. They must be felt with the heart." (Helen Keller, blind and deaf educator)

MAY 6

FIGHT POVERTY

* Bruce Wydick wrote an article in *Christianity Today* (February 17, * * 2012) called "Cost-Effective Compassion: The 10 Most Popular Strategies for Helping the Poor." Here are those strategies.

1. Get clean water to rural villages.
2. Fund de-worming treatments for children.
3. Provide mosquito nets.
4. Sponsor a child.
5. Give wood-burning stoves.
6. Give a microfinance loan.
7. Fund reparative surgeries.
8. Donate a farm animal.
9. Drink fair-trade coffee.
10. Give a kid a laptop.

DAILY SEED: Let us fight poverty in the best ways possible.

"Let us be the ones who say we do not accept that a child dies every three seconds simply because he does not have the drugs you and I have. Let us be the ones to say we are not satisfied that your place of birth determines your right to life. Let us be outraged, let us be loud, let us be bold." (Brad Pitt, actor/producer)

MAY 7

GET CLEAN WATER TO RURAL VILLAGES— STRATEGY #1

✳
✳ ✳ I was in Mexico. The village's water was delivered by a truck once a week. It was poured into a big barrel—a big, *open* barrel. No filters. No cover. No protection.

Fact: 748 million people in the world do not have access to safe water.[37] But lest we get bogged down by statistics, think of it this way. What if you knew of just *748* people who didn't have clean water, their children dying of diarrhea? What if they lived nearby?

You'd be outraged and so would I. It seems like a fixable problem. The water organizations have great hope, but they need our help. This is one of the main ways we can help change our world for the better.

Have you ever had giardia after traveling abroad? Yeah, me too. Let's let our stomachaches remind us to support clean water worldwide—with our prayers, advocacy, and money.

DAILY SEED: Pray for permanent water coverage for everyone, forever.[38]

"Water and sanitation problems have reached [the] boiling point: children are dying unnecessarily at the rate of twenty jumbo jets crashing every single day." (Ravi Narayanan, Chair of the Asia-Pacific Water Forum Governing Council)

MAY 8

FUND DE-WORMING TREATMENTS FOR CHILDREN— STRATEGY #2

✳
✳ ✳ Worms can cause blindness, elephantiasis, kidney damage, death, and so many other awful things that are hard to read about. Over 1.5 billion people are infected, according to the World Health Organization. That

means about a fourth of the world's people are in severe discomfort or are dying *right now*, from worms alone.

And they are amazingly easy to treat . . . in some cases, through one annual pill. The causes, on the other hand, are a bit more complex, but basically boil down to hygiene, sanitation, and clean water.

DAILY SEED: Pray for elimination of the most prevalent neglected diseases among the world's poorest and most vulnerable people by 2020.[39]

"Together we can see the end." (www.end.org)

MAY 9

PROVIDE MOSQUITO NETS—STRATEGY #3

* ** "I suspect that while we plan to fight malaria, the mosquitoes are also planning different tactics to attack, because they find us a delicacy!" This was written by Tumusiime K. Deo of Kampala, Uganda, who suffered from malaria (and the side effects of malaria meds) several times.[40]

I've never had malaria but I've heard a recurring theme about it—*don't get it*. It kills millions. Mosquito nets save lives.

DAILY SEED: Consider providing mosquito nets and pray for global eradication of malaria.

"It's estimated that Africa loses about 13 billion dollars a year to the disease [malaria]. Five dollars can save a life." (Jacqueline Novogratz, founder of global venture capital fund, Acumen)

SPONSOR A CHILD—STRATEGY #4

Raj is from a Dalit background in India. He was relegated to a life of menial, backbreaking, and filthy work. He had no choice. It's been that way for thousands of years. However, he received a sponsor through an agency that provided food and an education.

One day, Raj tried to befriend a boy of another caste. As a result, he was tied to a pole and beaten. He filed a complaint with the government. This could have cost him his life, but people from his village petitioned the government office. He was then freed and eventually became a Project Manager for the same sponsorship agency. Today he works for one of the leading Christian ministries in India as a field director for children.

Raj said, "I never met my sponsor, but he changed my life. In fact, he touched my whole village (500 families). I wish I could tell him thank-you."[41]

According to the *Christianity Today* article, child sponsorship is *the* most cost-effective long-term development intervention for fighting poverty.

DAILY SEED: Do you sponsor a child? If so, write him/her a letter today. If not, will you consider it? Child sponsorship websites abound.

"Because of Compassion International [child sponsorship agency], I was freed from the chains of poverty." (Beguen Theus, a Compassion alumni, who was elected to the Haitian parliament in 2011)[42]

GIVE WOODBURNING STOVES— STRAGEGY #5

In India, the air is thick with smoke from dung fires. Dung fires. Women and children make dung patties with their bare hands. Respiratory problems and disease are rampant. Wood-burning stoves are obviously better, with caveats. Efficient ones with chimneys need to be used. And wood burning creates deforestation and air pollution.

So what's the answer? People need fuel for heating and cooking. Cost and availability of biomass fuels are factors. A quarter of humanity lives without electricity because coal, oil, wind, nuclear, and renewable energy sources are out of reach for so many.

Just because a strategy is *popular* among givers doesn't necessarily make it effective. Sometimes we just have to go with the best option available, and for the folks in India, a wood-burning stove might trump a dung fire. But "necessity is the mother of invention" and effective energy for the masses is a necessity.

Oh, and then there's the climate change factor . . .

DAILY SEED: Answers, anyone?

"I'd put my money on the sun and solar energy. What a source of power! I hope we don't have to wait 'til oil and coal run out before we tackle that." (Thomas Edison, 1847–1931)

MAY 12

GIVE A MICRO-FINANCE LOAN— STRATEGY #6

Almost half the world lives on less than $2.50 a day. The women suffer horribly. Saving enough to start a small business is almost impossible so people live in poverty . . . for generations.

However, there are life-changing answers. One of them is to provide a micro-finance loan. An infusion of funds from the outside makes the leap from poverty possible. And we're talking a *loan*, not a grant. It gets paid back. That's the beauty.

A $50 micro-loan enables a woman to buy a flock of chickens. A $300 micro-loan trains a woman to sew and in some cases, buy a sewing machine. A $600 micro-loan helps install sewer lines in a home.

DAILY SEED: Have you ever provided a micro-loan? It doesn't take a lot of money to make a big difference. With Kiva, it's $25.[43]

"To me, the poor are like bonsai trees. When you plant the best seed of the tallest tree in a six-inch deep flower pot, you get a perfect replica of the tallest tree, but it is only inches tall. There is nothing wrong with the seed you planted; only the soil-base you provided was inadequate. Poor people are bonsai people. There is nothing wrong with their seeds. Only society never gave them a base to grow on." (Muhammad Yunus, *Creating a World Without Poverty: Social Business and the Future of Capitalism*)[44]

MAY 13

FUND REPARATIVE SURGERIES— STRATEGY #7

Facial deformity repair. Pediatric cardiac repair. Cleft palates. Cataracts. The list is long. The surgeries are generally successful and often easy.

Ravonna started a program in the Democratic Republic of Congo called the Ida Lee Project.[45] In addition to creating a pattern for reusable "bloomers" for women during their menstrual cycles, the clinic will provide fistula repair. Women suffering urogenital fistula due to rape during the civil war are disowned by their husbands.

If I had to narrow down my seed-planting options to the top ten, this one would make the list.

Can you imagine the joy of a repaired life?

DAILY SEED: Consider supporting reparative surgery organizations or physicians who perform the operations (e.g., Doctors Without Borders).

"As He passed by, He saw a man blind from birth. And His disciples asked Him, 'Rabbi, who sinned, this man or his parents, that he would be born blind?' Jesus answered, 'It was neither that this man sinned, nor his parents; but it was so that the works of God might be displayed in him. We must work the works of Him

who sent Me as long as it is day; night is coming when no one can work. While I am in the world, I am the Light of the world.' When He had said this, He spat on the ground, and made clay of the spittle, and applied the clay to his eyes, and said to him, 'Go, wash in the pool of Siloam' (which is translated, Sent). So he went away and washed, and came back seeing." (John 9:1–7)

MAY 14

DONATE A FARM ANIMAL— STRATEGY #8

Dan West was a farmer from the American Midwest, a member of the Church of the Brethren and an aid worker. His mission was to provide relief for Spanish Civil War refugees, but he discovered the ration of a daily cup of milk was not enough. And then he had a thought: What if they had not a cup, but a cow?

To make a long story short, Dan West founded Heifer International, which has now served over twenty million families. Impoverished families are provided with a farm animal and training. The core of the model is called Passing on the Gift. This means families share the training they receive, and pass on the first female offspring of their livestock to another family. This allows a once-impoverished family to become donors and full participants in improving their communities.[46]

DAILY SEED: Interested in the gift that keeps on giving? Check out Heifer International or other farm animal donation programs.

"Do what you can, with what you have, where you are." (Theodore Roosevelt, *Autobiography*)

MAY 15

DRINK FAIR-TRADE COFFEE— STRATEGY #9

✳
✳ ✳ According to the article, fair-trade coffee isn't a scam but has little real impact, like *zero* average impact on coffee grower incomes in a fair-trade network. This is due to flawed program design: growers must pay for certifications and bear the cost of compliance with fair-trade standards.

This is unfortunate because Americans alone drink four hundred million cups of coffee per day.[47]

And I do my part . . .

I think impact is an important consideration as we think of our pocketful of seeds. I'd rather focus my time, efforts, and money on the *most* effective ways to make a difference in the world. Wouldn't you? Yet the following is also a factor. "Fair trade" is defined as an organized social movement whose stated goal is to help producers in developing countries achieve better trading conditions and to promote sustainability. That *is* important, selfless, and teeming with possibility. Like all important endeavors, it might take time to work the kinks out.

DAILY SEED: As you sip your wake-up coffee, consider your consumption. It's a big part of your health and the health of the world economy. Consume well.

"It hit me very early on that something was terribly wrong, that I would see silos full of food and supermarkets full of food, and kids starving. . . . In Fair Trade, we see ourselves as this infinitesimal part of the world economy. But somebody's got to come up with an alternative model that says children eating is No. 1." (Medea Benjamin, co-founder, Global Exchange, and former U.N. nutritionist)

GIVE A KID A LAPTOP— STRATEGY #10

✳ ✳ ✳ For the cost of one laptop (also according to the article), you could pro-vide clean water to twenty people or de-worm a school of four hundred children for an entire year. Elsewhere, however, you'll hear glowing things about giving a child a laptop. So which is it? Maybe Richard Rohr is on to something, that "everything belongs." In other words, good works are good works, and we can get so hung up on being perfect that we do nothing. Notice that the all of these entries made it to the article's Top Ten list.

Do you want to be effective and efficient? I do too, but God seems to work on us over the course of a lifetime. If we ask, God *will* reveal our place in His plan. Some of us will give kids a laptop, others will give in different ways. The common denominator? That little word "give."

DAILY SEED: How does God want you to give today?

"Each one must do just as he has purposed in his heart, not grudgingly or under compulsion, for God loves a cheerful giver." (2 Corinthians 9:7)

FORGIVE PEOPLE

✳ ✳ ✳ So what does forgiving others have to do with planting seeds of change into the soil of the world? Well, I somehow think being effectively seedy is tied to being unstuck. Forgiveness means putting down that 10,000-pound gorilla you've been carrying around, which frees up a lot of time and energy to get on with other things. And God says that if his people who are called by his name humble themselves and pray and seek his face and turn from their wicked ways, then he will hear from heaven, will forgive their sin and will *heal their land* (see 2 Chronicles 7:14).

In other words, I think forgiveness of others *and ourselves* is a key to life. It *must* be included in learning true seedy-ness.

Frank forgave the drunk driver who killed his wife and children. I can't fathom the depth of that forgiveness, but I wouldn't wish the 10,000-pound gorilla of unforgiveness on Frank (or anyone). Frank was a world-changer before the accident and Frank is even more of a world-changer now, probably in large part because he was able to forgive.

DAILY SEED: Let us choose to forgive someone today.

"Forgiveness is not about forgetting. It is about letting go of another person's throat. You may have to declare your forgiveness a hundred times the first day and the second day, but the third day will be less and each day after, until one day you will realize that you have forgiven completely. And then one day you will pray for his wholeness." (William Paul Young, *The Shack: Where Tragedy Confronts Eternity*

MAY 18

FORM A HABIT

It takes twenty-one days to change a habit. Think "bad" habits, something to overcome, like nail-biting or overeating. New patterns solidify at about the three-week mark. The same is true of "good" habits.

If we want to change the world, we can make a concerted effort to do so for twenty-one consecutive days. But warning: stuff like this is habit-forming.

DAILY SEED: What new habit would you like to work on for the next twenty-one days?

"Watch your thoughts for they become words. Watch your words for they become actions. Watch your actions for they become habits. Watch your habits for they become your character. And watch your character for it becomes your destiny." (Margaret Thatcher)

MAY 19

FOSTER OR ADOPT A CHILD

Project 1:27 was started out of the conviction that no child should be without a forever family. James 1:27 calls Christians to "look after orphans in their distress." Project 1.27 is about helping Christian parents foster and adopt children in Colorado's foster care system.

In December 2004 there were 875 children legally available for adoption in the Colorado foster care system. Project 1:27 knew there were over 3,000 churches in Colorado with members called to care for children. Their mission— to assist in connecting the children waiting for a forever family with church members wanting to foster and adopt.

As of today, 582 children have been placed into foster families through Project 1:27 and 266 have been adopted. Yet in the United States today, there are almost 400,000 children in the foster care system with 100,000 waiting to be adopted.

My son, who is adopted, spoke to a group of college students when he was about twelve. He said, "I could have been aborted but my birth parents chose life for me, and here I am!"

Hard to argue with that.

DAILY SEED: Say a prayer for children in your community who need their forever family. Some need to return to their original families. Others need to be fostered/adopted. If this stirs your heart, look into it.

"Because now I know what I have been waiting for. I know exactly why the other processes didn't work. I know I was supposed to wait for this little girl." (Nia Vardalos, *Instant Mom*)

MAY 20

FUND SOCIAL JUSTICE

The Dalit Freedom Network is built on four pillars—education, healthcare, economic development, and social justice. All are part of a larger church planting movement. Some criticize the weaving of social justice with evangelism/church planting. *I can't imagine them as separate.*

The influence of Jesus flows through the corridors of political offices worldwide. Places of power. Places that impact generations. Places that can promote justice Without God's touch, those same places might promote oppression.

Institutional justice is hard to take on alone, but we can unite with others and create justice movements. One vital way is to *fund* justice. I believe one of the strongest ways we can make a difference in the world is to support social justice in the name of Jesus.

The Hebrew word for justice is *mishpat.* It means to treat people equitably. It's used over two hundred times in the Old Testament. Justice is important to God.

DAILY SEED: Look for a way to support a justice movement.

"How blessed are those who keep justice, who practice righteousness at all times!" (Psalm 106:3)

MAY 21

GARDEN (LITERALLY)

We can plant seeds, literally. We can prepare the soil, till the soil, sow the seeds, water, fertilize, weed, eradicate pests/diseases, thin the sprouts, weed some more . . . and more . . . and a few weeks later, harvest. We can enjoy the fruit of our labor.

The Book of Ruth speaks of gleaning. Likewise, we can give away a percentage of our garden's yield—to local food banks, homeless shelters, etc.

DAILY SEED: Plant something today if you can, even if it's a bean in a paper cup. Watch it grow. Learn from it.

"The entire fruit is already present in the seed." (Tertullian)

"Anyone can count the seeds in an apple, but only God can count the number of apples in a seed." (Robert H. Schuller, pastor and author)

MAY 22

GARDEN (FIGURATIVELY)

Being seedy, planting seeds of positive change into the soil of the world, can take many forms. During some seasons of life, we wait . . . like a newly-planted seed. During other seasons, we poke our heads out from our own soil . . . and look around at the world. And then, as we see need, as we choose to respond, and as a result of staying connected to the Vine (see John 15) . . . *we bear fruit.*

God has a lot to say about seeds and the fruitful (seedy) life. "Seed" scriptures have been scattered throughout this book. Here are some other examples:

"For as the soil makes the sprout come up and a garden causes seeds to grow, so the Sovereign Lord will make righteousness and praise spring up before all nations" (Isaiah 61:11, NIV).

"Very truly I tell you, unless a kernel of wheat falls to the ground and dies, it remains only a single seed. But if it dies, it produces many seeds" (John 12:24, NIV).

"The promises were spoken to Abraham and to his seed. Scripture does not say 'and to seeds,' meaning many people, but 'and to your seed,' meaning one person, who is Christ" (Galatians 3:16, NIV).

"If you belong to Christ, then you are Abraham's seed, and heirs according to the promise" (Galatians 3:29, NIV).

"No one who is born of God will continue to sin, because God's seed remains in them; they cannot go on sinning, because they have been born of God" (1 John 3:9, NIV).

As you know, I take my inspiration for planting seeds of positive change from Jesus. His words and example were so radically world-changing that they got him killed. Death, however, wasn't the end of the story. He rose again and was at first mistaken for the gardener (see John 20). Isn't that interesting? The gardener. He truly was, and is, the master seed-planter.

DAILY SEED: To be truly seedy, we need God. God, the Life-Giver.

"For you have been born again, not of perishable seed, but of imperishable, through the living and enduring word of God." (1 Peter 1:23, NIV)

MAY 23

GARDEN (PREPARE THE SOIL)

My husband prepares the soil of our garden by composting and fertilizing. He even has a manure spreader! He clears out the weeds and thorns and rocks. He sends a soil sample to our local agri college to make sure the chemical proportions are correct. Why all this work? Well, it's all about the fruit (or vegetables in this case).

I'm reminded of the parable of the sower and seed in Matthew 13 when I think about soil. The seed is God's word. The ground is us. We may be shallow or rocky or thorny . . . or well-prepared to receive the seed. Maybe it behooves us to think about the soil of the world. Some places are so impoverished and violent and rocky and thorny, the people barely survive. Millions don't survive. Maybe we would do well to think about *that* soil.

My heart breaks for people in failed states like Somalia who commit violence. Their children are starving. Violence is perpetrated all around them. They are trying to survive. What can we do to enhance the soil of Somalia, symbolically-speaking?

And how can we prepare the soil of the world closer to home? Create a more loving, welcoming atmosphere in our homes and churches maybe? It *is* hard to resist love.

It will take a lot of work, but enhancing the soil is one of the keys to good fruit. And it's all about the fruit.

DAILY SEED: Think figuratively for a moment. How can you prepare the soil of your world to better receive the seeds God wants to sow?

"And the one on whom seed was sown on the good ground, this is the man who hears the word and understands it; who indeed bears fruit, and brings forth, some a hundredfold, some sixty, and some thirty." (Matthew 13:23)

MAY 24

GARDEN (PROTECT THE SPACE)

We live in an area full of rabbits and other critters. They *love* fruit and vegetables, so we built a fence around our garden. It has tightly-spaced wire down low to keep the rabbits out and barbed wire up high to keep the deer out. Without those boundaries, the garden wouldn't survive.

But a gate is needed too. We gardeners need access to the garden. And once the vegetables are ready, they must be ushered from the garden to the kitchen.

We also need "life" boundaries with appropriate gates. We need to protect the seeds we sow in people's lives. We need to protect our children and the vulnerable in our midst. We need to know our enemies and not let them in. Otherwise, the seeds we sow won't survive.

We need to know "when to say *yes* and how to say *no*, to take control of our lives" in the words of Dr. Henry Cloud, author of *Boundaries*. We can get overwhelmed with need, but as Charles E. Hummel has said, "the need itself is not the call." Appropriate boundaries teach us when to say yes and when to say no.

DAILY SEED: What boundaries are needed to protect your space?

"'No' is a complete sentence." (Anne Lamott, writer and political activist)

MAY 25

GARDEN (SOW THE SEEDS)

✳ A couple of Ws come into play with seed-sowing. What and when.
✳ ✳ What seeds will be sown? Beets, peppers, corn, squash? When will they be sown? In Colorado, the rule is "after Mother's Day."

Figuratively, what seeds of change do you wish to sow? Working with children in China or adults with Alzheimer's or ??? And when will those seeds of change be sown? Timing can be a tricky thing. You know what they say about tomorrow—it never comes.

DAILY SEED: Decide what seeds to sow and when.

"When you sow, you do not plant the body that will be, but just a seed, perhaps of wheat or of something else. But God gives it a body as he has determined, and to each kind of seed he gives its own body." (1 Corinthians 15:37–38, NIV)

MAY 26

GARDEN (TEND TO THE SEEDLINGS)

✳ So the seeds are sown and lo and behold, a few days later, they sprout!
✳ ✳ Those little dedicated seedlings push through. Along with weeds.

So we weed and feed and water and cover (if there's a frost) and water some more and weed some more and . . . it's never ending.

The same is true of planting positive seeds of change into the soil of the world. Imagine—sprouts! Young, vulnerable change that must be nurtured and protected.

Then, after weeks and weeks, the seedlings grow into mature plants. And that's the *promise* of this book, that the probable outcome of seed-planting is fruit. Things can happen along the way, like hailstorms or grasshoppers, but we must plant anyway, because one thing is certain—no seedlings will emerge if they are never sown.

DAILY SEED: Let us tend to the seedlings of change we have planted.

"I say, if your knees aren't green by the end of the day, you ought to seriously re-examine your life." (Bill Watterson, *Calvin & Hobbes*)

"Gardening requires lots of water — most of it in the form of perspiration." (Lou Erickson)

". . . Slave to a springtime passion for the earth./ How Love burns through the Putting in the Seed/ On through the watching for that early birth/ When, just as the soil tarnishes with weed,/ The sturdy seedling with arched body comes/ Shouldering its way and shedding the earth crumbs." (Robert Frost, "Putting in the Seed," 1920)

MAY 27

GARDEN (HARVEST THE CROP)

Harvest time arrives. It took a lot of blood, sweat, and tears working on the garden, but oh, those tomatoes! There's *nothing* like a homegrown tomato.

Here's what Jesus said about the harvest.

"Do you not say, 'There are yet four months, and then comes the harvest'? Behold, I say to you, lift up your eyes and look on the fields, that they are white for harvest. Already he who reaps is receiving wages and is gathering fruit for life eternal; so that he who sows and he who reaps may rejoice together" (John 4:35–36).

He was referring to some people sowing into the lives of others, and others reaping, meaning we share the load. We might reap what was sown many years ago, but it really doesn't matter who does what, as long as each of us does our part—to prepare the soil, to protect the space, to sow the seeds, to tend to the seedlings, or to harvest.

DAILY SEED: The seed you plant today may be harvested many years from now. You may not see the end result, but plant anyway.

"Don't judge each day by the harvest you reap, but by the seeds that you plant." (attributed to Robert Louis Stevenson)

MAY 28

GARDEN (PRUNE THE PERENNIALS)

I'm glad I'm not a rose bush, because they have to take a whacking every fall. But wait, we humans have to take a whacking too. Yet the end justifies the means.

Jesus said in John 15:2, "Every branch in Me that does not bear fruit, He takes away; and every branch that bears fruit, He prunes it so that it may bear more fruit."

DAILY SEED: Regard pruning and discipline for what it is, a means to a better end.

"My son, do not reject the discipline of the Lord or loathe His reproof, for whom the Lord loves He reproves, Even as a father corrects the son in whom he delights." (Proverbs 3:11–12)

MAY 29

GARDEN (MARVEL AT THE MIRACLE)

Seeds are miraculous, even the tiniest of them. Recall what Jesus said about tiny mustard seeds in Matthew 17:20, that *"if you have faith the size of a mustard seed, you will say to this mountain, 'Move from here to there,' and it will move; and nothing will be impossible to you."*

So we can plant a tiny seed. The miracle is that even the tiniest of actions can have monumental impact, because God brings the increase anyway.

DAILY SEED: Think of some seeds of change that you have planted. Marvel at the miracle.

"Gratitude for the seemingly insignificant—a seed—this plants the giant miracle." (Ann Voskamp, *One Thousand Gifts: A Dare to Live Fully Right Where You Are*)

MAY 30

GET ANGRY

* I remember the first time it dawned on me that the Bible says to *be* angry
* * (and yet do not sin). (See Ephesians 4:26a.) Be angry! Anger's not the culprit; wrong responses to anger are the problem. We *should* be angry over slavery, pornography, those in Africa who force child soldiers to kill their parents.

But the mature know that vengeance doesn't heal. Even vengeance toward ourselves doesn't heal us internally. Love heals.

Where would black Americans be apart from the anger of Lincoln, Harriett Tubman, Rosa Parks and Martin Luther King? We *must* be angry—then pursue correct solutions and peace.

DAILY SEED: What makes you fighting mad? *Be* angry (but don't sin). Ask YBH (Yes, But How?). *"Do not let the sun go down on your anger"* (Ephesians 4:26b).

"Love implies anger. The man who is angry at nothing cares about nothing." (Edward Abbey, author and environmental advocate)

MAY 31

_____

GET DIRTY

Did you ever make mud pies as a kid? There's something so *satisfying* about getting dirty. And sometimes we can get muddy and dirty for a cause. We can roll up the sleeves, paint, plant flowers, build a Habitat house, work on a neighborhood makeover, rent a plot in a community garden, help with an equine therapy center. There are a lot of muddy, manure-y, sweaty options as we plant seeds of change into the soil of the world.

Extreme Community Makeover[48] and Habitat for Humanity[49] help create/improve homes and beautify neighborhoods. (Just make sure you're working *with* the neighborhood instead of *for* the neighborhood.)

DAILY SEED: Are there any tasks that require getting dirty, or tasks nobody else wants to do, that you might do as a love offering?

"Sometimes you just have to get a little bit muddy." (Farm Girl Faithism #52, by blogger Sara at https://hewittfarmsinc.wordpress.com, the ramblings of a young woman on faith, farming, and real life in rural Minnesota)

JUNE

GET INVOLVED IN CHURCH WORK

✳ ✳ ✳ I think the concept of *church* is genius. Church is (in part) a "natural affinity group or community development organization"—secular terminology for what the Church already does.

Church provides ways to get involved in the world. Mission teams are often on the cutting edge. Prayer teams bring two or more people together around important topics, and we know what God says about gatherings of two or more people (Matthew 18:20).

And Church does so much more. When we are too weary to give, Church teaches us to crawl into the arms of Jesus and rest. Work. Rest. Church. It's all good.

DAILY SEED: Are you involved in a great church? If so, dig in. If not, dig in to help make it so, or search for another—it's worth it. Church is *way* too important to just coast.

"Let us hold fast the confession of our hope without wavering, for He who promised is faithful; and let us consider how to stimulate one another to love and good deeds, not forsaking our own assembling together." (Hebrews 10:23–25a)

GET PUBLICITY FOR YOUR CAUSE

✳ ✳ ✳ The best time to get publicity for your cause is when the cause "happens" to be newsworthy. Be poised for action. Know who to contact. Make it a priority to be ahead of the curve.

Examples:

If your cause is fighting sex slavery, expose the sex trade during the Super Bowl.

If your cause has to do with a certain country, get press if there is a big event (or disaster) there.

If your cause is highlighted in a documentary, get press just before or after the Academy Awards.

DAILY SEED: Get to know media people. They can open doors for you.

"Without publicity there can be no public spirit, and without public spirit every nation must decay." (Benjamin Disraeli, British politician and writer)

JUNE 3

GET THE ATTENTION OF YOUR ELECTED OFFICIALS

Get on your congressmen's email lists. Sign up on their websites. Periodic emails will arrive from their offices. In other words, you don't have to seek them out. They come to you, electronically.

On our senators' websites, there are lists of the top issues, where they stand, and what they are working on. And you can weigh in on issues that are important to you. Every contact counts, even if it's just a few words. They represent us. How can they know how to vote if they don't know what we want?

In contacting your legislator, "be as specific as possible. Keep it brief. Identify your subject clearly, give the name and bill number of the legislation you are concerned about. Be reasonable; don't ask for the impossible or engage in threats. Ask that your legislators state their positions on the issue; you are entitled to know."[50]

DAILY SEED: Get on your congressional and senatorial email lists today.[51]

"There are many wonderful things that will never be done if you don't do them." (Charles D. Gill, Senior VP of United Technologies Corp.)

GET TO KNOW SOMEONE OF A DIFFERENT RACE OR SOCIO-ECONOMIC LEVEL

* This is one of the most important ideas in this book.
* * Knowing a person from China changes the way you filter news about China.

Knowing a person in subsidized housing changes the way you view poverty.

Knowing a person of another race changes your stereotypes.

Suddenly it's not about "those people," it's about Kumar or Mrs. Mitchell or Chin.

DAILY SEED: Do you have friends who are different from you? If not, how can you make that happen?

"We don't see things as they are, we see them as we are." (Anais Nin, essayist born to Cuban parents in France)

GIVE

* Joel Stein wrote an article in *Time* (December 2, 2013) with the sub-
* * title of "How can we fight income inequality without giving up any money?" Love the tongue-in-cheek.

God's heart wants us to give. Giving solves a multitude of problems. It helps take care of those who suffer, but it also helps take care of our own greed.

Giving is power. Dr. Mark Brewer says this, "God can do more with 90% than you can do with 100%." Pastor Robert Gelinas, Pastor of Colorado Community Church, says, "Give, but don't give it all here!!! Break your giving in half—give half to the church and half to bless others." Jesus said it's more blessed to give than to receive.

DAILY SEED: How does giving make you feel? I hope it makes you soar.

"What we spend, we lose. What we keep will be left for others. What we give away will be ours forever." (David McGee, author)

JUNE 6

GIVE BRICKS AND MORTAR GIFTS

* If you were to walk the halls of a particular school in Bangalore, you'd see plaque after plaque with the names of some very special people. The plaques are at the doors of the classrooms sponsored in honor or memory of loved ones. The sponsorships paid for bricks and mortar (construction).

Capital giving can be a great way to make a gift. Funding a building or classroom (or even a brick!) often comes with naming rights. You might not have the means to name a wing of a hospital in the United States, but you just might be able to do so in another country.

DAILY SEED: Consider giving the enduring gift of bricks and mortar in honor or memory of someone special to you.

"If you have built castles in the air, your work need not be lost; that is where they should be. Now put the foundations under them." (Henry David Thoreau, *Walden*)

JUNE 7

GIVE DURING A DISASTER

* The Center for International Disaster Information provides information on giving during a disaster. The information below is excerpted from the USAID CIDI website:[52]

"Cash is the best way to help people affected by international disasters. Our goal is to ensure that America's generosity results in the most effective relief, and we focus on helping donors make informed decisions about how to help."

Monetary Contributions to Established Relief Agencies Are Always the Best Way to Help

". . . Financial contributions allow professional relief organizations to purchase exactly what is most urgently needed by disaster survivors, when it is needed. Cash donations allow relief supplies to be purchased near the disaster site, avoiding the delays, and steep transportation and logistical costs that can encumber material donations. . . . Cash purchases also . . . support local merchants and economies, ensure that commodities are fresh and familiar to survivors, that supplies arrive expeditiously and that goods are culturally, nutritionally and environmentally appropriate.

". . . . In-kind and material donations require transportation, which is often prohibitively expensive and logistically complicated. . . . Further, shipments of material donations require an identified recipient on the ground— someone willing to receive, sort and distribute the material.

". . . . Unsolicited household donations can clog supply chains, take space required to stage life-saving relief supplies for distribution, and divert relief workers' time. . . . Before collecting goods, consider transportation expenses, storage/distribution challenges, and the real-time needs."

Know What Relief Experts Know

"Every disaster is unique and every disaster response is carefully tailored according to population needs that are assessed by relief professionals on the ground . . . who coordinate with each other, government entities and local groups. . . . These appraisals evolve daily. . . . Relief organizations that request material donations through public appeals will communicate specifically what items are desired in order to avoid problems."

Before Items Other Than Cash Are Collected,
Confirm That There Is a Need

"Some people feel a strong desire to give material donations in addition to cash. Opportunities to do this are rare but do come up, usually through appeals by relief organizations. . . .Visit www.InterAction.org for more information on relief and development agencies, where they work and how they're responding to a specific disaster.

"Any call for material donations must meet each of these criteria, or will risk burdening the relief effort it seeks to support:
- A credible relief organization has identified a need for items being requested.
- An organization is prepared to receive, manage and distribute the items.
- Costs of transportation, shipping, warehousing, and distribution are covered.
- Management of customs tariffs, fees and other cross-border requirements are covered.
- Quality assurance requirements from the host government and the recipient are met and are available for disclosure."

DAILY SEED: Give during a disaster . . . wisely.

Regarding sending bottles of water to devastated people, Juanita Rilling, director of the CIDI, as reported by CBS News April 24, 2016, said this, "100,000 liters [of water] will provide drinking water for 40,000 people for one day. This amount of water to send from the United States, say, to West Africa—and people did this—costs about $300,000. But relief organizations with portable water purification units can produce the same amount, 100,000 liters of water, for about $300."

JUNE 8

GIVE GIFTS THAT MULTIPLY

✳ Give during matching gift campaigns. Match other people's donations.
✳ ✳ (Match your children's donations!)

Give at year-end, particularly if your state has a program similar to Colorado Gives Day. (Colorado's Community First Foundation spearheaded a year-end giving day a few years ago.

In 2013, almost $21 million was raised, benefitting over 1400 nonprofits. The Foundation also raises funds to enhance the amount to each nonprofit on a percentage basis, so the original gift results in *even more* funding to the organization.) Over $155 million has been raised for Colorado nonprofits since 2007 through Colorado Gives Day.

Give through your employer if your company has a workplace giving plan. Many match employee donations.

Give gifts that multiply. According to World Vision, "Each year more than 6 million children die of preventable diseases before their fifth birthday. Gifts, in partnership with supplies from top pharmaceutical companies, multiply ten times to provide lifesaving medicines and other care to children and their families in the world's poorest countries."

Give to an endowment. Endowments accrue interest AND spin off funding to the nonprofit yearly—perhaps 5 percent per year. The principle remains year after year. In short, the original gift keeps on giving for decades and decades.

DAILY SEED: Give gifts that multiply.

"It is the heart that does the giving; the fingers only let go." (Nigerian saying)

JUNE 9

GIVE IMPACTFULLY

Boaz, in the Book of Ruth, made quite an impact in helping Ruth and Naomi. He was likely just being a "nice guy" when he first met Ruth, but his niceness, his giving heart, had an eternal impact. Boaz and Ruth eventually married, and their offspring was the forerunner of the Messiah, Jesus.

We may never know the impact of our help, but we can choose to *help impact-fully.* One way is through our giving of assets beyond cash. There are people and organizations that can facilitate donations of *appreciated assets* like stocks, mutual funds, real estate, oil and gas interests, commodities, etc. These include WaterStone, whose passion is to honor God by serving givers and ministries at the intersection of faith and finance,[53] the National Christian Foundation, whose task is to help us simplify our giving and multiply our impact,[54] and the many financial planners, large nonprofits, and denominational financial services organizations that can set up charitable gift annuities and legacy gifts through wills.

In addition, in-kind gifts are enormously helpful to ministries, nonprofits, and churches—gifts like office furniture, printers and other office equipment that's not obsolete, and services such as accounting or website development.

DAILY SEED: Consider maximizing your impact by donating stocks, real estate, or in-kind gifts to a ministry, nonprofit, or church.

"Be determined that you are making an indelible impact with great change. Now, dress up and go to make it happen!" (Israelmore Ayivor)

JUNE 10

GIVE RESPECTFULLY

A local Denver ministry created a Christmas Store. Churchgoers who can afford to do so buy new gifts and donate them to the store. The gifts are wrapped and sold to the needy for twenty-five cents on the dollar.

A family might be able to afford a $50 bike for their child, but not a $200 bike. (I get that!)

It's respectful and helpful. Romans 12:17 speaks of respecting what is right in the sight of all men.

Respect is a *big deal*. We want it for ourselves so we should offer it to others.

On a similar note about giving, there was a family who drew names for their Christmas gift exchange with a $50 limit on the purchase. Problem was, one family member insisted on giving $100 gifts. And do you think that person was loved or loathed? Well, maybe not *loathed*, but the practice was unfair, uncomfortable, and disrespectful to the others.

In giving to each other, we can be lavish but careful about unintended consequences, which can cause more harm than good. Giving large amounts of money to impoverished people in poor countries can cause serious unintended consequences—jealousy, fighting, etc. It's usually much better to give to an organization earmarked for that family or individual, so the distribution can be made in a culturally-appropriate way.

DAILY SEED: Give gifts . . . and give respect at the same time.

"It's not how much we give but how much love we put into giving." (Mother Teresa)

JUNE 11

GIVE THROUGHOUT THE YEAR

India Transformed started a fundraising campaign for a time of the year associated with reflection, fasting, repentance, sacrifice, moderation, and discipline—Lent. The gist of the campaign was to give church families tabletop banks so family members could contribute the value of their sacrifice to missions. For example, if someone were to give up coffee for Lent, the cost of the coffee during the Lenten period could be donated.

People loved it.

Giving can be more than a Christmas-y thing.

DAILY SEED: Consider how you can give in small, creative ways throughout the year.

"No act of kindness, no matter how small, is ever wasted." (Aesop, *The Lion and the Mouse* fable)

JUNE 12

GO FOR THE GOLD

Kintsugi is the Japanese art of fixing broken pottery with lacquer mixed with powdered gold. The breakage and repair become part of the object's history. The gold makes the pottery even more beautiful rather than something to disguise.

We are all "cracked pots" as Patsy Clairmont says. We have all sinned and fallen short of the glory of God, so we can either mourn the cracks or let them make us more beautiful and useful in the world. We can let God use us *not in spite of* our flaws, but *because* of our flaws.

I've heard that the best teachers were "C" students. If you are imperfect, you are the perfect candidate to go for the gold.

DAILY SEED: What imperfections do you want to give to God so He can fill them with gold?

"But we have this treasure in earthen vessels, so that the surpassing greatness of the power will be of God and not from ourselves." (2 Corinthians 4:7)

JUNE 13

GO ON A MISSION TRIP

If you've ever been on a mission trip, what was your first impression of the place you visited?

My first *India* impression was while sitting on a dusty bus in the middle of the night. We passed rows of sleeping people, inches from the bus wheels. We skirted cows and mangy dogs and beggars and trash heaps and Hindu temples and roadside shops and bent Dalit women sweeping the dirt and . . . well, that was the first block.

A few days later, after a bout of delhi belly, jet lag, extreme heat, moments of depression . . . oh, and colorful experiences, delightful new friendships, and amazement at God's work there, I knew I had fallen in love with India.

What's your mission trip story? If you've never taken one, I do hope you can go. Falling in love is a wonderful thing.

DAILY SEED: If you could go on a mission trip, where would you want to go?

"Perhaps travel cannot prevent bigotry, but by demonstrating that all peoples cry, laugh, eat, worry, and die, it can introduce the idea that if we try and understand each other, we may even become friends." (Maya Angelou)

JUNE 14

GO ON AN EXTENDED MISSION TRIP

* * * Terri lives in India. She's from Colorado and decided to dip her toe into India culture, originally for a one-two year stay. That was about eight years ago. She works with AIDS patients and pastors-in-training. She has an amazing ability to capture India in story.

If you've ever considered using your professional skills for an extended period in an overseas setting, you might want to take this quiz. http://www. ideasworld.org/quiz/. IDEAS has skilled Christian professionals working in many disciplines in over thirteen countries.

If you've ever considered using your professional skills for an extended period in an overseas setting, you might want to take this quiz: http://www. ideasworld.org/quiz/. IDEAS assists skilled Christian professionals working in many disciplines in over thirteen countries. You can also check out other sending agencies for information on long-term assignments. But first, go short-term.

DAILY SEED: Does living abroad kindle something within you? Pay attention to that and consider an extended stay or contribute to a fellow pilgrim's extended stay.

"The World is a book, and those who do not travel read only a page." (attributed to Saint Augustine)

JUNE 15

GO THE DISTANCE

* * * Some solutions are relatively easy and some are not. We must be willing to go the distance.

Millions of children around the world die of preventable diseases . . . still. Getting vaccines to them is a relatively easy solution but the delivery system is complex. We must go the distance.

My dad has cancer. The cure will be built on the backs of countless researchers, at great expense, but those researchers will go the distance.

I believe *all* of us can change the world daily, in countless small, easy ways. Some people, however, are called out to go the distance over a lifetime, to deal with the complex, to pound the fist on the table one more time, to die trying.

DAILY SEED: What, in your life, is calling you to go the distance?

"If the word quit is part of your vocabulary, then the word finish is likely not." (B.G. Jett, author and songwriter)

JUNE 16

GROW

The body is constantly regenerating itself—the lungs every six weeks, the taste buds every ten days. [55] If we stop growing, we die.

A counselor friend once told me that the main cause of marriage failure is that one of the spouses stops growing. If we stop growing, we die.

St. Peter said this, "Be on your guard lest, being carried away by the error of unprincipled men, you fall from your own steadfastness, but grow in the grace and knowledge of our Lord and Savior Jesus Christ." If we stop growing . . .

And growth is, of course, the point of the seedy life. We plant seeds of change so they'll grow. That growth makes a difference in the world.

Consider the ways we grow. We get better at what we do.

If we cook a lot, we get better at it.

If we run a lot, we get better at it.

If we bless people and help people and go out on a limb for people, we get better at it.

DAILY SEED: Grow a little today. Start reading through Galatians, Ephesians, Philippians or Colossians for "gardening tips."

"Life is change. Growth is optional. Choose wisely." (Karen Kaiser Clark, motivational speaker)

JUNE 17

GUARD AGAINST GOING TO SEED

"Going to seed" is a euphemism for deteriorating—losing vigor, losing productivity, losing heart, giving up, or falling into sin which sends us off course.

Think about the visual of going to seed. Things go to seed when they overstay. They aren't harvested in time. They droop. In other words, they burn out.

We must guard against not taking that vacation, burning the candle at both ends, pushing through doors that maybe God didn't intend for us to open.

The Bible speaks of burnout . . . *"Don't burn out; keep yourselves fueled and aflame. Be alert servants of the Master, cheerfully expectant. Don't quit in hard times; pray all the harder. Help needy Christians; be inventive in hospitality. Bless your enemies; no cursing under your breath. Laugh with your happy friends when they're happy; share tears when they're down. Get along with each other; don't be stuck-up. Make friends with nobodies; don't be the great somebody. Don't hit back; discover beauty in everyone"* (Romans 12:11–17, MSG)

There have been times when I've looked in the mirror to see bags under my eyes and exhaustion on my face, but I needed to push on and be valiant! How noble! I wish I had known I was just going to seed.

DAILY SEED: Are you (or have you ever been) at the burn-out point?

"The leader who tries to do it all is headed for burnout, and in a powerful hurry." (Bill Owens, American politician)

JUNE 18

HANG OUT WITH THE DIFFERENTLY-ABLED

✳ ✳✳ According to the 2012 Annual Disability Statistics Compendium, 12.3 percent of the U.S. population suffers from a disability.[56] That's more than California's entire 2012 population. Chances are you know a person with a disability.

Consider that person for a moment. Consider his/her challenges. Mobility? Employment? Stigma? Some, like Amy Purdy, choose to live inspired. She contracted bacterial meningitis at age 19 which led to amputation of both legs below the knee. And . . . she took bronze in Snowboard Cross at the 2014 Winter Paralympics in Sochi, Russia. She's also authored a book called *On My Own Two Feet—From Losing My Legs to Learning the Dance of Life.*

Am I that inspired?

I think one key to living a good life is hanging out with inspiring people. Many with disabilities are overcomers. And yes, some are stuck, angry, or too ill to be able to choose, but regardless, this is yet another call to making new friends. Friends of various colors, creeds, socio-economic levels, and abilities.

DAILY SEED: Make or contact a differently-abled friend today.

"Disability is not inability." (Ban Ki-moon, Secretary-General of the United Nations)

JUNE 19

HARNESS THE WISDOM OF SENIORS

✳ ✳✳ Retirement homes are *bastions* of wisdom. I direct the Holly Creek Retirement Community Choir. The median age is eighty. The oldest member (and strongest soprano) is ninety-five. Many were professionals before retirement, even CEOs.

What if we got better at tapping the wisdom of the elderly? In many cultures the elders are venerated, and for good reason. They've "been there, done that" and gained precious, hard-earned wisdom along the way. The Indian culture can't understand why our parents and grandparents don't live with us. It *is* an interesting thing to ponder.

We so often think of the elderly as *needing care* (and often they *do* need care), but oh, how much they have to give. A lifetime of wisdom . . . that's what they have to give.

I'm advocating for a culture shift regarding our elders. A shift toward monumental respect on the part of the juniors. A shift toward intentional mentoring on the part of the seniors.

We can ask our elders to come alongside us in planting seeds of change into the soil of the world. I wonder how many are never even *asked*. What a tragedy, but one that can be reversed.

DAILY SEED: What elder friend comes to mind? Can you ask him/her for wisdom . . . or for help?

"Coming from an Asian culture, I was always taught to respect my elders, to be a better listener than a talker." (Lisa Ling, American journalist)

JUNE 20

HAVE A BUCKET LIST

What do you want to do before you die? Go on that wished-for trip? Go skydiving? Make amends with someone? What seeds of change do you want to plant before you die?

DAILY SEED: Jot down your bucket list items. Maybe the last act can be the best act.

"Though no one can go back and make a brand new start, anyone can start from now and make a brand new ending." (attributed to Carl Bard via Zig Ziglar)

HAVE FUN

Steve was my youth director in the 1970s. (Am I that old?) Anyway, he was the kind of youth director always on the verge of getting in trouble with the church administration. Translation: *Best youth director ever!*

Now he's on staff with one of the biggest churches in the United States. His blog is called "Big God, Big Things." One of his recent ventures was to sponsor a "Dance Your Shoes Off" event. Think 2000 people on a football field, dancing a choreographed song, praising God in a big way, and at the end walking off the field, leaving behind thousands of pairs of new shoes for the needy.[57] To use a 70s term, that's just *cool*.

Steve taught us that Christianity isn't a list of don'ts, it's a list of *dos*. He taught us to follow Jesus *and* have fun. He's now suffering from cancer and is in constant, excruciating pain. And wouldn't you know it? Somehow, remarkably, he's still having fun . . . and making a more of difference in the world than ever.

DAILY SEED: Have fun today!
"Fun is good." (Dr. Seuss)

HEAL THE SICK

Once upon a time, Jesus spit on some clay, put it on a blind man's eyes, and then the man could see. Once upon a time, a friend prayed for a woman's compound-fractured arm, and the bone slipped back into place. Once upon a time, a doctor zeroed in on a tumor with a beam of radiation, and now the tumor is gone.

I believe in healing. I believe Jesus healed the sick and lame when He was God in the flesh, and I believe He still can . . . and does . . . as God in the heavenlies. Yet I also believe in the medical profession. Both the miracle workers and medical workers heal the sick.

I knew my daughter was destined for the medical world when we happened upon a rollover accident. I pulled over. She jumped out and ran to the driver who (miraculously) was shaken but OK. While she was *there*, I was just shaking and praying and marveling at her immediate reflex to offer care and healing.

DAILY SEED: Are you called to heal the sick?

"And all the people were trying to touch Him, for power was coming from Him and healing them all." (Luke 6:19)

The Declaration of Geneva, adopted by the World Medical Association in 1948, states this:

"At the time of being admitted as a member of the medical profession: I solemnly pledge to consecrate my life to the service of humanity; I will give to my teachers the respect and gratitude that is their due; I will practice my profession with conscience and dignity; The health of my patient will be my first consideration; I will respect the secrets that are confided in me, even after the patient has died; I will maintain by all the means in my power, the honour and the noble traditions of the medical profession; My colleagues will be my sisters and brothers; I will not permit considerations of age, disease or disability, creed, ethnic origin, gender, nationality, political affiliation, race, sexual orientation, social standing or any other factor to intervene between my duty and my patient; I will maintain the utmost respect for human life; I will not use my medical knowledge to violate human rights and civil liberties, even under threat; I make these promises solemnly, freely and upon my honour."[58]

HELP AN OUTSIDER

Kristine teaches kindergarten to twenty children from refugee families. Nine different languages are spoken in her classroom. I asked her how we can help refugee families and she had immediate answers. (Note that these are refugees, meaning they are protected here. They've fled their countries for refuge and safety due to political upheaval, war, and other horrors.)

She said the local resettlement agencies need volunteer help, usually *desperately*. They provide training. They can pair us with refugee families to assist them. Imagine—trauma, fear, language barriers, endless paperwork, standing in a grocery store not knowing which cleaning product washes what—dishes, clothes, or floors?

Imagine the joy of helping out.

DAILY SEED: Consider the refugees or other "outsiders" in your community.

"Do not neglect to show hospitality to strangers, for by this some have entertained angels without knowing it." (Hebrews 13:2)

HOLD ON TO HOPE

Hope is "the feeling that what is wanted can be had or that events will turn out for the best."

1 Peter 3:15 tells believers to be prepared to answer those who ask about why we have *hope*, which begs the question, "Do you have hope?" So many seem to believe Murphy's Law over 1 Peter 3:15.

I sat in a meeting recently and almost every idea I had was met with "we can't do that . . . or that . . . or that." I wanted to scream, "Where's the can-do attitude? Where's the hope?"

Romans 8:28 is a great promise to believers in Christ, but is also considered by some to be a very misused Scripture. *"And we know that God causes all things to work together for good to those who love God, to those who are called according to His purpose."* Not everything works out according to our wishes, but everything works out for our *good* from God's perspective. Letting God teach us *the more important thing* trumps a bitter disappointment or un-granted wish any day. In other words, in Christ, we win, *always*, if we define the win according to His purpose.

What hope! Hope for a valuable life and valuable contribution to the world.

DAILY SEED: Do you need a renewed sense of hope?

"Therefore, having been justified by faith, we have peace with God through our Lord Jesus Christ, through whom also we have obtained our introduction by faith into this grace in which we stand; and **we exult in hope of the glory of God.** *And not only this, but we also exult in our tribulations, knowing that tribulation brings about perseverance; and perseverance, proven character; and proven character, hope; and* **hope does not disappoint,** *because the love of God has been poured out within our hearts through the Holy Spirit who was given to us."* (Romans 5:1–5)

JUNE 25

HONE YOUR COMMUNICATION SKILLS

Lee Iacocca, known for engineering the Ford Mustang and reviving the Chrysler Corporation, said, "You can have brilliant ideas, but if you can't get them across, your ideas won't get you anywhere."

Being a world-changer includes communicating in a compelling way. We don't have to be the most gifted speakers in the world. After all, some speakers have glitz but no message. (And others have no earthly beauty but you can't take your eyes off them.) We should just perfect our presentation as much as possible, whether we're glitzy or otherwise.

It's likely that the world needs to hear your message. Take classes on public speaking or writing or blogging. Get someone's ear. Communicate. Use stories. Make it compelling. Make it *irresistible*. Challenge your audience to take action on your message.

DAILY SEED: Practice your "elevator speech" (fifteen-second message) on a topic close to your heart. Hone it so that people take notice.

"Good communication is as stimulating as black coffee, and just as hard to sleep after." (Ann Morrow Lindbergh, author of *Gift from the Sea*)

JUNE 26

HONOR THE SERVANTS IN YOUR MIDST

. . . servants such as members of branches of our military, teachers, pastors, parents, store clerks. They *serve* us. And if you've tasted the servant side of life, it can be challenging.

Think of how many people served you yesterday. Did you go to a mall, school, or restaurant? Church, library, or convenience store?

DAILY SEED: Look the servants in your midst in the eye and say thanks . . . or slip them a note or a flower.

"Feeling gratitude and not expressing it is like wrapping a present and not giving it." (William Arthur Ward, American writer)

JUNE 27

HOST A FOREIGNER

✳ ✳✳ WorldDenver's mission includes opportunities to house, show hospitality toward, and interact with international leaders. I'm guessing there are similar opportunities in your city, like hosting Up With People students, or international students, or foreign missionaries, or visiting professionals from other countries.

Hanging out with a foreign person helps you crawl out from your own little corner. We only have *our* perspective on the world unless we get the perspective of someone else.

Part of my job at the Dalit Freedom Network was to drive our Indian leaders around the United States for speaking engagements. Seeing the States from Kumar's eyes was a delight. "Wow! Your country is so appreciative. See that McDonald's trash can? It says "thank you" just for putting my trash there! And your country is so tolerant. See those yards? One has a political yard sign for a Democrat and right next door there's one for a Republican! And . . . your people treat me with respect."

I wanted to weep with thanksgiving for our country.

And the flip side is true too. Kumar and his family have spent many hours hosting me in Incredible India. It works both ways.

DAILY SEED: If you have opportunity, host someone from another country. Serve your favorite dish. Listen and learn.

"Hospitality means primarily the creation of free space where the stranger can enter and become a friend instead of an enemy. Hospitality is not to change people, but to offer them space where change can take place. It is not to bring men and women over to our side, but to offer freedom not disturbed by dividing lines." (Henri J.M. Nouwen, *Reaching Out)*

JUNE 28

HUG YOUR LOVED ONES

* I come from a long line of seed-planters.

* *   My dad taught me to be involved in my world.

My mom (who passed away in 1991) taught me to love my neighbors and to sew. (OK, just kidding about that last part. She *tried* to teach me to sew.)

My stepmom, Jo, teaches me to stay positive and laugh often.

My sister, Jill, teaches me to create things of beauty out of ordinary life.

My sister, Nita, teaches me to celebrate with one's kids every chance you get.

My son, Coy Austin, teaches me to live life out loud with gusto, passion, and meaning.

My daughter, Morgan, teaches me to play even if the dishes aren't done, to major on the major.

My husband, Irnie, teaches me to help people at every turn (and to plant lots of trees).

To Hannah, Jesse, Emmy, Meg and family, Emily and family, extended family, and so many friends . . . thank you for being you. Thank you for teaching me about the seedy life. I wish I could hug each of you so much more often.

DAILY SEED: Hug a relative or friend today.

"If you live to be a hundred, I want to live to be a hundred minus one day so I never have to live without you." (A.A. Milne, *Winnie-the-Pooh*)

JUNE 29

IGNITE SMALL GROUPS WITH SEED-PLANTING

Small groups are like families. (And I'm talking about intentional fellowship or study groups.) They bring people together to study, talk out issues, and grapple with life.

I've been in several small groups over the years. The group members are to this day some of the dearest people in my world. I've watched them start foundations, impact gang members, raise great kids, bury great kids, pastor churches, ride out crippling diseases. The joy and pain we've shared . . .

And small groups are also a great place for getting *practical* about impacting the world, studying books as a group, doing projects as a group, going on mission trips as a group.

There's something about group dynamics that makes us bolder. Jesus' disciples tended to work in groups of two to twelve. There's a lot of seedy power in our groups of two or more.

DAILY SEED: If you are part of a small group, take the Seed Challenge together.

"And if one can overpower him who is alone, two can resist him. A cord of three strands is not quickly torn apart." (Ecclesiastes 4:12)

JUNE 30

IMPLEMENT YOUR DENOMINATION'S MISSIONS STRATEGIES

In September 2000, world leaders committed their nations (through the United Nations) to these eight Millennium Development Goals (MDGs) to be achieved by 2015.[59]

1. Eradicate extreme poverty and hunger.
2. Achieve universal primary education.
3. Promote gender equality and empower women.
4. Reduce child mortality.
5. Improve maternal health.
6. Combat HIV/AIDS, malaria and other diseases.
7. Ensure environmental sustainability.
8. Global partnership for development.

The Cooperative Baptist Fellowship[60] took these eight goals and created a denomination-wide strategy to aid in their implementation. The power of thousands of churches joining hands with the United Nations in a unified way is *brilliant*, but probably unusual. Hopefully your denomination (or your individual church) has missions and justice strategies. Wouldn't it be wonderful if they connected to a greater strategy, such as current Sustainable Development Goals (SDGs) adopted at the UN Sustainable Development Summit in September 2015? The 17 SDGs are part of the 2030 Agenda for Sustainable Development to end poverty, fight inequality and injustice, and tackle climate change.[61]

Victor Hugo, author of *Les Miserables,* said, "It was darkness which produced the lamp. It was fog that produced the compass. It was hunger that drove us to exploration." Let the world's ills and inequalities drive you, your church, your denomination, or your network to solutions.

DAILY SEED: Explore your denomination's missions strategies. Explore your own church's missions strategies. Explore thoughts on teaming up with others to work on the current MDGs.[62]

"Coming together is a beginning; keeping together is progress; working together is success." (Henry Ford)

JULY

INCREASE GIVING YEARLY

* Around 1980, several what-later-became-mega-churches began in Den-
* * ver. The missions team of one of those, Cherry Creek Presbyterian, had
the idea to increase mission giving yearly up to 25 percent of the incoming
funds. And for many years, that yearly increase indeed happened. I think it
made it to 19 percent, which is remarkable . . . almost double a tithe (tenth).

Conventional wisdom says to grab as much wealth as possible. Gain,
gain, gain.

God, however, isn't exactly known for His *conventional* wisdom. His wisdom turns the world's wisdom upside down.

DAILY SEED: Give and then give some more. God loves a cheerful giver.

"The difference between self-love and being in love with yourself is that one
results in giving and the other in taking." (Jeffrey Fry, author and businessman)

INNOVATE

* Lori is innovative. She tutors underperforming students by pre-testing
* * them and writing a "prescription" much as a doctor would. She then
fills the prescription by helping them master phonics or multiplication, etc.,
according to their prescription. It's called Plumfield Learning Systems.

Most tutoring programs help kids with homework, but this is more targeted. She was willing to break free of established structures.

The risk of innovation is that few of us have the innovative vision *and* the
administrative skills *and* the fundraising ability to take the vision to fruition. It

takes a village, so to speak. Some innovate; others develop; others refine; others maintain. Lori is building the Plumfield village, but the innovation was her idea.

Innovation doesn't necessarily mean a massive paradigm shift. It might just mean doing the common thing differently. George Washington Carver said, "When you do the common things in life in an uncommon way, you will command the attention of the world." Carver, an innovator, certainly did. He was born into slavery but was so innovative with agriculture that *Time* magazine dubbed him a "Black Leonardo da Vinci."

DAILY SEED: Take your innovative ideas seriously. Pray about them. Maybe they are God's ideas and He planted the discovery seeds into your mind.

"Discovery is seeing what everybody has seen and thinking what nobody else has thought." (Dr. Albert Szent-Gyorgyi, discoverer of Vitamin C)

JULY 3

INTERN

An intern is a person who works as a trainee in a profession to gain practical experience. Sort of like an apprentice. DenverWorks was blessed to have interns from Denver Seminary. The interns needed the credit and we got graduate-level people who were enthused about the project as co-workers. It's a *great* way to build a team. I ended up hiring some of them. One is still there to this day.

Internships often provide training in a particular aspect like grant writing or event planning, good things for seed-planters to know. Internships get you into the thick of an issue. And according to www.internships.com, seven out of ten internships turn into full-time jobs.

Interested in interning? One website has over 78,000 internship postings. And if an organization you wish to work with doesn't offer internships, ask to intern anyway, especially if you can work for a time without pay or with a small stipend.

DAILY SEED: If your heart is set on a particular issue, seek to intern in that field.

"Be brave. Take risks. Nothing can substitute for experience." (Paulo Coelho, Brazilian novelist)

INVENTORY BARRIERS

What's holding you back from involvement? Too little time? Too little money? Too little energy? Compassion fatigue?

We all have barriers from time to time. Real barriers. We may be overwhelmed or broke.

And exhausted people need to rest, not pedal harder. If, however, the barriers are excuses, I urge you to do some soul-searching.

I've been all over the map on this one. I've asked God to show me the *balanced* life He desires for me. I think a vibrant seed is better than an old, battered, worn-out seed. But the seed never sown because "I was just too busy" never yields any fruit.

DAILY SEED: What are you barriers and what does the balanced life look like for you?

"You can focus on things that are barriers or you can focus on scaling the wall or redefining the problem." (Tim Cook, CEO of Apple)

INVEST

Hope Communities had a "benevolent investment" strategy for its affordable housing renovations. People of means were given opportunities to invest. There was a strong possibility of some return. And . . . there was the possibility of no return. However, the investors were stakeholders. They were involved in the projects. They lent their business wisdom. They created projects far more viable and successful than projects funded in other ways.

Matthew 25 speaks of the parable of the talents, which is about investing what we've been given—putting our money to work to make more money. And investing also means digging into the soul of the thing.

As a church or small group experiment, give some folks ten dollars. Have each invest it, according to Matthew 25:14–30, over a period of a week or two. Come together and report on results. Whose ten dollars yields the most?

"The one who had received the five talents came up and brought five more talents, saying, 'Master, you entrusted five talents to me. See, I have gained five more talents.' His master said to him, 'Well done, good and faithful slave; you were faithful with a few things, I will put you in charge of many things; enter into the joy of your master'" (Matthew 25:20–21).

God wants us to be smart and savvy, investing what we have been given to produce far more. What a lesson to learn.

DAILY SEED: What can you invest to yield even more?

"Financial peace isn't the acquisition of stuff. It's learning to live on less than you make, so you can give money back and have money to invest. You can't win until you do this." (Dave Ramsey, financial author)

JULY 6

INVITE "OTHERNESS"

Inviting other-ness (elevating another culture) builds friendships, trust, and respect . . . and it's good for the soul of a community.

Ask Indian students to teach your group how to play cricket. Host an international food festival. Learn an African dance. Study another language. Hold a fashion show featuring the clothing of another country.

I saw an Indian fashion show in a Nebraska church, of all places. The youth group girls modeled Indian saris brought over by a missionary. (If you've never seen saris or salwar kameezes or the gold jewelry worn by Indian brides, you are in for a treat!) This fashion show included Indian desserts. Clay cups were distributed. The missionary spoke. Seeing the beauty and meaning of Indian fashion helped me understand India.

DAILY SEED: Consider ways you can elevate another culture in your community.

"Respect for others guides our manners." (Laurence Sterne, Irish novelist and Anglican clergyman)

JULY 7

JOIN GROUPS

There are so many groups that change the world, like Amnesty International or Love146 or Oxfam or One.org or ... (this could go on for a long time). Joining groups is like going shopping—only in reverse. I don't really "need" new clothes unless I see cute ones at the mall. Then, *I can't get them off my mind.*

Conversely, when I'm a member of a group that sends me information about suffering people, *I can't get them off my mind.*

And then I can *do something* about it.

DAILY SEED: Join a group today, on-line or in person.

"Growth is never by mere chance; it is the result of forces working together." (J.C. Penney)

JULY 8

KEEP IT HELPFUL

Some giving harms. Some *helping* harms. An example is doing for others what they can do for themselves. America's welfare system was ushered in by Democrats, then reformed by a Democrat (Clinton). Our country has a soft heart for those who need a helping hand.

Unfortunately, however, good intentions created dependency among some recipients, so a course correction was made. The safety net is there, but it's smaller now, to keep helping from harming.

Our DenverWorks board consists of strong Republicans *and* strong Democrats. Why? Because there's a strong bi-partisan ethic for keeping help *helpful*. For empowering the jobless with skills and dignity so *they* can land the jobs.

We must make sure our help is wanted, needed, and doesn't create dependency. Good intentions aren't enough.

DAILY SEED: Evaluate the help you give others to ensure it isn't inadvertently harming.

"Until we embrace our mutual brokenness, our work with low-income people is likely to do more harm than good. I sometimes unintentionally reduce poor people to objects that I use to fulfill my own need to accomplish something." (Steve Corbett, *When Helping Hurts: How to Alleviate Poverty Without Hurting the Poor . . . and Yourself*)

JULY 9

KEEP IT MUTUAL

Once I was driving along a downtown street with my children. A homeless guy came over to our car. I rolled down the window (a bit) and he handed *me* a dollar and said to buy my kids a treat. *I looked him in the eyes.* Yep, he was a real person.

Sometimes we give; sometimes we receive. You or I might need that food bank, or a daughter might need that domestic violence shelter, or a neighbor might need some legal counsel but can't afford it. It is *so* important to not set up an "us & them" mentality. We all need the Savior. We all need each other.

We are to esteem others more highly than ourselves. We can't know each person's story unless we've walked in their moccasins.

I've heard a lot of stories in my time. Many of those storytellers are my heroes. I feel like a wimp compared to them. Sure, a lot of people have made bad decisions and a few are downright scary, so I'm not being "Pollyanna." I'm just suggesting that we keep it mutual, that we do unto others as we would have them do unto us.

DAILY SEED: Strive for mutual respect in today's interactions.

"I speak to everyone in the same way, whether he is the garbage man or the president of the university." (Albert Einstein)

JULY 10

KEEP IT SIMPLE

Years ago I read Richard Foster's *Freedom of Simplicity: Finding Harmony in a Complex World,* then checked it off my long to-do list. I wasn't ready for simplicity. I didn't understand it. I found it terribly illusive, unproductive, and unsatisfying.

Now busy-ness, *that* was a different story!

But I'm finding that the older I get, the more I like simplicity. I give myself permission to do a few tasks a day rather than a hundred! I get the fact that I'm a human *being* more than a human *doing* (well, most of the time). I'm finding joy and "enough-ness" in planting the garden, going for a run, trading puns with my kids on Facebook, sitting on a rock to think. In fact, those have become choice times rather than squeezed-in times.

I can listen to my grandkids better if I'm not multi-tasking. I can stop to pray for a friend if I'm not in a frenzy of activity.

I can remember Jesus' words to Martha: *"Now as they were traveling along, He entered a village; and a woman named Martha welcomed Him into her home.*

She had a sister called Mary, who was seated at the Lord's feet, listening to His word. But Martha was distracted with all her preparations; and she came up to Him and said, "Lord, do You not care that my sister has left me to do all the serving alone? Then tell her to help me." But the Lord answered and said to her, "Martha, Martha, you are worried and bothered about so many things; but only one thing is necessary, for Mary has chosen the good part, which shall not be taken away from her" (Luke 10:38–42).

If Jesus came to my home, would I sit at his feet and listen to him, or would I fret over what to fix him for dinner?

What I *really* want is simplicity. Leftovers for dinner. Great chat. Apparently Jesus wants the undistracted me, too.

DAILY SEED: How can you find the freedom of simplicity today?

"Simplicity and purity are the two wings by which a man is lifted above all earthly things. Simplicity is in the intention—purity in the affection. Simplicity tends to God; purity apprehends and tastes Him." (Thomas à Kempis, author of one of the best-known books on Christian devotion, *The Imitation of Christ* [c. 1418–1427])

JULY 11

KEEP IT VITAL

Going on a mission trip to an impoverished country can kind of wreck your life. Once, after I returned from India, I was visiting a friend who was complaining about her trash compactor being broken. In India, there are piles of trash higher than buildings . . . everywhere. And people defecating on the sidewalks. And dead people . . . on the sidewalks.

I'm not mad at my friend. I have no room to point fingers.

I'm just inviting us to do *something* to make a difference in the world rather than spending our lives fretting over our broken appliances. I'm inviting us to do vital work. "Vital" means "necessary for the well-being of something."

God will show you what is necessary to the well-bring of someone or some group. And he will equip you to provide. He says that if you provide a cup of cold water for someone, you are doing it for him. And that is definitely keeping it vital.

DAILY SEED: It's never too late to live a vital life.

"The major value in life is not what you get. The major value in life is what you become." (Jim Rohn, motivational speaker)

JULY 12

KNOW YOURSELF AND USE YOUR STRENGTHS

I like to play "What's Your Favorite?" on road trips. (Just ask my family.) What's your favorite movie? What's your favorite high school memory? What's your favorite ice cream? . . . which usually leads to an ice cream stop in the next town, alas. It's a fun way to get to know others.

It's important to know yourself too, however. It's good to look inside and identify your strengths, interests, and "sweet spots," i.e., when you are your most authentic self. It can be formal or informal.

A personality test or a "what's my favorite" game helps us find our way, because God made us the way we are on purpose.

DAILY SEED: What's your favorite way to help others?

"For we are His workmanship, created in Christ Jesus for good works, which God prepared beforehand so that we would walk in them." (Ephesians 2:10)

JULY 13

LAUGH AND CELEBRATE

A few days ago I was at the deli counter of the grocery store. The clerk came over with smiles and a lilting voice. "What can I get for you, Lovely?" (Believe me, I wasn't lovely. It was one of those days when I tried to sneak to the store without seeing anyone I knew—in my sweats and mussed-up hair.) But she called everyone Lovely. And I *couldn't help* but smile because she was so contagious.

Contagious laughter is seediness.

Making a difference in the world includes smiling at the future. The description of a worthy woman in Proverbs 31 is possibly a metaphor for *wisdom:* *"She extends her hand to the poor; and she stretches out her hands to the needy."* *"Strength and dignity are her clothing, and **she smiles at the future**."*

If we believe God will use us in spite of our flaws and shortcomings and mussed-up hair, we can smile at the future. And I don't know about you, but sometimes life is tough and laughter doesn't come easily, but when it does come, it helps ease the pain, one's own pain and that of others.

DAILY SEED: Laugh today. Be contagious.

"When the Lord brought back the captive ones of Zion, we were like those who dream. Then our mouth was filled with laughter, and our tongue with joyful shouting; Then they said among the nations, "The Lord has done great things for them." The Lord has done great things for us; We are glad." (Psalm 126:1–3)

JULY 14

LEAD THE WAY

Volumes have been written on leadership. One of my favorites is called *Servant Leadership: A Journey Into the Nature of Legitimate Power and*

Greatness. Author Robert Greenleaf asks, "Why would anyone accept the leadership of another except that the other sees more clearly where it is best to go?"[63] Walt Whitman wrote, "We convince by our presence." Elisa Morgan says, "We are all influencers. We can influence by accident or we can influence by effort."[64]

DAILY SEED: Who is influenced by you? Lead that person.

"If your actions create a legacy that inspires others to dream more, learn more, do more and become more, then you are an excellent leader." (Dolly Parton, singer, possibly originally from John Quincy Adams)

JULY 15

LEARN HOW TO FUNDRAISE

People sort of bow down to professional fundraisers. They think fundraisers can grow money on trees. Hmm . . .

Fundraisers *are* highly-valued. They're often key to the success of a cause, but fundraisers are regular people who know a few secrets like these.

Have a balanced fundraising strategy—a three-legged stool. For instance, 1/3 grants, 1/3 individuals, 1/3 events . . . or whatever three work for your cause.

Have some skill with writing, but more importantly, have skills with people. People give to people!

Have the ability to follow directions precisely. If you need to write a grant proposal, many foundations use their state's common grant form. See www.coloradocommongrantforms.orgas an example. The formula is there. And virtually every foundation can be located at www.foundationcenter.org for a nominal fee.

DAILY SEED: Do you need to raise money for your cause? Dig in and learn the ropes.

"In good times and bad, we know that people give because you meet needs, not because you have needs." (Kay Sprinkel Grace, fundraising professional)

JULY 16

LEAVE A LEGACY AND MAKE END-OF-LIFE PLANS

Somebody once said, "It's never too late to live happily ever after." Some of us have made mistakes in life. OK, *all* of us have. Some of those mistakes have been minor; others have done massive damage. It's never too late, however, to turn to God. Let Him forgive. Let Him turn the rest of your life into one of blessing. In the words of Zig Ziglar, "Where you start is not as important as where you finish."[65]

And consider the legacy you want to leave. Our imprint on society can continue after we're gone. So live well . . . from this moment on.

And end well.

DAILY SEED: Make end-of-life plans. Leave a legacy. Finish strong.

"I am of the opinion that my life belongs to the whole community and as long as I live, it is my privilege to do for it whatever I can. I want to be thoroughly used up when I die, for the harder I work the more I live." (George Bernard Shaw, playwright)

JULY 17

LIGHTEN SOMEONE'S LOAD

1991 was a year of great heaviness for me. I lost my marriage, then my mother. Dear friends helped me carry the load, including Gary and Arlene. Gary wrote this extraordinary poem for me.

To Debbie~
The wind upon the grass was harsh
and blew from ridge through vale and marsh.
It drifted up within its hands
the people's fears through which life spans;

and grasped them with unyielding strength
to hold each life through breadth and length.
Until all hope within them failed
and even strong among them quailed.
Yet here and there a small spark blazed
as one, then two saw through the haze.
And there, though dim, the Way was lit
so each one now could break the bit,
which held them down and weighed their soul
with bitter pain and broken goal.
Yet as they watched; the Way grew bright.
And as they moved; each step grew light.
Until they found the peace once lost
and newness there, beyond all cost
of anyone; but from God's grace,
which brings us freely to His place.
And those who make the stand with Him,
find strength to live, and heal within. —Gary Glatthar

To this day, Gary's poem hangs above my desk. It still lightens life's loads.

DAILY SEED: How can you lighten the load of another today?

"Sympathy is two hearts tugging at one load." (Charles Henry Parkhurst, clergyman and social reformer)

JULY 18

LISTEN TO THE YOUNG

The Millennials and Gen Z kids are lining up to lead into the next era. It makes sense to listen to them. Maybe you *are* one of them. They don't yet have the wisdom gained from age, but they have fresh ideas. They have techie ability I can only wish for. They are entrepreneurial and seek meaning in their work. We need them . . . and they need us.

Wouldn't it be fascinating to ask a youth group to design the perfect church for their generation?

I wonder what they would change. I wonder what they would keep. I wonder what would be most important to them?

I think world-changing would be near the top.

DAILY SEED: If you are older, listen to the young. If you are young, let no one look down on your youth, but be wise enough to listen. To listen is to honor.

"Most of the successful people I've known are the ones who do more listening than talking." (Bernard M. Baruch, American financier)

JULY 19

CAMEO (by Emily Strickfaden[66])

My generation gets excited about the possibility of planting seeds into the generations below us because we trust that they have a long time to develop. Personally, I love working with the generations below me because I realize how many small acts, kind notes, and big prayers have been imbedded in me from such a small age. I am intrigued by the unique qualities of each person and in turn, plant purposeful and specific plants into each individual. Sammy, a student from my church, is a sweet girl who now also shares this vision because of a transformative experience.

Every winter my church goes to downtown San Diego to be a part of the Christmas Blessing. The Christmas Blessing is an event put on by City of Refuge, an urban mission that holds a heavy presence on the streets of San Diego. Christmas time is a heartening time for City of Refuge because close to 1,000 kids will receive a Christmas gift. The families that come are underprivileged and cannot afford presents for their children. They will wait hours in a roped-off line to receive the gifts. For many of the children, this is the only gift they will receive this Christmas. While families wait in line, we give out hot chocolate and cookies, have crafts, coloring, balloon animals, and face painting. When it is their turn, they enter a Winter Wonderland Warehouse, listen to a Christmas story and then receive their gift! One year Sammy came along to experience the joy. In the car ride she was not sure what the Christmas Blessing was or what she would be doing, but she was excited to be serving alongside her church in any way possible. She painted little faces and cut red paper into the shape of ornaments and shared her contagious smile with the children. But one hour in, it was apparent that Sammy was struggling. My pastor noticed her sitting alone by the vans, tears running in to the palms of her hands. My pastor gently asked what was wrong.

"I've been here before," she said almost with disbelief. My pastor inquired further, trying to understand what she meant. "I've been here before on the other side of the rope."

Sammy had waited in line for hours one year with her family while she had her face painted. She was one of the children that would only receive one Christmas gift that year.

The people that poured into Sammy years ago may not have realized that they were planting seeds of change that would one day foster a tangible difference. Instilling a sense of worth into an individual can provide them with the encouragement needed to plant seeds into others. Sammy made the choice to let her tribulation change her life to have purpose.

When we come from a place where we can say that we've been here before, we know that it is time to plant a seed of change.

DAILY SEED: Think about what you have received in life. Consider how you can pay it forward, like Sammy.

"I would have despaired unless I had believed that I would see the goodness of the Lord in the land of the living." (Psalm 27:13)

JULY 20

LIVE ACCORDING TO YOUR PRINCIPLES

✳
✳ ✳   Here's Gandhi's list of Seven Deadly Social Sins:
      Politics without Principle.
      Wealth without Work.
      Commerce without Morality.
      Pleasure without Conscience.
      Education without Character.
      Science without Humanity.
      Worship without Sacrifice.

That's quite a list to chew on. As we go about our lives, we can use reminders like this to monitor ourselves and the issues to which we attach.

Are we abiding by our principles? Are we promoting work? Are we conducting business ethically? Are we leading healthy lives physically and psychologically? Are we helping our schools build character into the students? Are we speaking up on scientific issues if we differ? Are we saying yes to a life of faith even if it means sacrifice?

DAILY SEED: Let's live according to our principles today.

"A people that values its privileges above its principles soon loses both." (Dwight D. Eisenhower, in his first inaugural address)

JULY 21

LIVE ON LESS AND GIVE MORE

✳
✳ ✳   My favorite cookbook as a young wife was called *More-with-Less Cookbook: Suggestions by Mennonites on How to Eat Better and Consume Less of the World's Limited Food Resources.* Yeah, we were a little hippie-ish that way.

Today, the obsession is getting the next expensive phone. There's not so much of a bent toward living on less. It seems our society ebbs and flows between the two. For me, it's a conscious choice. I can always live on a little less and give a little more.

A friend of mine went on a clothing fast. She chose not to buy any new clothes for a year. She re-purposed her current clothes. She smiled as she told me about how many more compliments she got on the latter. She lived on less and it worked really well for her. Love that.

DAILY SEED: Try a grand experiment. Simplify.

"The secret of happiness, you see, is not found in seeking more, but in developing the capacity to enjoy less." (Socrates)

"Fear less, hope more; eat less, chew more; whine less, breathe more; talk less, say more; love more, and all good things will be yours." (Swedish proverb)

JULY 22

LOAN YOUR EXECUTIVE SKILLS

✳ ✳ ✳ Once I asked one of the top fundraisers in the country if we could hire her. She said, "Nope, you can't afford me. So here's the deal, you buy me a cup of coffee, and I'll meet with you monthly and teach you the ropes." So I bought those cups of coffee and we met regularly. *And* she became our board president. *And* she helped us secure our endowment, six AmeriCorps volunteers, and a *lot* of funding. She loaned her executive skills, all for a cup of coffee.

Chambers of Commerce offer great programs such as CEO Exchanges and mentoring for younger or nonprofit executives.

Not much has been more valuable to me than *mentoring from someone older and wiser.*

DAILY SEED: If you are an executive, who needs your wisdom?

"Remember that mentor leadership is all about serving. Jesus said, 'For even the Son of Man came not to be served but to serve others and to give his life as a ransom for many' (Mark 10:45)." (Tony Dungy, *The Mentor Leader: Secrets to Building People and Teams That Win Consistently*)

JULY 23

LOOK UNDER YOUR NOSE

A roundtable of nonprofit "hall of famers" sat in a room giving input on a government grant. Also at the table was a rep from a church. She was a little wisp of a thing—young, smart, beautiful, but not one of the mucky-mucks. The topic was how to gather groups of young Hispanics to access the benefits of this grant.

Form affinity groups! Go to the high schools! Access the leadership skills of gang members!

Then she spoke up. "We already have a huge group of young urban Hispanics at our church."

Nobody listened . . . or at best, they symbolically patted her on the head, meaning "that's not really what we had in mind."

It was the best idea in the room and I've never forgotten her. The answer was right under the noses of the mucky-mucks.

DAILY SEED: Are there answers to your questions within your own network (right under your nose)?

"Hey, I don't have all the answers. In life, to be honest, I've failed as much as I've succeeded. But I love my wife. I love my life. And I wish you, my kind of successes." (from the movie, *Jerry Maguire*)

JULY 24

MAKE A BIG DIFFERENCE

Cailey K. is founder and president of Colorado Kids 4 Kids which is a kid-run nonprofit with the mission of helping sick, disabled, underprivileged and homeless kids. She started off by giving away her birthday presents when she was six.

Now she's twelve.

Cailey K. is making a big difference . . . from a middle-school classroom.

Madame Curie made a big difference . . . from a laboratory.

Dietrich Bonhoeffer made a big difference . . . from a concentration camp.

Jane Goodall made a big difference . . . from the wilds of Tanzania.

Joni Eareckson Tada makes a big difference . . . from a wheelchair.

Dwight L. Moody made a big difference . . . from a pulpit.

Nelson Mandela made a big difference . . . from twenty-seven years in prison.

Maybe you're a stay-at-home mom and you can make a big difference . . . from your kitchen.

Maybe you're a business person and you can make a big difference . . . from your office.

Maybe you're a student and you can make a big difference . . . from your laptop.

Maybe you're old . . . or young . . . or overweight . . . or underweight . . . or happy . . . or depressed . . . but consider your circumstances and how God might use you from your unique vantage point.

You and I can make a big difference by blooming where we are planted. We can give, in the words of Dr. Mark Brewer, "all that we know of ourselves to all that we know of God."

Maybe the world needs your God-inspired message. *All* God-inspired messages make a big difference in the world.

DAILY SEED: Where are you planted? What message do you have for the world?

"Be who God meant you to be and you will set the world on fire." (St. Catherine of Siena)

JULY 25

MAKE A DAILY DIFFERENCE

The Sioux battle-cry, "Nake nula waun welo," means "I am ready for whatever comes." It has apparently been wrongly translated to "Today is a good day to die" and wrongly attributed to Crazy Horse or Low Dog. That being said, we think of it as an expression of internal warrior strength and willingness, even eagerness, to give one's life in the name of one's cause.

What if we modified the phrase to "Today is a good day to live?" What if it became an expression of willingness (and even eagerness) to *live* one's life in the name of one's cause?

Motivational speaker Steve Maraboli said, "Today is yours to shape. Create a masterpiece!" What if we woke up every morning with a fresh start and the desire to make a difference? Although some are captives of things like illness or prison, part of life is about choice. We can choose to make a difference daily. Even the captives. May God help them and all of us.

DAILY SEED: "Today is a good day to live." Live well . . . and make a difference in someone else's life too.

"'What day is it?' asked Pooh. 'It's today,' squeaked Piglet. 'My favorite day,' said Pooh." (A.A. Milne)

"We are what we repeatedly do. Excellence, then, is not an act but a habit." (author Will Durant, summarizing Aristotle's words, "these virtues are formed in man by his doing the actions")

JULY 26

MAKE A PRODUCTION

✳
✳ ✳   Andrew Brown produced the gendercide documentary *It's a Girl: The Three Deadliest Words in the World* through Shadowline Films. Shadowline's byline is "to know is not enough." Andrew and friends, fresh out of college, just jumped in and did it.

The movie starts with an Indian woman standing over the seven graves of her newborn girls—girls she had to kill. Your heart breaks not only for the babies, but for that mom, who had so little choice.

The power of a production. How else would we even know, much less *feel* the pain?

On a similar note, I once met with a missions leader who showed me an impressive video of his ministry on his laptop. He said he'd taught himself how to use software and filmed it himself. I said, "Oh I could never do that," but then I priced taking a videographer to India and changed my words to, "Well, maybe I could do that." And I did. The result wasn't award-winning but I could tell the story with a simple slide show and background music.

Sometimes we just have to jump in and do it.

DAILY SEED: Consider telling your story through a production.

"You may tell a tale that takes up residence in someone's soul, becomes their blood and self and purpose. That tale will move them and drive them and who knows that they might do because of it, because of your words. That is your role, your gift." (Erin Morgenstern, novelist and multimedia artist)

JULY 27

MAKE A SMALL DIFFERENCE

"If you think you're too small to make a difference, you've never spent the night with a mosquito." (African saying)

Some are called to be Nelson Mandelas or Mother Teresas. Others of us are called to ordinary-ness. We can make small differences that aren't even noticed, except maybe by the recipient.

We can ask our favorite waiter about his sick child.

We can send a "thinking of you" card to a friend.

We can speak our spouse's love language.

My husband loves for me to hang out with him while he fixes the tractor. It's a small thing I can do that means a lot to him, even if I'm useless on that tractor-fixing part.

Mother Teresa said. "It is not how much we do, but how much love we put in that action."

Small actions matter. The "widow's mite" story made it into the best-selling book in the world!

It all counts.

DAILY SEED: Read the story of the widow's mite in Mark 12:41–44. Do a little act of kindness today.

"Few will have the greatness to bend history itself, but each of us can work to change a small portion of events. It is from numberless diverse acts of courage and belief that human history is shaped. Each time a man stands up for an ideal, or acts to improve the lot of others, or strikes out against injustice, he sends forth a tiny ripple of hope, and crossing each other from a million different centers of energy and daring those ripples build a current which can sweep down the mightiest walls of oppression and resistance." (Robert F. Kennedy)

JULY 28

MAKE DEPOSITS

In the context of relationships, I love the concept of making deposits into each other's lives.

For example, we can agree with a spouse's opinion rather than criticize it. That brings a little lift to the spirit! It's a deposit rather than a withdrawal from the bank account of love, so to speak.

We can look for ways to say "yes" to our children rather than the too-frequent "no." Deposits.

We can look for ways to help neighbors or friends. Deposits.

We can look for ways to say a gracious word or donate to a cause. Deposits.

DAILY SEED: Consider making a deposit into someone's life today.

"Each day of our lives we make deposits in the memory banks of our children." (Charles R. Swindoll)

JULY 29

MAKE MIDCOURSE CORRECTIONS

I once hiked the Canyonlands of Utah with friends. We got off the beaten path. It was about 110 degrees. In the middle of the day. And we ran out of water. We literally had to get together and strategize and calm each other down. So, we made midcourse corrections. We checked our maps. We backtracked. We looked for landmarks. And obviously, we made it.

More often than not, the path isn't clear. We go to college or get a job, not knowing the final destination. We open a door, then close it and try another door. Life is just one big midcourse correction.

Smart mission work has the same path of midcourse corrections. At DenverWorks, we considered starting a car ministry because our clients needed cars.

Didn't work. But computer training and professional clothing closets and mentoring worked. (Our clients needed those things too.)

We must stay *on mission*, but not fear making tweaks along the way.

DAILY SEED: Need to correct any mistakes or make any adjustments today?

"Mistakes are made to be corrected, not to be insulted." (Nishan Panwar, writer)

". . . mistakes are inevitable, but what is not, and what will set us apart, is our ability to learn from them." (Nick Trout, *Tell Me Where It Hurts: A Day of Humor, Healing and Hope in My Life as an Animal Surgeon*)

JULY 30

MAKE SACRIFICES

Jacob loved Rachel. He made a commitment to her father, Laban, to work for him seven years in exchange for Rachel's hand in marriage. At the seven-year mark, Laban gave him . . . Leah, Rachel's older sister. After a series of events, Jacob worked seven *more* years to marry Rachel.

Fourteen years . . . now that's sacrifice. Some sacrifices are small, like giving up coffee to redirect the money to missions. Some sacrifices are large, like giving up a kidney to save someone else's life.

A lot of this book is about small sacrifices, but what if we Americans chose significant sacrifice as part of our corporate "seed-planting?" I know this is radical, but when I hear about the inequities in the world, I wonder if *we* are called to limit ourselves for the sake of the world.

In 1997, David Pimentel, professor of ecology at Cornell University, stated, "If all the grain currently fed to livestock in the United States were consumed directly by people, the number of people who could be fed would be nearly 800 million."

We as a nation have worked *hard* for our prosperity, but where do we draw the line? (This topic would stoke a lively discussion around our dinner table!) Jesus said, *"From everyone who has been given much, much will be required; and*

to whom they entrusted much, of him they will ask all the more" (Luke 12:48b).
What if we were to share our wealth with the hungry?

I mean, seriously, could you survive on 10 percent less food?

Yeah, so could I.

DAILY SEED: What does the word "sacrifice" stir up for you?

"WL's [White Liberals] think all the world's problems can be fixed without any cost to themselves. We don't believe that. There's a lot to be said for sacrifice, remorse, even pity. It's what separates us from roaches." (Dr. Paul Farmer,[67] *Mountains Beyond Mountains: The Quest of Dr. Paul Farmer, a Man Who Would Cure the World*)

JULY 31

MAKE SELECTIONS ACCORDING TO YOUR BELIEFS

Years ago, we became friends with my doctor and his wife. So when it occurred to me that he did abortions, I knew I needed to speak up. (I'm unashamedly pro-life with a soft heart for those who have had abortions.)

So I talked to my doc/friend in a quivery voice, telling him I needed to change doctors to stay in line with my beliefs. Then this happened, seriously. He said, "You know, I only do a few, but even those have been bothering me. I think I'll just quit doing them."

I was stunned.

We can speak up, even in shaky voices. We can make choices based on our convictions.

DAILY SEED: Have you considered choosing doctors, vendors, goods/services, even food sources according to your beliefs?

"There are two primary choices in life: to accept conditions as they exist, or accept the responsibility for changing them." (Denis Waitley, author of *The Psychology of Winning*)

AUGUST

MAKE OVER A COMMUNITY OR CLASSROOM

For Dalit children, going to school is in itself a delight, but imagine trading wooden benches and bare walls for bright colors, murals of alphabets and numbers, smart boards, and school supplies? (Visit www.dalitnetwork.org for ideas.)

For some blighted U.S. neighborhoods, graffiti removal is in itself a delight, but imagine more extensive fix-up and beautification like tree-planting, weatherization, painting, and home repair? (Visit www.extremecommunity-makeover.orgfor ideas.)

The key is working *with* communities, not *for* communities.

DAILY SEED: If you're the hands-on type, consider working on a beautification or makeover project.

"Every living person and thing responds to beauty. We all thirst for it. We receive strength and renewal by seeing stirring and satisfying sites." (Lady Bird Johnson, former First Lady)

MARKET PRODUCTS AND SERVICES

Frank helps ladies in Guatemala sell the scarves they make on looms. The Guatemalans in this area survive on tortillas, so utterly malnourished their growth is stunted. The hope is that this condition won't last forever. Maybe there's a market for their wares.

Micro-enterprise products have traditionally needed foreign markets, but that approach relies on customs regulations and changing fads. Another compelling approach is to build local markets, such as landing contracts to make school uniforms. It's more stable and cost-effective.

If you have marketing skills, you can help market micro-enterprise products, here *and* there.

DAILY SEED: If you are a marketer, get those advertising juices flowing on behalf of micro-enterprise in developing countries. If you are a shopper, buy those products at fair trade shops, online, or from the Franks of the world.

"Doing business without advertising is like winking at a girl in the dark. You know what you are doing, but nobody else does." (Steuart Henderson Britt, marketing management author)

AUGUST 3

MATCH YOUR INTERESTS AND SKILLS WITH VOLUNTEER AND JOB OPPORTUNITIES

First, identify your interests, strengths, and skills. Use inventories like StrengthsFinder.[68]

Secondly, match them with available volunteer or job opportunities. For volunteer opportunities, try www.volunteermatch.org or www.synergyscape.com. For job or internship opportunities, try your state or city's nonprofit website. Colorado's list of nonprofit job and internship postings is at www.coloradononprofits.org. Check with your church. Check with your friends-and-family network.

Know who you are. Invest who you are. Like your favorite sweater, there's nothing like a perfect fit.

DAILY SEED: Do you know your strengths and skills? Match them to volunteer or job opportunities. Seek the perfect fit.

"If your senses are numbed with delusion and denial, you will stop looking for these true strengths and wind up living a second-rate version of someone's life rather than a world-class version of your own." (Donald O. Clifton, *Now, Discover Your Strengths*)

AUGUST 4

MAXIMIZE IMPACT

Medical professionals sometimes return from mission trips feeling the way my friend Cindy put it, "We were just able to put Band-Aids on cancer" so they explore other ways to make a difference in the world medically, like training indigenous Community Health Workers, or raising funds for immunizations, or outfitting a mobile medical clinic to travel to remote areas. They want to *maximize impact.*

Inevitably, when I return from India, someone will ask me if I get discouraged because the poverty is so pervasive. And the answer is no, because a lot of organizations are on the same path of education, healthcare, economic development (and for the Christian ones, starting churches). Because they agree on a model, they *maximize impact.*

Yes, we must seek the best ways to tackle big problems! I believe this strongly, but I also believe we must avoid doing *nothing* for fear of getting it "wrong." *Love may be misguided, but it is never wrong.* Sometimes we maximize impact; sometimes we impact one or two lives, but those one or two lives are just as important as your life and mine. It all helps.

But why live less than "to the max" if we can see how something can be done better?

DAILY SEED: Do you know of a situation that could be handled better, to maximize the impact?

"I would rather be ashes than dust! I would rather that my spark should burn out in a brilliant blaze than it should be stifled by dry rot. I would rather be a superb meteor, every atom of me in magnificent glow, than a sleepy and permanent planet. The proper function of man is to live, not to exist. I shall not waste my days in trying to prolong them. I shall use my time." (Jack London, author of *Call of the Wild*)

AUGUST 5

MEET BASIC NEEDS (FOOD, CLOTHING, SHELTER)

"'I was hungry and you fed me,
I was thirsty and you gave me a drink,
I was homeless and you gave me a room,
I was shivering and you gave me clothes,
I was sick and you stopped to visit,
I was in prison and you came to me.'
"Then those 'sheep' are going to say, 'Master, what are you talking about? When did we ever see you hungry and feed you, thirsty and give you a drink? And when did we ever see you sick or in prison and come to you?' Then the King will say, 'I'm telling the solemn truth: Whenever you did one of these things to someone overlooked or ignored, that was me—you did it to me.'" (Matthew 25:35–40, MSG)

If we provide food, water, a room, or clothes for anyone . . . or visit those who are sick or in prison . . . that's a big deal. The God of the Universe says that it's doing those things to him. Not that it's *like* doing it to him, it *is* doing it to him. Here are his words from verse 40 in the New American Standard version: "Truly I say to you, to the extent that you did it to one of these brothers of Mine, even the least of them, you did it to Me."

Regardless of one's opinions about immigration, it's a fact that people die of thirst in the northern Mexican desert trying to make it to the border. That's desperation for a better life.

And Christians set out water in strategic places.

If I were starving or dying of thirst, I would be eternally grateful to the "angels" who met my need. And I would listen to their message.

Please don't get hung up on the immigration issue. Get hung up on the thirst issue.

DAILY SEED: Meet basic life needs through food pantries, water projects, prisoner visitation programs, etc. There are many options.

"When people were hungry, Jesus didn't say, "Now is that political or social?" He said, "I feed you." Because the good news to a hungry person is bread." (Desmond Tutu)

"I never look at the masses as my responsibility. I look at the individual. I can love only one person at a time. I can feed only one person at a time. Just one, one, one. So you begin . . . I began. I picked up one person. Maybe if I didn't pick up that one person I wouldn't have picked up 42,000. Just begin . . . one, one, one." (Mother Teresa)

AUGUST 6

MEET INFRASTRUCTURE NEEDS

Doug's an engineer. He spent much of his career working on water *infrastructure* around the world. Not isolated projects for isolated villages (which are also important), but infrastructure.

Organized systems of connecting sources with delivery across whole countries. Systems like water, electricity, irrigation, sanitation, communication, technology.

Question: Should we spend our time passing out flashlights in Africa or working on the passage of the Electrify Africa Act, helping Africa bring electricity to 50 million people? Or both? (The Act passed, by the way.)

DAILY SEED: Evaluate projects. Think to scale. Is there a way to be more effective and efficient?

"One of the great mistakes is to judge policies and programs by their intentions rather than their results." (Milton Friedman, Nobel Laureate economist)

MENTOR A TEEN

✳
✳ ✳ The value of mentoring at-risk teens is undisputed. Mentoring benefits young people in ways like increased high school graduation rates, improved behavior, decreased likelihood of initiating drug and alcohol use, etc.[69] It's pretty plain and simple. I'd love to see the stats on the value to the *mentor*. I'm guessing they're equally compelling.

I mentored Diane when she was a teen. Or she mentored me. I keep getting that confused. But our paths probably wouldn't have crossed had it not been for the mentoring agency. So at the end of our official mentoring year, we decided to continue our relationship a bit longer.

That was thirty-five years ago.

DAILY SEED: Consider mentoring . . . or being mentored.

"Mentoring brings us together—across generation, class, and often race—in a manner that forces us to acknowledge our interdependence, to appreciate, in Martin Luther King, Jr.'s words, that 'we are caught in an inescapable network of mutuality, tied to a single garment of destiny.'" (Marc Freedman, author of *The Kindness of Strangers: Adult Mentors, Urban Youth and the New Voluntarism*)

MINIMIZE

✳
✳ ✳ Dan White Jr. blogged about a meeting he had had with a young PhD Kenyan pastor. "I was expecting a delightful spiritual conversation, but I received a gentle but pointed rebuke on American Christianity. The classic memorable line from my new pastor friend was "we don't want your overstuffed Jesus.

Ouch."[70]

The pastor went on to describe how the Christians in his village cared for each other in their poverty and extended care to other villages.

They didn't need consumerism to make them happy or giving. (Consumerism is, after all, a pit that can never be filled. Ugh.) Instead, they happily gave out of their poverty. They apparently had something so many Americans don't have—contentment with the minimal.

DAILY SEED: What would minimalism look like for you?

"Edit your life frequently and ruthlessly. It's your masterpiece, after all." (Nathan W. Morris, author and advocate of debt-free living)

AUGUST 9

OFFER A HOME-AWAY-FROM-HOME TO VISITORS

Sarah lives close to the Immigrant Detention Center. She offers her guest bedroom to families of immigrants who are being detained and those released from detention, people who may only have the clothes on their backs, no phone, and no money. This idea could be used for anyone needing a safe, free, warm home-away-from-home.

My husband and I traveled in Europe years ago. After spending several days camping in a cold rain, we longed for refuge, a home-away-from-home, so we went to L'Abri in Switzerland, a study center founded by Dr. Francis and Edith Schaeffer. People from all over the world were there seeking answers to honest questions about God and the significance of human life. Our room was simple, the meals hot, and the conversations glorious.

L'Abri means "shelter." I've never forgotten how thankful I was for l'abri from the cold rain.

Sarah provides l'abri from far more than an inconvenient rain.

DAILY SEED: Do you have space to spare? Might it become l'abri to visitors?

"It is in the shelter of each other that the people live." (Irish proverb)

AUGUST 10

ORGANIZE

✳ ✳ ✳ I'm not talking about closets here. I'm referring to community organizing—the intentional coming together of people in a community to unify and act on chosen issues.

Communities organize around mutual self-interest on issues like graffiti-removal, crime, solidarity in Poland. A community organizing mantra is "FW-FWFLFH" (Fight, Win, Fight, Win, Fight, Lose, Fight Harder). Communities often organize around issues that need attention but aren't resolved by more conventional means.[71]

Community organizing often gets branded as liberal and radical, but I think it's better described as the American way in its purest form. People often lose faith in the political system, but they can unite and organize for healthy change. It may take blood, sweat, and tears, but it works.

DAILY SEED: Who can you join forces with for positive change?

"Don't agonize. Organize." (Florynce Kennedy, a founder of the National Organization for Women)

AUGUST 11

OVERESTIMATE THE IMPORTANCE OF MENTAL HEALTH

✳ ✳ ✳ One of the seeds we can sow is the mental health seed. We can encourage the health insurance industry to adequately cover it. We can encourage the unstable in our midst to seek it.

We can remind ourselves to practice it, daily.

I believe many of our society's ills are rooted in mental distress. We've seen it in workplace and school violence. I also believe addictions are wreaking havoc.

Addiction is "the state of being *enslaved* to a habit or practice." Mental illness and addictions are forms of slavery, imprisoning people, people we love.

These words from Isaiah 61:1–3 could easily be referring to mental health, i.e., the afflicted, the brokenhearted, captives, prisoners . . . you get the picture:

The Spirit of the Lord God is upon me, / Because the Lord has anointed me / To bring **good news to the afflicted;** */ He has sent me to* **bind up the broken-hearted,** */ To proclaim* **liberty to captives,** */ And* **freedom to prisoners** */ To proclaim the favorable year of the Lord, / And the day of vengeance of our God; / To* **comfort all who mourn,** */ To grant those who mourn in Zion, / Giving them a* **garland instead of ashes,** */ The* **oil of gladness instead of mourning,** */ The* **mantle of praise instead of a spirit of fainting.** */ So they will be called* **oaks of righteousness,** */ The* **planting of the Lord, that He may be glorified.**

DAILY SEED: What does mental health look like to you and those you love?

"If there is a single definition of healing, it is to enter with mercy and awareness those pains, mental and physical, from which we have withdrawn in judgment and dismay." (Stephen Levine, *A Year to Live: How to Live This Year as if it Were Your Last*)

AUGUST 12

PARTNER AND COLLABORATE

DenverWorks and the Denver Rescue Mission put together a partner-ship—part collaboration, part space-sharing, but not quite a merger (for now). You might say the two organizations are "dating." It's proving to be a great idea for both sides. *"Two are better than one because they have a good return for their labor"* (Ecclesiastes 4:9).

I like to think of it as "specializing and referring." DenverWorks can specialize in the jobs and professional clothing piece; Denver Rescue Mission can specialize in the housing and emergency services piece. Then both can have bulls-eye referrals to each other's specialty areas. Partnerships and collaborations often save money, time, and wheel-reinvention (not to mention that funders like to support partnerships).

DAILY SEED: Think about potential partners for your cause.

"As Christians, we should be the best collaborators in the world. We should be quick to find unlikely allies and subversive friends, like Jesus did." (Shane Claiborne, *Red Letter Revolution: What If Jesus Really Meant What He Said?*)

AUGUST 13

PAY IT FORWARD

One day, I had to go to the Motor Vehicle Department, which can be, um, challenging. The lady at the counter was crabby. For some reason, I decided not to capitulate. I decided to pay a moment of patience forward. *"See that no one repays another with evil for evil, but always seek after that which is good for one another and for all people"* (1 Thessalonians 5:15)

So I asked her sincerely, "Are you having a bad day?" She started crying, seriously. We were able to share a moment.

DAILY SEED: Pray this with me: "Lord, give me the grace to make kindness more of a habit. You've been so kind and forgiving to me. Your mercies are new every morning. Help me to pay kindness forward today."

"Kindness is in our power, even when fondness is not." (Samuel Johnson, 18th-century English writer)

AUGUST 14

─────────

PITCH AN IDEA

*** If you know a restaurant owner, pitch the idea of inviting your friends there on a particular night in exchange for 10 percent of the proceeds for your cause.

If you know a business owner, pitch the idea of a corporate sponsorship for your cause. The business gets publicity; the cause gets financial support.

If you're a sportster, pitch the idea of forming a team to raise funds for your cause.

Like Babe Ruth, make the pitch.

DAILY SEED: To whom can you pitch an idea for support for your cause?

"You can't stand in your corner of the forest, waiting for others to come to you. You have to go to them sometimes." (A.A.Milne, *Winnie the Pooh)*

AUGUST 15

─────────

PLAY A GAME

*** I played World Vision's board game many years ago. It was about people who lived in poverty. The problem was, no matter what move you made, it was almost impossible to get ahead. Talk about frustration!

Fast forward a few decades. Now, more "moves" can enable people to bust out of dire poverty.

The "Half the Sky Movement" has a game. World Vision has games. Compassion has games. There's even an event in cities across America called "Compassion Games: Survival of the Kindest." The challenge to play the Compassion Games came from Louisville, Kentucky. Louisville's mayor asked his citizens to perform acts of service during a one-week period. His goal was 55,000 acts of service. Instead, more than 90,000 acts of service were recorded, and Mayor

Greg Fischer proclaimed his city "the most compassionate city in the world." This year's Compassion Games will be held in twenty cities around the world.

DAILY SEED: Play a board game . . . or get your city on board to play the Compassion Games.

"What was the result when inmates at the California Institution for Women competed in last year's annual Compassion Games? For the first time in the institution's history, 11 days went by without a single violent incident." (Jon Ramer, co-founder of the Compassionate Action Network)

AUGUST 16

PLEAD FOR THE WIDOW

* The Burundi "adopt-a-widow" program is different. Really different. * * Both the sponsor *and* the widow check each other out before making the commitment. I *love* that. Yes, the sponsor has funding to assist the widow, but the widows seem to have dispositions made of *velvet steel*, and I don't know about you, but I need role models made out of velvet steel. I need their inspiration and skill. The mutuality of this model is something to consider.

We must always remember widows and orphans. God seem to have a special place in His heart for them.

DAILY SEED: If you know a widow, give her a call.

"*Defend the orphan, plead for the widow. Come now, and let us reason together, says the Lord.*" (Isaiah 1:17b–18a)

POST-IT

✳ Keep a pad of sticky notes handy. Write notes of thanks or encour-
✳ ✳ agement to behind-the-scenes people—bus boys, repair people, hotel
employees, bus drivers, co-workers, lonely people, mail carriers, neighbors.
Or write to in-front-of-the-scenes people. Odds are they get more complaints
than compliments.

DAILY SEED: Plant a smile seed. Post a note to someone today.
  "You smile. I smile." (Unknown)

PRACTICE

✳ I can't resist that "practice random kindness and senseless acts of
✳ ✳ beauty" thing. Maybe it's because I don't do it enough. Or maybe
it's because it doesn't seem world-changing enough, but when I think of my
world-changing friends, they *delight* in kindness and beauty. So I guess what
it comes down to is this: planting seeds of change can be life-giving and *fun*.

And in case you or I get stuck on random acts of kindness ideas, here are
a few . . .

Bake cookies and take them to work. Wash someone else's car. Meet the
new neighbor. Offer to babysit for a single mom. Invite someone lonely to
your home on a holiday. Organize a coat drive. Give a compliment

And who knows? That random or senseless act just might change the world.

DAILY SEED: Make today a RAK day.
  "Unexpected kindness is the most powerful, least costly, and most underrat-
ed agent of human change." (Bob Kerrey, governor and senator from Nebraska)

AUGUST 19

PRACTICE GIVING THANKS

✳ Several times in my life I've had to endure insufferable and finger-point-
✳ ✳ ing people. (Do I sound upset?) It *was* hard to be around them day
after day. So once upon a time, every time I had a "here-we-go-again" thought,
I would substitute a nice thought. And I've made it a practice, except when I
forget . . . sigh.

Instead of "he's compulsive and blaming," I substituted "he's organized and
I appreciate that." Instead of "she's being unfair," I substituted "she's just going
with the information she has."

I certainly don't think we should evade what bothers us. We should be
proactive in dealing with difficult people and situations, but it's awfully easy
to dwell on the negative without ever getting to solutions. Then the negativity
grows into an imprisoning habit.

Giving thanks first helps. *"In everything give thanks."* (1 Thessalonians 5:18)

A solution to forgetting is practicing. And practicing. And practicing.

DAILY SEED: Look around. Name ten things for which you're thankful.

"I'm actually muttering to myself, 'Thank you. . .thank you. . . thank you.'
It's an odd way to live. But also kind of great and powerful. I've never before
been so aware of the thousands of little good things, the thousands of things
that go right every day." (A.J. Jacobs, *The Year of Living Biblically: One Man's
Humble Quest to Follow the Bible as Literally as Possible*)

AUGUST 20

PRAY

✳ One of the definitions of prayer is "spiritual communion with God."
✳ ✳ When I have a spiritual communion with other people, I lean forward

to hear what they're saying. I study their eyes. I take them into my soul. I trust them with mine. We seek something higher and magnificent together.

Do I do that with God? Mmm, well . . . I usually do most of the talking. And then a little later, after I've jabbered and vented, I ask God to fix things. And He does, eventually and always, usually in ways I hadn't expected. But leaning forward and listening and studying God's eyes and taking Him into my soul? And to think He does that with me? That He leans forward listens and studies my eyes and takes Me into His soul? Breathtaking.

Communion. I want more of that with God. Quiet, sacred filling.

DAILY SEED: Commune with God.

"I pray because I can't help myself. I pray because I'm helpless. I pray because the need flows out of me all the time, waking and sleeping. It does not change God—it changes me." (C.S. Lewis)

"Prayer is not asking. Prayer is putting oneself in the hands of God, at His disposition, and listening to His voice in the depth of our hearts." (Mother Teresa)

"I have so much to do that I shall spend the first three hours in prayer." (Martin Luther)

AUGUST 21

PRAY FOR FIVE PEOPLE OR ISSUES A YEAR

Our church in Tucson had a great year-end tradition. On the last Sunday of the year, we each brought a five-person list to the altar. Those were the five people we committed to pray for during the coming year. It was amazing to see the results. Out of the many thousands of people I've met over the years, I particularly remember those groups of five.

Praying in depth for five issues a year would have the same effect—having a targeted rather than vague expectation of God's intervention. Powerful.

DAILY SEED: Choose your five and commit the rest of the year to pray for them, intensely.

"Therefore, confess your sins to one another and pray for one another, that you may be healed. The prayer of a righteous person has great power as it is working." (James 5:16, ESV)

AUGUST 22

PRAY FOR ENEMIES

Philip Yancey spoke on prayer and described a tactic used by soldiers in the Gulf War. On the backs of their decks of cards were pictures of the top fifty-two "bad guys," the most dangerous terrorists they were fighting. It kept the enemy before them constantly.

Philip mused, "What if those cards were used for prayer? What if those soldiers prayed for those fifty-two? Could the fifty-two really have a change of heart?"

And what would happen to us if we prayed for our enemies instead of killing them in our hearts?

DAILY SEED: Pray for an enemy.

"You have heard that it was said, 'You shall love your neighbor and hate your enemy.' But I say to you, love your enemies and pray for those who persecute you, so that you may be sons of your Father who is in heaven; for He causes His sun to rise on the evil and the good, and sends rain on the righteous and the unrighteous." (Matthew 5:43–45)

"Do I not destroy my enemies when I make them my friends?" (Abraham Lincoln)

AUGUST 23

PRAY FOR THE DEPRESSED

✳
✳ ✳ That word "depression" bothers me. It can mean anything from having an off day to having a near-suicidal day. Or year.

As a young bride, I was on the Pill and it messed with my head (although I didn't know what was causing the head-messing at the time). I was seriously depressed, yet happily married with a great career ahead. My advisors told me to "choose joy." I'm sorry to say that I couldn't *choose* anything other than what was. Inwardly, it was dark. Very dark.

Today marks the most advanced day in human history. Tomorrow will be even more advanced, yet depression still lurks, seeking to devour people. That being said, God has answers. For me, it was as simple as getting off the Pill. For others, meds. For others, counseling. For others, forgiving or letting go. For still others, a miracle. I believe in miracles. Pray for answers for the depressed.

DAILY SEED: Who do you know who is/might be depressed? Stop now and pray.

"Here is the tragedy: when you are the victim of depression, not only do you feel utterly helpless and abandoned by the world, you also know that very few people can understand, or even begin to believe, that life can be this painful." (Giles Andreae, British artist and poet)

"He heals the brokenhearted and binds up their wounds." (Psalm 147:3)

AUGUST 24

PRAY THROUGH THE NEWS

✳
✳ ✳ Today's news has to do with terrorism, invasion, privacy fears, a mass abduction, a domestic violence death. It's like yesterday's news. And tomorrow's. And you and I can pray through that news.

Some prayers come easily. Others are *"Kyrie . . .* Lord, have mercy" because we don't know how to pray *specifically* on complex matters. Sometimes we just have to *groan* to God, cry for his help on behalf of the world.

DAILY SEED: Pray through *today's* news.

"'Help' is a prayer that is always answered. It doesn't matter how you pray—with your head bowed in silence, or crying out in grief, or dancing. Churches are good for prayer, but so are garages and cars and mountains and showers and dance floors. Years ago I wrote an essay that began, 'Some people think that God is in the details, but I have come to believe that God is in the bathroom.'" (Anne Lamott)

"And in the same way the Spirit also helps our weakness; for we do not know how to pray as we should, but the Spirit Himself intercedes for us with groanings too deep for words; and He who searches the hearts knows what the mind of the Spirit is, because He intercedes for the saints according to the will of God. And we know that God causes all things to work together for good to those who love God, to those who are called according to His purpose." (Romans 8:26–28)

AUGUST 25

PRAY THROUGH YOUR NETWORK

A network is "an interconnected group or system." Your network's common denominator is . . . you. Your family, your friends, your social media friends, your neighbors, your co-workers.

What can you bring to them that *only you* can provide? Shared history? A certain gift or service? *Prayer?* It's possible you're the *only* person who prays for a certain someone.

DAILY SEED: Walk or drive through your neighborhood. Pray for the people. Especially the crotchety ones.

"God never gives us discernment in order that we may criticize, but that we may intercede." (Oswald Chambers, author of *My Utmost for His Highest*)

PREACH AND TEACH

Some are *called by God* to preach or teach. Both preaching and teaching are spiritual gifts, but read James 3:1—*"Let not many of you become teachers, my brethren, knowing that as such we will incur a stricter judgment."* Yikes! The privilege of speaking comes with the great responsibility to bridle the tongue, to keep it in check, to guard against blessing *and* cursing from the same mouth.

Later in verse 13 we read this: *"Who among you is wise and understanding? Let him show by his good behavior his deeds in the gentleness of wisdom."* And verses 17–18: *"But the wisdom from above is first pure, then peaceable, gentle, reasonable, full of mercy and good fruits, unwavering, without hypocrisy. And the seed whose fruit is righteousness is sown in peace by those who make peace."*

All of us who desire to be wise and understanding can *act* in the wisdom from above, whether or not we verbally preach or teach. For those called to preach or teach, *do.*

Guard the tongue. Sow the seeds. Make a difference.

DAILY SEED: Are you gifted to preach or teach? What are some ways to plant seeds of change through your preaching or teaching?

"Teaching might . . . be the greatest of the arts since the medium is the human mind and spirit." (John Steinbeck, author)

PRIORITIZE

* A friend with four little children recently quit her job. She asked herself
* * that question, "What can *only I* provide to certain people or in certain
situations?" It illuminated a lot of things that others could do. It pared down her
priorities and freed her of the guilt monster. Other people could take over. She
didn't have to be Super Woman after all. Only a few things were essential and
the *most* essential was time with her kiddos.

She prioritized. She did it! She wrote about it. And I'm guessing a lot of
other women are also finding the courage to fold that Super Woman cape and
put it away (or burn it).

Prioritizing liberates. Bra-burning represented women's liberation in the 60s.
Maybe cape-burning could liberate women of today.

DAILY SEED: Regarding the ideas in this book, we must prioritize. What's
your priority way to plant seeds of change into the soil of the world?

"You have to decide what your highest priorities are and have the courage—pleasantly, smilingly, non-apologetically—to say 'no' to other things. And
the way to do that is by having a bigger 'yes' burning inside." (Stephen Covey,
author of *The 7 Habits of Highly Effective People*)

PROMOTE DEMOCRACY

* As imperfect as we are as a country, I want the values and freedom of
* * democracy for others around the world. But freedom is non-existent in
parts of the world. Non-existent. Some democracies have a long way to go in

moving from theory to practice. And with all democracies, a certain amount of garbage has to be tolerated in the name of freedom. Sometimes a lot of garbage.

But all in all, I choose to fight for democracy. I choose to support organizations that work to advance democracy and human rights. And I'm on-my-knees thankful for those who have given their lives for my freedom.

DAILY SEED: Plant a freedom seed today.

"A democracy, that is, a government of all the people, by all the people, for all the people; of course, a government after the principles of eternal justice, the unchanging law of God; for shortness sake, I will call it the idea of freedom." (Theodore Parker, American abolitionist)

"Lord, make me an instrument of Your peace." (St. Francis of Assisi)

AUGUST 29

PROTECT THE YOUNG AND VULNERABLE

Yesterday I visited friends and their three-pound-eight-ounce baby boy in the hospital. He's perfect, but way too early . . . so vulnerable. I wanted to put my arms around the incubator and sing to him. The protection urge was strong, and I'm not even his mommy.

Collectively, we want to protect our young. There's even a code among prisoners to shun (or harm) other prisoners who have hurt children.

Can we do more as a society to protect our young and vulnerable? Can we intervene when a child is bullied? Can we guard children's hearts and minds from violence? Seems they see it everywhere. Can we let them be children long enough to develop skills to deal with the bad stuff of life?

There's nothing like the laughter of a child. If you have children, treasure those laughs.

If it's been a while since you've heard it, listen for it as you go about your days. Let it be a reminder to protect our young and vulnerable.

DAILY SEED: How can you protect the young and vulnerable in your world?

"Defend the weak and the fatherless; uphold the cause of the poor and the oppressed." (Psalm 82:3, NIV)

"We owe our children, the most vulnerable citizens in our society, a life free of violence and fear." (Nelson Mandela)

AUGUST 30

PROVIDE IMMUNIZATIONS AND VACCINATIONS

✳ The first time I visited a Dalit school, five of the children had mumps.
✳ ✳ The physicians on the team jumped into action, possibly saving the fertility (or even the lives) of many. The parents didn't know that mumps is contagious, so they sent their children to school.

Mumps is preventable by vaccines. Providing immunizations and vaccinations can change the world. Period. Unfortunately, however, the vaccination cost has skyrocketed. In 2001, $1.37 provided vaccinations against six diseases. In 2011, the eleven-disease package cost was $38!

In the United States, the federally-funded Vaccines for Children program provides free vaccines for uninsured children, but worldwide, a child dies every twenty seconds from a disease that could have been prevented by vaccinations.[72]

We mustn't give up. Vaccinations have been called the best buy in public health.

DAILY SEED: If this public health issue interests you, do some research on where to give. Imagine a world where nobody dies of preventable diseases.

"Treatment without prevention is simply unsustainable." (Bill Gates, co-founder of Microsoft, philanthropist)

PROVIDE UNGLAMOROUS SUPPORT

✳ ✳ ✳ I've spent many years as an executive director, so you can trust me on this. "General Operating" support is usually the most helpful to nonprofits. It's pretty unglamorous compared to the good feeling of funding something tangible, but the organization knows its needs and most of them are unglamorous—utilities, health insurance, ink cartridges. And the organization might be short on one fund for a particular month because so many have given to another fund. General Operating support keeps things balanced and moving forward. It's not as much fun for the giver but it is lifeblood for the organization.

DAILY SEED: Consider giving "general operating" or "wherever most needed" support.

"Little minds are interested in the extraordinary; great minds in the commonplace." (Elbert Hubbard, American writer and philosopher)

SEPTEMBER

PUT A LASER BEAM ON POLICY

 Our efforts are less effective if public policy negates our cause. We must fight for changes to misguided or downright evil policies. We (the Davids of the world) must turn our sights on the giant (Goliath). And we all know how that David and Goliath thing turned out. What sounds like an impossibly monumental task *can* be done.

An example of policy negating the cause would be the practice of untouchability in India. Prior to 1950, denying Dalits basic human rights was *legal*. There were restrictions in sharing food, access to public places, entry into temples and denial of access to drinking water sources. The Untouchability (Offences) Act of 1955 was enacted, but it put the burden of proof for law-breaking on the accused. The punishments awarded under the Act were not adequate. So the issue was studied for years. The committee's report was submitted in 1969.

Today, untouchability, though illegal, still exists. Policy change rarely means immediate culture shift. I believe all African-Americans would agree that their civil rights didn't immediately change after the Civil Rights Act of 1964.

For the Dalits of India and African-Americans in the United States, the battles for equality continue.

However, policy change is the essential start. Without it, we would be fighting battles that had no legal basis. It's hard enough to fight battles that *have* a legal basis.

DAILY SEED: If there is a cause important to you, is a public policy shift on the issue needed?

"Thus David prevailed over the Philistine with a sling and a stone, and he struck the Philistine and killed him; but there was no sword in David's hand." (1 Samuel 17:50)

"Giants are not what we think they are. The same qualities that appear to give them strength are often the sources of great weakness." (Malcolm Gladwell, *David and Goliath: Underdogs, Misfits, and the Art of Battling Giants*)

SEPTEMBER 2

PUT ON ARMOR

Ephesians 6 tells us to put on the full armor of God so we can stand firm against the world forces of darkness and the spiritual forces of wickedness. It also says our struggle is not against fresh and blood, meaning there's bigger evil going on than that of mere people. This is such a deep truth . . . and one that a lot of people would dismiss as religious nonsense, but I believe it. Do you? I also believe God is love . . . and love conquers all, including evil. Do you believe it?

So what's a "spiritual force of wickedness" anyway? I'm not sure of the nature of pure evil and our enemy Satan, but I've experienced waves of despair and I've vomited in fear. I've looked into the faces of my middle school students, pretty sure some had been abused. I've seen the movies about the Holocaust. I refuse to watch horror movies. They're just too . . . real.

Evil lurks, but we have battle plans. God instructs us to put on the belt of truth, breastplate of righteousness, footwear of the gospel of peace, shield of faith, helmet of salvation, and sword of the Spirit.

My point is that in the battle for your cause or issue or people group, you'll face resistance. Put on the armor. Win the battle.

DAILY SEED: What battles are you fighting? Put on the belt, breastplate, footwear, shield, helmet, and sword.

"The humblest citizen of all the land, when clad in the armor of a righteous cause, is stronger than all the hosts of error." (William Jennings Bryan, American orator and politician)

SEPTEMBER 3

RAISE FUNDS

✳ OK, now for some practical fundraising ideas to try. (This is a long
✳ ✳ one.) For each one, you can attach a fundraising component like selling tickets, suggesting a donation amount, etc.

Host Something. Host an international food fest . . . or a mystery dinner[73]
. . . or a cook-off . . . or a bake sale and cake walk[74] . . . or a non-event (sending
out lovely invitations, of course).

Sponsor Something. Sponsor a raffle (checking on permits first) . . . or an
exchange of books, tools, toys, children's clothes, cookies! . . . or a household
goods bazaar . . . or a live auction . . . or a silent auction . . . or an online auction[75] . . . or a skills auction (of music or cooking lessons, consultation on any
topic, housecleaning, babysitting, home organization, car detailing, yard work).

Put on a Show. Put on a talent show . . . or karaoke night . . . or concert . . . or
dance-a-thon . . . or golf tournament . . . or car wash . . . or read-a-thon or joke-a-
thon or poetry slam.

Sell Something. Sell flowers . . . or cookbooks . . . or holiday cards . . . or
calendars . . . or customized cell phone covers . . . or symbols of hope (ribbons,
necklaces, wrist bands).

Create Something. Paint faces . . . or street numbers on curbs.[76] Create
wishing trees, hanging cards from branches depicting needed goods and their
cost . . . or art auctions (including children's art) . . . or craft shows . . . or
photo contests.

Throw Parties. Throw pizza parties . . . or board game tournaments . . .
or computer game tournaments . . . or pancake breakfasts (inviting a celebrity
for photo ops) . . . or trivia contests.

Do Drives. Collect vitamins, reading glasses, food, bikes, electronics.
Check on organizations in your area that work with nonprofits for the free collection of old electronics. The "payment" is an optional donation to the designated nonprofit.

Go Outdoors. Go caroling (and pass the hat) . . . or host an outdoor movie (Screen on the Green) or a community garage sale . . . or try to play cricket . . . or sponsor cardboard boat races or stargazing bonfires or snow or sand sculpture contests . . . or sidewalk chalk art contests.

Stay Indoors. Provide childcare for "parents' night out" . . . or wrap gifts . . . or sell nap vouchers at work or school (complete with a recliner) . . . or host milk/cookie/movie nights . . . or invite guest lecturers and donate the admissions profit . . . or buy loadable cards from stores that give a percentage to charity. (Our local grocery stores offer a free loadable card to use in their stores. If you sign up through one of their approved nonprofits, $5 of every $100 you spend goes to the charity. No hidden fees: fees.)

Have Fun. Have crazy fun with jail-and-bail events . . . or pink-plastic-flamingos-in-yard events . . . or flash mobs (passing the hat for the cause) . . . or penny challenges[77] . . . or pet parades.

Be Athletic. Walk, run, bike . . . or sponsor triathlons . . . or decathlons. (Consider creating your own decathlon [ten events] with friends. Choose events like running, swimming, biking, tennis, bowling, golf, a basketball shoot-out, archery, volleyball or softball, and, say, checkers. Hold it over a weekend. End it with a picnic!)

Climb Mountains. We Coloradans like to climb our 14,000-foot peaks. One group raised funds per each one "bagged." What activities are unique to your area?

Lose Weight. One friend self-sponsored her weight-loss program to promote her cause. People made a pledge for every pound she lost. Talk about incentive to stick to the diet!

Raise Funds Online. Individuals or groups can set up online fundraising campaigns at www.My.Fundraising.com. It's fast, easy, and *free*.

DAILY SEED: Do you need to raise funds for your cause? Get creative and proactive!

"No one has ever become poor by giving." (Anne Frank, from *The Diary of Anne Frank)*

SEPTEMBER 4

RAISE FUNDS (More Thoughts . . .)

✳ Nicole raises over $3000 a year for women's empowerment in India
✳ ✳ in an untraditional way, by selling apple pies. Sasha Dichter[78] wrote, "(Traditional) fundraising is about a transaction—I raise funds from you, you get nothing in return. I'd rather be an evangelist, a storyteller, an educator, a translator, a table-pounder, a guy on his soap box, a woman with a megaphone, a candidate for change. I want to talk to as many people as I can about my ideas, whether in person or in newsletters or on Facebook or in *The Economist* or at a TED conference, and capture their imagination about the change I hope to see in the world."

Nicole sells pies. Dichter pounds the table. Both are asking, "Are you with me?"

DAILY SEED: How can you tell your mission's story and invite others to join you in funding it?

"I'm proud to be a fundraiser for many reasons, but for one reason more than any other. Fundraising saves lives, and not just in the way you think it does." (Alan Clayton, creative director of Revolutionise)

SEPTEMBER 5

RAISE FUNDS (Still More Thoughts . . .)

✳ Not too long ago, I tried a bizarre fundraising idea. It was an experi-
✳ ✳ ment, because the conventional wisdom was that such ideas no longer work, but it raised over $30,000.

It was a direct mail piece. A letter in an envelope. With a stamp. So yep, mailings still work, at least for a while longer. So do grant-writing, events, auctions, corporate sponsorships, etc.—the traditionals. And never forget the old faithful—direct, person-to-person asks.

I wonder what's next in the always-evolving world of fundraising? It's important to stay ahead of the curve but also to remember the older and often more affluent generation, which (gasp!) still reads traditional mail.

DAILY SEED: List some traditional *and* cutting-edge fundraising ideas for your cause.

"Honor the Lord from your wealth and from the first of all your produce." (Proverbs 3:9)

"But you shall remember the Lord your God, for it is He who is giving you power to make wealth, that He may confirm His covenant which He swore to your fathers, as it is this day." (Deuteronomy 8:18)

SEPTEMBER 6

REACH THE UNREACHED

The Great Commission is clear. *"God authorized and commanded me (Jesus) to commission you: Go out and train everyone you meet, far and near, in this way of life, marking them by baptism in the threefold name: Father, Son, and Holy Spirit. Then instruct them in the practice of all I have commanded you. I'll be with you as you do this, day after day after day, right up to the end of the age"* (Matthew 28:19–20, MSG).

Jesus commissioned His disciples to go out and spread the Gospel, but most believe the commission also applies to *all* Jesus-followers.

Love is the most powerful tool in the world. God *is* love. Read 1 John 4:7–21. *We've been commissioned to reach the whole world with love.*

Could there be a more wonderful task?

DAILY SEED: How can you reach someone with Love today?

"In the midst of a turbulent, often chaotic, life we are called to reach out, with courageous honesty to our innermost self, with relentless care to our fellow human beings, and with increasing prayer to our God." (Henri J.M. Nouwen, *Reaching Out*)

SEPTEMBER 7

READ IMPORTANT BOOKS

Bill Hybels of the Willow Creek Association believes in reading important books. He said, "You're a leader. It's your job to keep your passion hot. Do whatever you have to do, read whatever you have to read, go wherever you have to go to stay fired up. " And . . . "If you lower the ambient noise of your life and listen expectantly for those whispers of God, your ears will hear them. And when you follow their lead, your world will be rocked."

I agree. Reading important books inspires me. Inspiration can mean *inhalation*. We can symbolically *breathe in* motivation, purpose, and passion through our reading.

DAILY SEED: Inhale an important book today.

"I find television very educating. Every time somebody turns on the set, I go into the other room and read a book." (Groucho Marx)

SEPTEMBER 8

READ THE BIBLE

Why change the world? Because the Bible tells us to. Here are a few examples.

"In everything, therefore, treat people the same way you want them to treat you, for this is the Law and the Prophets" (Matthew 7:12).

"Vindicate the weak and fatherless; Do justice to the afflicted and destitute" (Psalm 82:3).

"If there is a poor man with you, one of your brothers, in any of your towns in your land which the Lord your God is giving you, you shall not harden your heart, nor close your hand from your poor brother; but you shall freely open your hand to him, and shall generously lend him sufficient for his need in whatever he lacks. Beware that there is no base thought in your heart, saying, 'The seventh year, the year of remission, is near,' and your eye is hostile toward your poor brother, and you give him nothing; then he may cry to the Lord against you, and it will be a sin in you. You shall generously give to him, and your heart shall not be grieved when you give to him, because for this thing the Lord your God will bless you in all your work and in all your undertakings. For the poor will never cease to be in the land; therefore I command you, saying, 'You shall freely open your hand to your brother, to your needy and poor in your land'" (Deuteronomy 15:7–11).

I grew up with these messages. They're imbedded in me, so I consider the "seedy" life to be the normal Christian life. Sure, I fall short in implementation, but I know the foundation I want my life to be based upon.

What messages did you receive? What's their source?

DAILY SEED: Read James 2 for some world-changing instruction.

"For the word of God is living and active and sharper than any two-edged sword, and piercing as far as the division of soul and spirit, of both joints and marrow, and able to judge the thoughts and intentions of the heart." (Hebrews 4:12)

"I put a New Testament among your books, for the very same reasons, and with the very same hopes that made me write an easy account of it for you, when you were a little child; because it is the best book that ever was or will be known in the world, and because it teaches you the best lessons by which any human creature who tries to be truthful and faithful to duty can possibly be guided. As your brothers have gone away, one by one, I have written to each such words as I am now writing to you, and have entreated them all to guide themselves by this book, putting aside the interpretations and inventions of men." (Charles Dickens in a letter to Edward Dickens [1868], published in *The Selected Letters of Charles Dickens*)

SEPTEMBER 9

READ THE U.N. DECLARATION OF HUMAN RIGHTS

Have you read the United Nations' Universal Declaration of Human Rights? Take a few minutes and check it out at www.un.org/en/documents/udhr. (Truly, I encourage you to do that.)

In 1948, the General Assembly of the United Nations put it forth as a common standard of achievement for all peoples and all nations. It's chock-full of words like freedom, equality, and protection as well as a lot of "anti" sentiments like anti-slavery, anti-torture, and anti-discrimination. Sound familiar? Likely so, if you're an American.

But what if you're not? Hundreds of millions of people in the world can't own property, can't send their children to school, can't use the community well. They can't even read this!

Think about it for a minute. Do you own your home (or might you be able to purchase one someday)? Are your kids able to get a free K-12 education? Can you walk to a tap right now for a glass of water without someone shooing you away?

In Matthew 10, Jesus sent his twelve buddies out to the wider community with these words, "Freely you have received; freely give." I think about this a lot. Even the poorest American among us can walk up to a water fountain and get a drink of cold water. We have received much.

What can you (and I) freely give today?

DAILY SEED: Keep the Declaration on the forefront as you consider the nations. How can you speak out for the rights of others?

"First they came for the Socialists, and I did not speak out—because I was not a Socialist. Then they came for the Trade Unionists, and I did not speak out—because I was not a Trade Unionist. Then they came for the Jews, and I did not speak out—because I was not a Jew.

"Then they came for me—and there was no one left to speak for me." (Martin Niemoller, German anti-Nazi theologian)

RECEIVE

✳   I would be so offended if I gave someone a gift and he/she said, "Oh no,
✳ ✳ I can't take that. You can't afford it and I just wouldn't feel right about
taking it." I'd just take it back and give it to someone who would appreciate it.

It's honoring to the giver to receive their gifts. One of my most treasured
gifts is one I received from Ruth, my sponsored child. It's on my "to grab" list
if my house were on fire. I'm so thankful she gave it to me. It reminds me to
pray for her every time I see it (which is daily) . . . and it makes me smile.

DAILY SEED: Be aware of opportunities to receive graciously.

"Gracious acceptance is an art—an art which most never bother to cultivate. We think that we have to learn how to give, but we forget about accepting things, which can be much harder than giving. . . . Accepting another
person's gift is allowing him to express his feelings for you." (Alexander Mc-
Call Smith, *Love Over Scotland*)

RE-CALIBRATE

✳   If we fall down, we can get back up. If we've never started down the
✳ ✳ right path, we can start today. If we've sown seeds of destruction, we
can repent and start sowing seeds of positive change. If we sin, we can be forgiven. It's the beauty of the Gospel.

It's interesting (and more than coincidental) that today's entry falls on
September 11. Remember where you were on September 11, 2001? I was glued
to the TV and saw the Twin Towers fall in real time. I sat there stunned, sick,
and crying, but at some point during the morning I had to pull away and re-
calibrate. I had to cancel a board meeting and change the day's plans for my

children. The whole world had to re-calibrate.

A personal or communal tragedy can show us what we're made of. It can give us opportunity to take a stand. Re-calibration can move us from stuck to unstuck.

DAILY SEED: Need to re-calibrate in some area of life?

"It's never too late to be what you might have been." (George Eliot, pen name for Victorian writer Mary Ann Evans)

SEPTEMBER 12

RECOGNIZE EVERYDAY HEROES

My Fab friends are . . . fabulous. They are my everyday heroes. They're four extraordinary women, but most of their heroism is quiet. Each would drop whatever she is doing, from wherever she happened to be, to help me if I had a need. And that wouldn't make the papers. They are extraordinary because they quietly care . . . and help . . . and sacrifice . . . and love.

These lifelong friends are my heroes, but others in my everyday life are as well—people like my stepmom, my son-in-law, and my brother-in-law. They are brave, consistent, and honorable. They serve even when nobody is looking. Their actions are like wildflowers in our field. Individually they may go unnoticed, but they are incredibly beautiful nonetheless. And to stoop down and marvel at one in the field is like recognizing an everyday hero.

DAILY SEED: Who are your everyday heroes? Tell them they are.

"A hero is no braver than an ordinary man, but he is braver five minutes longer." (Ralph Waldo Emerson)

REDIRECT THE NEGATIVE

I've stood quietly at a mass grave of three thousand people. They were killed in the tsunami of 2004.

A quarter of a million people died that day. Most of the people at this particular site were Dalits who lived on the India coast as fishermen. The tsunami led to worldwide focus on the Dalits.

Then in 2008, when many Christians were murdered in the Indian state of Orissa, the awareness seeds had already been planted because of the tsunami. The world was outraged. Change started happening.

Tragedies often bring a need to light. Think Komen (breast cancer) or MADD (drunk driving fatalities). Mourning can turn into action. Something negative can bring about something positive.

Joseph said to his brothers in Genesis 50:20, *"As for you, you meant evil against me, but God meant it for good in order to bring about this present result, to preserve many people alive."*

DAILY SEED: Turn something negative into something positive today.

"You build on failure. You use it as a stepping stone." (Johnny Cash, one of the best-selling music artists of all time)

REFUSE TO BECOME COMPLACENT

Although I see needs all around me all of the time (well, not so much when I am preoccupied), some days I'm an ugly American—arrogant, isolated, pretentious. And I have to fight my way back to caring.

Complacency is just so easy.

DAILY SEED: Has something been tugging at you? Choose action over complacency.

"Listen to Mr. Complacency long enough and he'll convince you that what you really, really need is a nap." (Alex and Brett Harris, founders of www.TheRebelution.com, popular Christian teen website)

SEPTEMBER 15

REFUSE TO GET WORTH FROM OTHERS

I've been criticized for not making much money. I've been criticized for sending my kids to inner-city schools. It's hard to disregard what people think. After all, feedback is important and the Bible advocates seeking wise counsel. And although some friends have scratched their heads over my decisions, most have supported and encouraged me on my unusual journey.

I was following John Perkins' 3 Rs[79] and sometimes they're not very popular.

I met Mr. Perkins once, in an elevator on our way to the same meeting. Over the course of that day, I told him about my desire to start DenverWorks. I'd been tentative about the venture because I'm white and a lot of the people we would be serving were not.

Mr. Perkins asked, "Did God tell you to do it?"

"Yes."

"Then do it."

I'm glad I listened to Mr. Perkins (and God). DenverWorks *works.*

Just stay true to your call, even if your upward mobility is defined differently than other people's. Like John Perkins, you and I can become ordinary radicals. And that's worth the choice to not listen to the naysayers.

DAILY SEED: Have you ever been shunned for "marching to the beat of a different drummer?" If your path is God's path, press on, and don't let the naysayers stop you.

"I have no right to say or do anything that diminishes a man in his own eyes. What matters is not what I think of him but what he thinks of himself. Hurting a man in his dignity is a crime." (Antoine de Saint-Exupéry, author of *The Little Prince*)

SEPTEMBER 16

REFUSE TO GIVE UP

✳ Giving up is not the same as *ending* something. We never give up on ✳ ✳ our children, although at some point, we *end* our financial support. We never give up on helping others, although we might *end* a particular helping job. We never give up on ourselves, although the pinnacle of Christian maturity is to *end* one's own efforts and surrender to God.

In fact, endings are often necessary, because there is an appointed time for everything. A time to give birth, and a time to die. A time to plant, and a time to uproot what is planted. But for the purpose of making a difference in the world, refuse to give up. For the purpose of love, never give up. Love never fails.

Winston Churchill said, "Never, never, never give up." He also said, "If you're going through hell, keep going."

DAILY SEED: Refuse to give up.

"There are times in life when people must know when not to let go. Balloons are designed to teach small children this." (Terry Pratchett, English author and supporter of Alzheimer's Disease research)

RELAX

Remember the Greek mythology character, Atlas, who carried the world on his shoulders?

Well, that's not you . . . or me.

A danger of writing this book is that I'd be perceived as recommending too much for each person to bear . . . "the Atlas Effect." And that can't be farther from the truth. My motto is "make a difference daily," not "do *everything* daily."

DAILY SEED: Set down that "world" you've been carrying. Give it to God . . . and relax.

"*. . . casting all your anxiety on Him, because He cares for you.*" (1 Peter 5:7)

RELEASE CAPTIVES

"*The Spirit of the Lord is upon Me, because He anointed Me to preach the gospel to the poor. He has sent Me to proclaim release to the captives, and recovery of sight to the blind, to set free those who are oppressed*" (Luke 4:18).

I don't think Jesus was telling us to spring guilty prisoners out of jail. He was sent to *proclaim* release to captives. In His name, we can also proclaim release to captives—captives of wrong thinking, captives of addictions, captives of human trafficking, captives of all sorts of evil.

So how does that work, exactly? Two things come to mind. One is internal release from captivity, expressed so well through Viktor Frankl's life message. "Everything can be taken from a man but one thing: the last of human freedoms—to choose one's attitude in any given set of circumstances, to choose one's own way." Many captives have been released this way. In fact, captivity can give birth to greatness. Nelson Mandela was held captive for twenty-seven years, *then* became the president of South Africa four years after his release.

The other thing that comes to mind has to do with external release—our help in releasing physical captives. We can support organizations like International Justice Mission. IJM's purpose is to spring victims of trafficking out of captivity.

Can you imagine the joy of release from captivity?

DAILY SEED: Do you know, or know of, any captives? Pray for their release. Act on their behalf.

"There are nations where people live in captivity, fear and silence. I believe, one day, from prison camps and torture cells and from exile, the leaders of freedom will emerge. The world should stand with those oppressed people until the day of their freedom finally arrives." (Tsakhiagiin Elbegdori, President of Mongolia)

SEPTEMBER 19

REMEMBER INDIVIDUALS

Remember the story of the young man walking along the beach with thousands of washed-ashore starfish? He saw an old man tossing them one by one back into the ocean. He asked the old man why, because such a small fraction of them could be saved and the old man's efforts wouldn't make any difference. To which the old man replied, as he tossed another one into the water, "It makes a difference to that one."

Each of the 7+ billion people on Earth is fearfully and wonderfully made. *Each* has 60,000+ miles of blood vessels. *Each* has needs and longings. *Each* is important and unique. *Each* has a purpose.

Treasure *each* person in your life.

DAILY SEED: Regard each person you see today as if he/she is the most important being on the planet.

"What man among you, if he has a hundred sheep and has lost one of them, does not leave the ninety-nine in the open pasture, and go after the one which is lost, until he finds it? And when he has found it, he lays it on his shoulders, rejoicing. And when he comes home, he calls together his friends and his neighbors, saying to them, 'Rejoice with me, for I have found my sheep which was lost!'" (Luke 15:4–6)

SEPTEMBER 20

REMEMBER THE POOR

Paul and Barnabas, according to Galatians 2:10, were sent to the Gentiles with one thing to remember—the poor.

In Kenya, if a poor woman is raped and reports it, she must get in line behind 149,000 other women awaiting their day in court.

We must never ever ever ever ever forget the poor.

DAILY SEED: Do you know a poor person? Remember him/her.

"Sometimes I would like to ask God why he allows poverty, famine and injustice in the world when he could do something about it . . . but I'm afraid he may ask me the same question." (Unknown)

SEPTEMBER 21

REPRESENT A MINISTRY OR NONPROFIT

When I walk into DenverWorks these days, few people know I started the ministry. The new staff and volunteers don't have a clue about that, but *they* have taken up the cause. I *love* that.

They represent the ministry. *They* help the clients prepare their resumes. *They* put on fundraising events. *They* represent DenverWorks as they chat in grocery store lines or over lunch.

Every cause needs champions.

DAILY SEED: Hoist the flag for a ministry or nonprofit that is making a difference in the world.

"Give us clear vision that we may know where to stand and what to stand for—because unless we stand for something, we shall fall for anything." (Peter Marshall, former Senate chaplain, *Prayers Offered by the Chaplain*)

SEPTEMBER 22

REQUEST A SPEAKER

Steve Jobs gave one of the top graduation speeches of all time at Stanford in 2005, just after his 2004 cancer diagnosis. Gradspot.com gave it an award for the "Best Ironically Uplifting Comment About Death." He died in 2011.

There was only one Steve Jobs, but there are many other world-changers. Invite one of them to speak to your group. Check out speaker cost-sharing with a group with similar interests. Check out author book tours. An author visiting your area might be interested in multiple speaking engagements.

And one other thing . . . might the speaker be you?

DAILY SEED: Who do you know, or know of, who would make a great speaker for your cause (including yourself)?

"If you have an important point to make, don't try to be subtle or clever. Use a pile driver. Hit the point once. Then come back and hit it again. Then hit it a third time—a tremendous whack." (Winston Churchill)

SEPTEMBER 23

RESCUE (OR NOT)

When I think of rescue efforts, I think of sinking ships. Rescuers endanger their own lives to retrieve those who are drowning. Who do you know who is drowning in sorrow or problems? Rescue can begin with hearing their cries for help.

That being said, sometimes we shouldn't rescue. Some among us are enablers, alas. Some are codependent. Some want to rescue even if it harms the person being rescued.

Should we rescue girls who have been kidnapped for sex trafficking? *Absolutely.*

Should we rescue those who make us feel guilty but can do for themselves? *Um, no.*

The Bible speaks to *both* sides of rescue in Galatians 6: *"Bear one another's burdens, and thereby fulfill the law of Christ"* (v. 2). *"But each one must examine his own work, and then he will have reason for boasting in regard to himself alone, and not in regard to another. For each one will bear his own load"* (vv. 4–5).

In *Starship Troopers,* Robert Heinlein asks, "How often have you seen a headline like this?—'Two Die Attempting Rescue of Drowning Child.' Poor arithmetic, but very human. It runs through all our folklore, all human religions, all our literature—a racial conviction that when one human needs rescue, others should not count the price."

In *The Language of Letting Go,* Melody Beattie says, "I used to spend so much time reacting and responding to everyone else that my life had no direction. Other people's lives, problems, and wants set the course for my life. Once I realized it was okay for me to think about and identify what I wanted, remarkable things began to take place in my life."

In other words, sometimes we rescue. Sometimes we don't.

DAILY SEED: Is someone in your life crying out for rescue? Should you say "yes, absolutely" or "um, no . . . "? Respond with wisdom and conviction.

"For He rescued us from the domain of darkness, and transferred us to the kingdom of His beloved Son." (Galatians 1:13)

SEPTEMBER 24

RESOLVE CONFLICTS

I used to teach life skills to gang members and incarcerated youth. (It was kind of humbling because they presumed that I was an expert on living an impeccable life. Right.)

One of our units was on conflict resolution—being clear on *what* the problem was, being clear on *whose* problem it was, using tools like "time-outs" for the rage to simmer down, etc.

And one time, a young man raised his hand and asked me if people really did that stuff. He was incredulous . . . and the others in the room nodded in agreement. So I asked them a question. "How many of you are locked up in here because you did something *in the heat of the moment*?" (I meant it to be a rhetorical question, but almost all the hands went up.) My point was that learning some conflict resolution skills could save jail sentences, family relationships, lives.

Many cities have Conflict Centers with programs and classes. Conflict resolution books abound. Like anything worth obtaining, study might be required. Conflict resolution isn't necessarily intuitive. Peacemaking might be one of the most useful seeds to plant.

Read James, chapter 4, for info on conflict resolution.

DAILY SEED: Think of a conflict needing resolution. Are you called to be the peacemaker?

The "peacemakers" are not simply those who bring peace between two conflicting parties, but those actively at work making peace, bringing about wholeness and well-being among the alienated." (Robert A. Guelich in *Sermon on the Mount: A Foundation for Understanding*)

SEPTEMBER 25

REST

*Resting at least one-seventh of the time was God's idea. It's called
* *Sabbath. Jesus seemed to have done a fair amount of hanging out with
friends and family, resting.

Do you know anyone who is frenetic? Trying to be God, Jr.? I think if we're
really following God, we'll take time to rest.

I couldn't have written this book when my children were young. Some
days, I felt like I'd already made nine thousand sandwiches and to make one
more was just too much. I certainly didn't have the luxury of writing. I didn't
have much money and I was tired. Rest was a treasure.

I don't think we should beat ourselves up if we're broke or exhausted.
Maybe that's a time to rest . . . and giving a cup of cold water is all we can do.
(See Matthew 25:35–45.) In fact, even if we're *not* broke or exhausted, we're
to rest. It's just part of the equation.

DAILY SEED: What is restful for you? Is rest part of your equation?

*"By the seventh day God completed His work which He had done, and He
rested on the seventh day from all His work which He had done. Then God blessed
the seventh day and sanctified it, because in it He rested from all His work which
God had created and made."* (Genesis 2:2–3)

SEPTEMBER 26

RE-PURPOSE, RE-USE, AND REPAIR

*On a mission trip to India a few years ago, we took craft projects for the
* *women. We parceled out thread, beads, and sewing tools into Ziploc
bags. The women were polite about the project but what they *really* valued were
the Ziploc bags. Imagine living in a slum with dirt floors and no protection

for your food. Imagine a miracle such as Ziplocs or Tupperware. Food safe from insects and rats. Another time in India, the zipper on my suitcase broke. It wouldn't make the trip back to the United States. I asked our Indian leader where I could discard it and she virtually lunged at it.

Things can be re-used and repaired.

I shop at Goodwill stores, where somebody's throwaway item makes a cute accessory for me . . . but our throwaway items are like *gold* there.

The disparities are staggering. I can do more to re-purpose, re-use, repair, or give to someone in need (rather than discard) . . . and really learn the lessons from my Indian sisters.

DAILY SEED: Are there things you can re-purpose, re-use, repair, or give to someone in need (rather than discard)?

"Use it up, wear it out, make it do, or do without." (Unknown)

SEPTEMBER 27

RUB ELBOWS WITH WORLD CHANGERS

If you could spend an hour with anyone in the world, who would it be? I think my hour would be with my world-changer buddies. Seems every time we get together, I *skip* back to my car. They motivate me. They make me want to shout from the rooftops. They give me ideas. They like me. That's what world changers do. They *like* people. And wouldn't you know it? Most of them are *happy* people.

DAILY SEED: Who are your world-changer friends? If you don't have any, get some. Have lunch together. Listen to their stories. Be inspired. Skip!

"Alone among unsympathetic companions, I hold certain views and standards timidly, half ashamed to avow them and half doubtful if they can after all be right. Put me back among my Friends and in half an hour—in ten minutes— these same views and standards become once more indisputable. The opinion of this little circle, while I am in it, outweighs that of a thousand outsiders: as Friendship strengthens, it will do this even when my Friends are far away. For we all wish to be judged by our peers, by the men 'after our own heart.' Only they really know our mind and only they judge it by standards we fully acknowledge. Theirs is the praise we really covet and the blame we really dread." (C.S. Lewis, *The Four Loves*)

SEPTEMBER 28

HELP A STUDENT IN NEED

Susan provides scholarships and mentors to women who need a break in life. The women are chosen for their aptitude, spunk, and financial need. Susan didn't need to *invent* new educational programs. Those abound. She just connects the students with resources, meeting practical needs in practical ways. And the women thrive.

Some of us can't furnish a scholarship, but we could contribute to a scholarship fund . . . or tutor a student . . . or mentor a student . . . or pray for students that face academic and peer pressure.

DAILY SEED: Consider the students in your life. Encourage them financially or otherwise.

"Education makes a people easy to lead but difficult to drive: easy to govern, but impossible to enslave." (Peter Brougham, British statesman, in a speech to the House of Commons, 1828)

SEPTEMBER 29

SEND STUFF (OR NOT)

Debbie P. organizes people to pack and send containers (those giant ones) to Africa. The cost? About the cost of a used car. The value? About the value of a really nice home in many parts of the United States. In other words, packing a container is *way* worth it for the Africa Coalition of which Debbie is a part.

However, it often *doesn't* pay to send a container. Our used clothes and cars may or may not be worth exporting. The Center for International Disaster Information encourages people *not* to send goods during disasters. The website gives ways to re-purpose donated goods for conversion to cash for disaster relief.

DAILY SEED: Do the homework before exporting goods. They might be a treasure trove . . . or there might be better ways to help those in dire need.

"To know the road ahead, ask those coming back." (Chinese proverb)

SEPTEMBER 30

SERVE FROM YOUR GOD-GIVEN DESIGN

One of my favorite things in life is to help people discover their God-given design—their strengths, their gifts, their purpose, that thing that lights them up. I remember one young DenverWorks client who came in with no life in her eyes. She was almost physically and spiritually comatose. The reason? She had been told she was utterly worthless.

So we started with a career test. She scored high in two categories—manual dexterity and helping professions. Bit by bit, we put together possibilities, like learning sign language to work with the deaf. And I got to see an amazing sight—the beginnings of twinkly eyes. The last time I saw her, I think she was walking about two feet off the ground. She was *not* utterly worthless. She was alive. She had found meaning and purpose. She just needed to discover her God-given design.

First Corinthians 12:14–15 says, *"For the body is not one member, but many. If the foot should say, 'Because I am not a hand, I am not a part of the body,' it is not for this reason any the less a part of the body."*

All of us have a design. All of us have a key part to play. All of us can serve. All of us can plant seeds of positive change into the world around us.

DAILY SEED: Whether you are in the arts or manufacturing or teaching or nursing or government or whatever, you are gifted to serve.

"Hide not your talents, they for use were made. What's a sundial in the shade?" (Benjamin Franklin)

"As each one has received a special gift, employ it in serving one another as good stewards of the manifold grace of God. Whoever speaks, is to do so as one who is speaking the utterances of God; whoever serves is to do so as one who is serving by the strength which God supplies." (1 Peter 4:10–11)

OCTOBER

SERVE THROUGH ART

✳ ✳ ✳ Our India ministry needed to raise funds for a new school. I could envision a courtyard of bricks that donors could purchase (with their name or a Scripture or whatever). You've seen those. But shipping bricks to India? No way—*way* too expensive.

Faith is an artist. We came up with a variation on the theme. A mosaic mural! Donors could purchase a brick-sized plywood unit which was one two-hundredth of the mural. Each unit had the donor's name or a Scripture and went together to form a fabulous picture of God's hands holding a jacaranda tree with doves. (Mind you, Faith is extraordinary.) It now graces the entryway to the school/children's home . . . and, by the way, made a lot of money for the project.

DAILY SEED: Are you an artist? You are gifted to serve.

"We artists are indestructible; even in a prison, or in a concentration camp, I would be almighty in my own world of art, even if I had to paint my pictures with my wet tongue on the dusty floor of my cell." (Pablo Picasso)

SERVE THROUGH DRAMA

✳ ✳ ✳ *Ruined* is a play by Lynn Nottage. It won the 2009 Pulitzer Prize for Drama. It's about the plight of women in the civil-war-torn Democratic Republic of Congo. After I saw it, I could hardly speak. Years later, tears still come to my eyes when I think of it.

Whether on the stage or screen, little communicates like drama.

DAILY SEED: Are you a dramatist? You are gifted to serve.

"The first step (especially for young people) to controlling your world is to control your culture. To model and demonstrate the kind of world you demand to live in. To write the books. Make the music. Shoot the films. Paint the art." (Chuck Palahniuk, American novelist)

OCTOBER 3

SERVE THROUGH MUSIC

✳ Bono of U2 is one of the "seediest" guys around (in the good sense).
✳ ✳ Check out www.one.org, which Bono co-founded. Check out his views on Jesus in *Bono* by Michka Assayas.

Many musicians use their platform for world change. Caedmon's Call advocates for the Dalits.[80] More Than Music does a presentation called "At the Table with Dr. King" which inspires students to listen for and respond to the unique call on their lives to serve others.[81] Brad Corrigan of the number-one-selling indie rock band, Dispatch, created a Kickstarter campaign to fight forced commercial sexual exploitation. The campaign was called "Ileana's Smile" in honor of a young girl from a trash dump community in Nicaragua who was forced into prostitution in order to make money for her family. Ileana contracted HIV and died in 2011.

DAILY SEED: Are you a musician? You are gifted to serve.

"The most powerful thing about this walk is to have the courage to look inside first. We must deal with the trash inside and have a transformed heart before we can deal with the trash out there, across the borders. What power there is in God's relentless love. Change starts here, in our own healed hearts." (Brad Corrigan)

OCTOBER 4

SERVE THROUGH SPORTS

✳ ✳ ✳ Njaka runs a soccer ministry in Madagascar. Gregg organized the legacy gift of Payne Steward (pro golfer who died in a plane crash) for a state-of-the-art golf course for inner-city kids. Jim went to India to conduct basketball clinics. They are missionaries . . . and they have a blast.

Interestingly, Jim was able to teach object lessons about God through basketball imagery. He couldn't have taught a traditional Bible study to the Hindu teens who attended the camp.

God doesn't use us *in spite of* our interests. He uses us *because of* and *through* those interests. Who said changing the world can't be fun?

DAILY SEED: Are you an athlete? You are gifted to serve.

"When you invest your time, you make a goal and a decision of something that you want to accomplish, whether it's make good grades in school, be a good athlete, be a good person, or go down and do some community service and help somebody who's in need." (Nick Saban, University of Alabama football coach)

OCTOBER 5

CAMEO (by Gregg Bettis[82])

✳ ✳ ✳ At 6:00 P.M. on June 10, 2004, on a "routine" final approach into a small private airpark on the beautiful shores of Table Rock Lake in Southwest Missouri, suddenly without warning, a powerful right quartering wind shear slammed into the rear of the high performance airplane I was piloting, forcing me sharply off course to the left.

Immediately after applying full power for a go-around and pushing full right rudder, my left wing tip struck the top of an eight-foot tree near the edge of the runway at 120 mph. I watched my propeller fold up like a paper clip as I crashed through the top branches of another nearby tree and then dove full speed into the ground.

The last thing I distinctly remember before the impact of the crash and waking up in the hospital was being in perfect peace. In a flash, the Holy Spirit brought to mind Psalm 91:1: *"He who calls out to the Most High, shall abide under the shadow of the Almighty"* . . . and I rapidly cried out to God three times, "Oh God help me, Oh God help me, Oh God help me."

I share my story with you because I am absolutely convinced that the power of heaven is unlocked on earth when we give ourselves to the intimacy of abiding in the very presence of the Almighty. God heard and answered my call and He is obviously not finished with me or with you yet.

My earnest prayer for all who reads my story, for all of my friends and family and for every precious young person who comes through our gates at Kids Across America Kamps is that you and they might gain a renewed momentum. I hope you experience a holy fascination to pursue the greatest pearl of human existence . . . a personal, intimate, passionate, living relationship with the glorious Creator of the universe.

In the next days, weeks, months and years, no doubt you or someone you know will need help. If so, call 9-1-1 . . . Psalm 91:1 . . . and I assure you that Jesus will hear you, and He will answer you. In addition, like me, you too will experience new dimensions of His kingdom power and glory!

DAILY SEED: When you need help, don't hesitate. Pray and believe in the greatest pearl of human existence.

Give me the Love that leads the way
The Faith that nothing can dismay
The Hope no disappointments tire
The Passion that'll burn like fire
Let me not sink to be a clod
Make me Thy fuel, Flame of God. (Amy Carmichael, missionary to India)

SERVE THROUGH YOUR PROFESSION

Some of the most valuable help a nonprofit can receive is from professionals who volunteer their service. Doctors can donate time at inner-city clinics. Lawyers can donate consultation to people in poverty struggling with family or civil matters . . . or help a nonprofit set up its 501(c)(3) status. Accountants can donate assistance in preparing audits or 990s. Elected officials can just show up at an event and provide their vote of confidence.

DAILY SEED: Are you a professional? You are gifted to serve.

"Give me a lever and a place to stand, and I will move the world." (Archimedes)

SERVE WITH YOUR HANDS-ON SKILLS

At our Tucson church, we called them SWAT Teams (Servants with a Trade). They fixed cars, repaired roofs, and unclogged sinks for widows, single moms, and others who just couldn't afford to pay. They were some of the happiest people in the church. They *loved* blessing people with their mechanical and construction skills.

DAILY SEED: Are you a laborer? You are gifted to serve.

"I would never want to reach out someday with a soft, un-calloused hand—a hand never dirtied by serving—and shake the nail-pierced hand of Jesus." (Bill Hybels, founding pastor, Willow Creek Association)

OCTOBER 8

SET UP A FOUNDATION

*** Think dinner table conversation where all of the family members can weigh in on the family giving, even the children. Donor-advised funds can be set up through community foundations (with small admin fees) or can stand alone.

If you're a person of means, check with your financial advisor about the advantages of setting up a foundation.

If you're a person with less net worth, just give. A dollar bill is a dollar bill, whether given through a foundation or slipped directly into the offering plate.

DAILY SEED: Check out www.foundationcenter.org to open your eyes to a whole world of possibilities.

"As you grow older, you will discover that you have two hands, one for helping yourself and the other for helping others." (Audrey Hepburn, actress)

OCTOBER 9

SET UP MUTUAL AID FUNDS

*** Charles Gray and friends came up with a great idea. They set up a mutual aid fund. Each member deposited a lump sum and contributed a small amount each month. It was called a FIN (Friend in Need) Fund which allowed its members to request money when an emergency arose. Monthly meetings determined distributions but also served as forums for non-cash creative solutions. What a terrific idea![83]

DAILY SEED: Might this be an idea for you and your friends (or your church or neighborhood)?

"A friend loves at all times." (Proverbs 17:17)

"I would rather walk with a friend in the dark than walk alone in the light." (Helen Keller)

OCTOBER 10

SHARE A MOMENT WITH SOMEONE DIFFERENT

If there could be a silver lining to the sickening school, workplace, and theater shootings since Columbine, it would be the launch of anti-bullying campaigns. Seems so many of the perpetrators are characterized the same way—as loners and "different," although *Time* called Eric Harris and Dylan Klebold "the monsters next door." The massacre sparked debate over the nature of high school cliques and bullying, among many other things like gun control. Being bullied doesn't justify the unspeakable suffering of the victims and their families, but we know bullying is real.

What can we do about that? It costs little to chat with the loners and the different, but interestingly, to do so takes intention and even courage.

The movie, *Silver Linings Playbook*, speaks of taking negativity and using it as fuel. Whether we're teens or adults, let's fuel up to share a moment, or lunch, with someone different today. It just might matter.

DAILY SEED: Who comes to mind that's a loner or different from yourself? Consider reaching out.

"There's a drive in a lost soul—in one that is searching for acceptance, companionship, belonging, whatever you want to call it. The slightest coincidence ignites a spark that one hopes will lead to something meaningful." (Doug Cooper, author of *Outside In*)

SHARE THE WELL

✳
✳ ✳ Caedmon's Call (the band), named a whole album *Share the Well* after seeing the discrimination against Dalits at the community well. That's a caste issue, but 10 percent of the world can't share the well because there's no clean water to be had. Over 1,400 children die *every day* from diarrhea caused by bad water and poor sanitation.[84] Even if you did nothing else, supporting clean water worldwide would change the world.

DAILY SEED: Do some research for water aid to learn how to "share the well" with your dollars.[85]

"And whoever in the name of a disciple gives to one of these little ones even a cup of cold water to drink, truly I say to you, he shall not lose his reward." (Matthew 10:42)

SHARE YOUR IDEAS

✳
✳ ✳ Sam Walton said that their best ideas come from clerks and stock boys (of Walmart or Sam's).

Ideas are priceless. None are inconsequential. Some make the world a better place. As soon as I put the last period on this book, I know I'll hear about another great *idea*. And another and another. And so might you.

Implement them. Share them. Send them to me if you'd like! And check out these world-changing ideas created by USAID (Development Innovations Ventures and Grand Challenges for Development).[86]

DAILY SEED: Share your ideas. Maybe they'll go viral!

"One resists the invasion of armies; one does not resist the invasion of ideas." (from *Histoire d'un Crime,* Victor Hugo)

OCTOBER 13

SHOW HOSPITALITY

* ** Nanci's home is always full of people—giggly young people, leaders huddled in a corner planning a meeting, friends of all sorts and colors. Don and Judy's home is quieter with homemade soup bubbling on the stove. Jacque's home is a "there's-the-frig-help-yourself-to-anything" home. I've been in a number of slum homes where chai and cookies are offered to guests. All are warm, hospitable places. They feel good.

Maya Angelou. "People may not remember what I said or did, but they'll remember the way I made them feel."

We can offer a couch or a sandwich or a hug. That's hospitality.

DAILY SEED: Who needs your couch or sandwich or hug?

"Be hospitable to one another without complaint." (1 Peter 4:9)

"Definition of Southern Hospitality—'A state of mind. More than where you were born. See also fried chicken, sweet tea, football, beer, acoustic guitars, hospitable. Being devoted to front porches, magnolias, the good Lord, and each other.'" (from Pinterest)

OCTOBER 14

SHOW YOUR SUPPORT

* ** The Dalit Freedom Network uses a clay cup as its symbol. Even to this day, some Dalits drink out of mud cups then smash them on the ground, because if an upper caste person were to drink after them, they (the uppers) would become "polluted." So, we've distributed the clay cups widely to stand in solidarity with the Dalits.

Once a friend was at the coffee shop in a U.S. congressional building. At the cash register was . . . a clay cup.

Symbols, displays, stickers, ribbons, clay cups = conversation and heightened awareness.

DAILY SEED: What tangible way can you show your support for a cause?

"Man's ultimate concern must be expressed symbolically, because symbolic language alone is able to express the ultimate." (Paul Tillich, Christian existentialist philosopher, from *Dynamics of Faith*)

OCTOBER 15

SHUN EXCUSES

Mrs. Shambarger had no tolerance for excuses. She was the director of our women's singing group in college. And we were *good* . . . in large part because Mrs. Shambarger had no tolerance for excuses. If one of us got "sort of" sick and needed to miss a performance, Mrs. Shambarger would say, "You can be sick some other time."

It's amazing what you can accomplish when you can't duck out easily.

DAILY SEED: Own your life. Shun explanations and excuses.

"To rush into explanations is always a sign of weakness." (Agatha Christie, *The Seven Dials Mystery*)

"He that is good for making excuses is seldom good for anything else." (Benjamin Franklin)

OCTOBER 16

SIGN PETITIONS; DECLARE EMPATHY

This Declaration of Empathy (petition) can be signed online, right now, at www.dalitnetwork.org. I would encourage that! Here's a portion . . .

"Whereas, The Dalit people of South Asia are considered history's longest standing oppressed population, subjected for millennia to discrimination, untouchability, bonded slavery, and social and economic segregation;

Whereas, This Declaration expresses our deepest concern and empathies for all Dalits everywhere who are subject to the scourge of human trafficking and modern day slavery;

Whereas, We the people of The United States of America are in a unique position to understand the suffering of slaves, the passion of abolitionists, and the path to freedom;

Now therefore, We the undersigned parties . . . assert that our nation should recognize modern day slavery . . . and should strongly oppose the continuing degradation, discrimination, oppression, and segregation of Dalits anywhere in the world."

In contrast, I was recently asked to sign a petition in favor of expanded legalized gambling to support public education. Of course, the gambling part was in *extremely* small print. I'm glad I read the fine print first.

DAILY SEED: Study the issue and if it passes muster, add your name to the cause.

"You will always be a puppet on someone else's line if you don't care enough about the big picture to let your tiny voice be heard. When it is combined with the tiny voices of millions of others that is the real power." (Kenneth Eade, *An Involuntary Spy*)

OCTOBER 17

SIT ON A NONPROFIT BOARD

Sometimes it's hard to find good board members. Granted, good board members need to take things very seriously, offer wisdom and guidance, commit a good amount of time, and raise funds (at least in a "give-or-get" way).

Oh . . . maybe that's why it's hard to find good board members.

But, if you're so inclined, you are needed.

DAILY SEED: Sit on a board . . . not on a fence.

"I've always respected those who tried to change the world for the better, rather than just complain about it." (Michael Bloomberg, former mayor of New York)

OCTOBER 18

SOW SEEDS OF A GIVING HEART IN CHILDREN

I grew up believing that giving isn't optional. It's just what you do. It helps the world work.

Dad sat at his desk every Sunday morning and made out the tithe check. The sense of giving was so positive it didn't occur to the "little girl me" that it was sacrificial for our parents.

Later, I realized that not every kid grew up that way. Some of those grown-up kids are shocked at such a strong emphasis on generosity. But there's hope! We can all discover or re-discover the joys of generous giving.

I'm grateful to my parents and my church for sowing seeds of giving into my spiritual DNA.

DAILY SEED: Teach a child to have a generous spirit. Show the way.

"Train up a child in the way he should go, even when he is old he will not depart from it." (Proverbs 22:6)

OCTOBER 19

SPEAK UP

I've spent countless hours on the sidelines of soccer matches, volleyball games, and track meets with other parents. Maybe you have too. That's a lot of time to chat. I've found that moms love hearing about other moms, so that's been a fun place to start. I can connect two worlds because of my personal journey—the Dalit mom world with the U.S. soccer mom world. In a casual shoulder-to-shoulder way, I can speak up.

I can also speak up (and turn up the heat) with people of power and influence. Maybe you can too.

As we say to our toddlers, "Use your words!"

DAILY SEED: What issue needs your words?

"Let the words of my mouth and the meditation of my heart be acceptable in Your sight, O Lord, my rock and my Redeemer." (Psalm 19:14)

OCTOBER 20

SPEAK

I know people who would rather jump into a shark-infested pool than speak in public. Me? I'll blab to anyone who will listen.

Speaking can take many forms, like talking to our kids while driving them to school or teaching a class or addressing a crowd. Some people, however, have speech issues, as Moses did. See below for God's solution. God wouldn't be deterred! There are other ways to speak.

DAILY SEED: What form does your speaking take?

"Then Moses said to the Lord, 'Please, Lord, I have never been eloquent, neither recently nor in time past, nor since You have spoken to Your servant; for I am slow of speech and slow of tongue.' The Lord said to him, 'Who has made man's mouth? Or who makes him mute or deaf, or seeing or blind? Is it not I, the Lord? Now then go, and I, even I, will be with your mouth, and teach you what you are to say.' But he said, "Please, Lord, now send the message by whomever Thou wilt. Then the anger of the Lord burned against Moses, and He said, 'Is there not your brother Aaron the Levite? I know that he speaks fluently. And moreover, behold, he is coming out

to meet you; when he sees you, he will be glad in his heart. You are to speak to him and put the words in his mouth; and I, even I, will be with your mouth and his mouth, and I will teach you what you are to do. Moreover, he shall speak for you to the people; and he will be as a mouth for you and you will be as God to him.'" (Exodus 4:10–16)

"Let your speech always be with grace, as though seasoned with salt, so that you will know how you should respond to each person." (Colossians 4:6)

OCTOBER 21

SPONSOR A CHURCH PLANTER

"Joseph," a church planter in India, met a Hindu lady in his village who had been diagnosed with cancer. She knew that death was imminent and was afraid of hell and what she would become in the next birth. She believed that her karma (good or bad deeds) would determine her reincarnation (next form of life). So Joseph shared the Good News of Christ with her and she became a believer. What a beautiful relief, to know that her sins were forgiven and her eternity would be spent with God.

Sponsorship of a church planter through various missions agencies often covers rigorous, academic Bible training, outreach materials, vocational and literacy training for the villagers, and in some cases, a bicycle to reach the people!

DAILY SEED: Sponsorship—what a way to reach nations for Christ. Consider a Church Planter sponsorship.

"The elders who rule well are to be considered worthy of double honor, especially those who work hard at preaching and teaching. For the Scripture says, 'You shall not muzzle the ox while he is threshing,' and 'The laborer is worthy of his wages.'" (1 Timothy 5:17–18)

OCTOBER 22

SPONSOR A COMMUNITY HEALTH WORKER

✳ A friend visited a hospital in India. One side was state-of-the-art; the
✳ ✳ other side had blood-stained mattresses with no sheets and limited supplies. Women about to give birth were turned away if they couldn't pay. Guess which side was the Dalit side?

Paul Farmer, MD and professor of medical anthropology at Harvard, was asked in 2007, "Which single intervention would do the most to improve the health of those living on less than $1 a day?" Dr. Farmer's reply: "Hire community health workers to serve them."

Operation Mobilization India/Dalit Freedom Network (DFN) has a four-tier healthcare delivery system—Community Health Workers, Regional Clinics, Mobile Clinics, and a Nurses Training College/Dalit Hospital Project. The Community Health Workers are most often hired from the villages they'll serve. They are trained in the basics. They receive an income. They are respected. They save lives.

DAILY SEED: Sponsorship—what a way to reach nations with healthcare. Consider a Community Health Worker sponsorship.

"You treat a disease, you win, you lose. You treat a person, I guarantee you, you'll win, no matter what the outcome." (Patch Adams, American physician, comedian, and social activist)

OCTOBER 23

SPONSOR A SCHOOL, CLASSROOM, OR TEACHER

✳ Sponsoring a school or classroom can include naming rights, of-
✳ ✳ ten in honor or memory of a loved one. The sponsorship may cover

construction or desks or science lab equipment or computers or library books or . . . a restroom. In poor areas of India, having Western toilets is a big deal!

Sponsoring a teacher can be done domestically (example, Teach for America) or globally (options abound).

DAILY SEED: Sponsorship—what a way to reach nations with education. Consider sponsoring a school, classroom, or teacher.

"True teachers are those who use themselves as bridges over which they invite their students to cross; then, having facilitated their crossing, joyfully collapse, encouraging them to create their own." (Nikos Kazantzakis, author of *Zorba the Greek*)

OCTOBER 24

SPONSOR A WOMAN

When "Grace" was a six-year-old Dalit child, both of her parents died within a year of each other. Not wanting the extra burden, her relatives sold her to the village headman for 400 rupees (about $9).

Later, her uncle, who had become a Christian, found her and took her to his city. The family cared for her and she too became a believer in Christ. She's now married and has a child.

But Grace was uneducated and the only one in the family who couldn't earn a living. One day, she met sewing instructors from a Christian ministry's vocational program. She joined the sewing class and did quite well. (A high percentage of such programs' grads get jobs, many making up to five times what they had previously earned.)

Can you imagine making five times what you currently earn? Sponsoring a woman in a vocational training is a great investment.

DAILY SEED: Sponsorship of a woman—what a great way to empower nations. Consider sponsorship of a woman in a developing country.

"You educate a man; you educate a man. You educate a woman; you educate a generation." (Brigham Young, pioneer leader of Latter Day Saint movement)

OCTOBER 25

SPREAD GOOD NEWS

A definition of the word "gospel" is "the *good news* of salvation in Jesus Christ." Who wouldn't want to spread good news? Jesus is the ultimate change maker. He changed the world a couple of thousand years ago and is still changing the world. That's good news. And here's more. *"Beloved, let us love one another, for **love is from God; and everyone who loves is born of God and knows God.** The one who does not love does not know God, for **God is love**"* (1 John 4:7–8).

Can you think of any better news than that? I mean, seriously?

Believe the gospel.

Spread the gospel.

DAILY SEED: Who do you know who needs some good news today?

"And then he told them, "Go into all the world and preach the Good News to everyone." (Mark 16:15, NLT)

OCTOBER 26

SPREAD GOOD WORKS

"What use is it, my brethren, if a man says he has faith, but he has no works? Can that faith save him? If a brother or sister is without clothing and in need of daily food, and one of you says to them, 'Go in peace, be warmed and be filled,' and yet you do not give them what is necessary for their body, what use is that? Even so faith, if it has no works, is dead, being by itself" (James 2:14–17).

Robert Gelinas says it this way: "Faith without works is dead, but works without faith is empty." And Micah 6:8 speaks *clearly* on doing good works. *"He has told you, O man, what is good; and what does the Lord require of you but to do justice, to love kindness, and to walk humbly with your God?"*

"Do," "love," and "walk" are verbs.

The daily seeds in this book are combinations of evangelism and social justice, good words and good works . . . a sacred pairing.

DAILY SEED: What good work(s) does God have in mind for you today?

"We are His workmanship, created in Christ Jesus for good works, which God prepared beforehand so that we would walk in them." (Ephesians 2:10)

OCTOBER 27

STAND FIRM

Remember the story from *The Odyssey* about Odysseus and his men approaching the island of the Sirens who sang so seductively and irresistibly? Odysseus had been warned about the Sirens, so he plugged his men's ears with beeswax and had them bind him to the mast of the ship. He alone heard the Sirens' song, promising to reveal the future. He begged to be released from his fetters, but his faithful men only bound him tighter. They could have removed the beeswax, but they *stood firm* and even went above-and-beyond to help their leader.

There's a message here. Can we make difficult decisions or resist temptation if we aren't first standing firm? Can we help others if we aren't first standing firm?

Odysseus and his men needed wax and ropes in order to stand firm. People in recovery need to rid their homes of temptation in order to stand firm. All of us need to be grounded in our beliefs in order to stand firm.

DAILY SEED: Do you need wax, ropes, accountability, a good housecleaning, or anything else to stand firm?

"He brought me up out of the pit of destruction, out of the miry clay, and He set my feet upon a rock making my footsteps firm." (Psalm 40:2)

"Be on the alert, stand firm in the faith, act like men, be strong." (1 Corinthians 16:13)

OCTOBER 28

START A CAMPAIGN OR MOVEMENT

✳ ✳ ✳ Check out www.change.org to start a petition, campaign, or movement. Millions of people are involved with change.org and there are victories daily, from suicide prevention on the Golden Gate Bridge to creating a chemo Barbie for kids with cancer to standing against date violence to . . . your choice.

Just now, while sitting at my computer, I paused. I leaned back in my chair. I mentally searched for the perfect story about a campaigner, but too many came to mind. So many of you carry a torch for something important. You rattle the bushes. You rally the troops. You move people.

DAILY SEED: Consider creating a campaign for your cause.

"We're working for a world where no one is powerless and where creating change is a part of everyday life." (www.change.org)

OCTOBER 29

START A FILM FORUM

✳ ✳ ✳ A few years ago, we started a humanitarian film forum called World-Views. We chose a film a month, invited a speaker on the topic, and invited nonprofits working on the topic to set up booths. We held the films at a local theater. And to quote the film *Field of Dreams*, "If you build it, they will come." They did. The movies have ranged from *The Lost Boys of Sudan* with local lost boys as speakers . . . to *Paper Clips* about the scale of the Holocaust . . . to *Osama* about the Taliban . . . to *Crash* about racism.

Later, our church started a film series called TransForums. They expected a handful of people at the first showing, and over three hundred showed up.[87]

DAILY SEED: Watch a documentary on an important topic. Consider starting a film series.

"No art passes our conscience in the way film does, and goes directly to our feelings, deep down into the dark rooms of our souls." (Ingmar Bergman, Swedish film director)

OCTOBER 30

START OR JOIN A STUDY GROUP

✳
✳ ✳ "Great Decisions" is America's largest discussion program on world affairs. It involves reading the Great Decisions briefing book, watching a DVD, and meeting in a discussion group. It's produced by the Foreign Policy Association and is non-partisan. Each year, eight topics are chosen by a panel of experts. This year's topics include the Israeli/US relationship, defense technology, the Islamic awakening, and China's foreign policy. [88]

I love this study. It brings us together, pushes us, empowers us, and improves us as world-changers.

And if this one isn't your cup of tea, there are *plenty* of other books to study, both secular and faith-based. World issues are multi-dimensional and have layers and layers of history/background. Frankly, I need to study unbiased sources to make up my mind. Study is to my growth as soil, light, and water are to plants' growth.

DAILY SEED: Check out study groups on global topics.

"It is a mistake to think that the practice of my art has become easy to me. I assure you, dear friend, no one has given so much care to the study of composition as I." (Wolfgang Amadeus Mozart, classical composer)

OCTOBER 31

STAY INFORMED DAILY

✳ Do you have a reliable news source? Is it balanced or outlandishly
✳ ✳ biased? I urge you to **use your own grid and filter out opinion/spin** in the news. (Spin disgusts me.) We need facts so we can create our own interpretations and responses.

This is called *thinking.*

I urge you to stay informed by both secular and sacred sources. This book has biblical underpinnings, but I've gotten some of my best stuff from USAID, Oxfam, One.org, Human Rights Watch, etc. If an organization has portions with which you don't agree, weed those portions out. And conversely, if you're not a Christian, I urge you to read what the Bible has to say about being a world changer. Radical ideas run rampant in the Bible, like turning the other cheek or esteeming others as higher than oneself.

And there are some remarkable words about living a seedy life in the Bible. Check out Luke 8 and John 15 about seeds and fruit and such.

DAILY SEED: Stay informed daily. Filter out spin. Think.

"The average American expends more time becoming informed about choosing a car than choosing a candidate." (George Will, Pulitzer Prize-winning political commentator)

NOVEMBER

STRIVE TOWARD ELIMINATION OF A DISEASE OR SOCIAL ILL

＊ ＊ ＊ The Carter Center tackled eradication of Guinea worm disease, an agonizing disease that affected 3.5 million people in the 1980s. Today, it's 99.9 percent obliterated.

The Dalit Freedom Network has tackled abolishment of the caste system. It's a tall order, affecting one-sixth of the world. Today, there is progress.

As I write, millions of people are fighting against something dreadful, like cancer. And someday there will be a cure. A couple of decades ago, cancer was a death sentence, but that's no longer true.

Every cause has champions. Think Jonas Salk (polio vaccine) or Neil Armstrong (first moonwalk) or B.R. Ambedkar (hero of the Dalits). But also consider the co-champions, those who stood *beside* Salk and Armstrong and Ambedkar . . . people who were *also* striving toward elimination of that disease or social ill. Consider being a part of the championship team in winning the war against a disease or social ill. And celebrate wildly when that war is won.

DAILY SEED: What illness or practice would you love to see eradicated? Join a team striving for change.

"Whether our task is fighting poverty, stemming the spread of disease or saving innocent lives from mass murder, we have seen that we cannot succeed without the leadership of the strong and the engagement of all." (Kofi Annan, seventh Secretary-General of the United Nations)

NOVEMBER 2

STUDY CULTURAL DIFFERENCES

Foreign to Familiar by Sarah Lanier starts with a story about Aida. Aida is Lebanese and had been in the United States eight years before she realized a cultural reality. She said, "I've been lonely since moving here. When people in the office would ask me if I wanted to go to lunch, I would say 'no' to be polite, fully expecting them to ask me again. When they didn't and left without me, I thought they didn't really want me along. In my culture it would have been too forward to say 'yes' the first time. For this reason, I have few American friends."[89]

Eight years! How terribly sad.

Years ago, we invited some Japanese students over for dinner. They ate our Southern delicacies politely, then seconds, and thirds, and fourths, until we realized it was impolite for them to decline if offered. Yikes! They were probably miserable.

A little study can make a big difference as we interact with other cultures. Books like *Foreign to Familiar* help. Spiritually-speaking, there are no distinctions between people, but cultural *norms* vary widely.

DAILY SEED: Do you know someone from a different culture? Ask him/her about cultural differences they experience.

"For there is no distinction between Jew and Greek; for the same Lord is Lord of all, abounding in riches for all who call on Him." (Romans 10:12)

NOVEMBER 3

STUDY WORLD RELIGIONS

We Westerners need to study Islam, not just out of curiosity, but out of necessity. And certainly the reverse is true as well. We (and they) need truth—not stereotypes, because world events are lining up for a showdown. Just today, I read that the sharia court of ISIS issued a fatwa that its jihadists should "empty the city of Al-Qamishli of all Christians, take their women; they are yours, and behead the Christian men." Does mainline Islam support this? How do everyday Muslims deal with terrorism in the name of Allah? How would everyday Christians deal with terrorism in the name of Christ? What are Muslims told about Christians—that they/we are moral-less infidels? And what are Westerners told about Muslims—that their women wear burkas covering suicide bombs?

Are Muslims and Christians enemies? Jesus addressed the issue of enemies. *"You have heard that it was said, 'You shall love your neighbor and hate your enemy.' But I say to you, love your enemies and pray for those who persecute you, so that you may be sons of your Father who is in heaven; for He causes His sun to rise on the evil and the good, and sends rain on the righteous and the unrighteous"* (Matthew 5:43–45).

Um, that kinda nails it.

So we need to study other religions from a trustworthy source. We need to understand other religions and formulate our response. If world events *do* line up for a showdown, what position will you take?

DAILY SEED: Seek out a world religions course from a reliable source. Then, find your voice on the topic. And *"beyond all these things put on love, which is the perfect bond of unity."* (Colossians 3:14)

"My experience of living with people of diverse religions and cultures taught me that one will never be at peace with the other if one is at war with oneself." (Tariq Ramadan, Swiss-born professor of Contemporary Islamic Studies at the University of Oxford)

NOVEMBER 4

SUBSTITUTE HEALTH FOR HARM

People who go to AA meetings *substitute* a meeting for a drink. People who go to the gym *substitute* a workout for a burger. People who are raging mad *substitute* a hefty run for throwing a chair through a window. Jesus *substituted* His death on the cross for all of us humans who fall short.

In other words, for *all* of us who don't have our act together *all* of the time, we can substitute a good act for our temptation to act badly.

DAILY SEED: Substitute a good act for a bad one today.
"Do not be overcome by evil, but overcome evil with good." (Romans 12:21)
"Love is the one option that is always open to you." (Unknown)

NOVEMBER 5

SUBSTITUTE IMPORTANT FIGHTS FOR STUPID FIGHTS

We've heard about church splits over things like the color of the carpet. How embarrassing!

We should be fighting on the *same* side for people who don't even have a church building, much less carpet.

Get over the stupid fights. Get on with the ones that matter.

DAILY SEED: Are you waging any stupid wars?
"Fight the good fight of faith; take hold of the eternal life to which you were called." (1 Timothy 6:12)

NOVEMBER 6

SUGGEST "IN LIEU OF" GIFTS

✳ If you don't need more dishes or clothes or *stuff*, suggest "in lieu of"
✳ ✳ gifts to your friends and fam.

"In lieu of a (Christmas, wedding, birthday) gift, please consider a dona-tion to XYZ charity or to a charity of your choice." My husband and I did this and raised several thousand dollars for a school in India. The nonprofit sent out tax receipts. Later, I sent school pictures and a report to those donors (which they loved!). Alternatively, you can set up an online wish list with links at gift-giving time, such as to a nonprofit's Christmas catalog.

On the flip side, giving and receiving tangible gifts is a big deal. "Receiv-ing Gifts" is one of the love languages in Gary Chapman's book, *The Five Love Languages*, so this idea isn't for everyone, but it might work for some.

DAILY SEED: Treasure gifts, both given and received, in whatever form they take.

"If instead of a gem, or even a flower, we should cast the gift of a loving thought into the heart of a friend, that would be giving as the angels give." (George MacDonald, Scottish clergyman and author)

NOVEMBER 7

SUPPLY A WISH LIST NEED

✳ Some nonprofits post wish lists on their websites. Our local alternative
✳ ✳ high school needs copy paper, gift cards, books—it's all on their web-site under "Fill a Need."

Sometimes our local food bank hands out "fill a need" cards to people entering the grocery store.

It's easy to pick up an item or two and put it in their basket on the way out.

Just make sure giving something tangible is on the wish list of the group in need, not *your* wish list for them. In other words, some giving, although well-intentioned, may not help.

According to the Center for International Disaster Information fact sheet, "frequently, clean water, food and clothing are available near the disaster site, and sending more can get in the way of staging and delivering life-saving supplies. Uninvited donations take relief workers' time to manage and may put local merchants out of business, creating a second economic disaster. They are also exponentially more expensive to send, incur more costs every time they change hands and leave a big carbon footprint in their wake. In addition to helping more people at lower cost, monetary donations are used to set up medical clinics, reunite family members and provide shelter and other services which are vital to survivors." [90]

DAILY SEED: If you wish to give something tangible, check with the recipient organization and give what it needs.

"I have a simple philosophy. Fill what's empty. Empty what's full. Scratch where it itches." (Alice Roosevelt Longworth, American writer and prominent socialite)

NOVEMBER 8

SUPPORT AFFORDABLE HOUSING OR HOMELESS SHELTERS

Do you ever feel guilty when you pass a homeless person with a sign? I heard the director of a big homeless shelter say the probability of alcoholism in the "sign-holding population" is about 99 percent. But we still feel guilty sometimes if we don't give. And there's always the chance the person is part of the 1 percent.

The shelter and affordable housing people know far better than the average Joe about how to meet the needs. Give to those organizations. Then hand out their cards (with a granola bar) to the sign-holders.

And don't get me wrong. I've given money. I've bought breakfast burritos and circled back to hand them to the person on the corner. I've handed out DenverWorks cards. And once I gave some money to a lady and later saw her on a nearby street, drunk.

I've felt wrong about *not* giving at times. And I've felt wrong about giving at times.

Tough call, but supporting affordable housing or homeless shelters or rescue missions is a sure-fire winner. They deal with the short-range *and* long-term needs of the homeless.

DAILY SEED: If you're not sure what to do next time you see a sign-holder, consider substituting your question mark with a donation to a shelter or mission. Really **see** the person on the street and meet the need in the best way possible.

"I mean, I don't think I'm alone when I look at the homeless person or the bum or the psychotic or the drunk or the drug addict or the criminal and see their baby pictures in my mind's eye. You don't think they were cute like every other baby?" (Dustin Hoffman, actor)

NOVEMBER 9

SUPPORT CHRISTIANS WORLDWIDE

Up to 500 Christians were killed by Hindu nationalists in the Indian state of Orissa in 2008. 50,000 were left homeless. Of the 827 reports filed, 75 ended in convictions, and nine people were convicted for their role in killing Christians. Nine.[91]

Open Doors has information on the persecuted church and the annual International Day of Prayer for the Persecuted Church. In some form today, 100 million Christians are being persecuted and it's estimated that 180 are killed each month for their faith. Christians are the most persecuted religious group worldwide.[92]

DAILY SEED: The first two Sundays in November are dedicated to prayer for the persecuted church. See www.idop.org for this year's details.

"And if one member suffers, all the members suffer with it." (1 Corinthians 12:26a)

NOVEMBER 10

SUPPORT INSTITUTIONS THAT MAKE A DIFFERENCE

✳   SAME Café's mission of *serving good food for the greater good* says it all.
✳ ✳ SAME (So All May Eat) is the first nonprofit restaurant in Denver. Its patrons set the price for their mostly local, organic cuisine. The café states, "If you can give more, please do. If you have a little less, pay what you can. If your pockets are empty, exchange an hour of volunteer work at SAME for a meal."[93]

DAILY SEED: Seek out institutions in your area that make a difference in your community.

"Is this not the fast which I choose, to loosen the bonds of wickedness, to undo the bands of the yoke, and to let the oppressed go free, and break every yoke? Is it not to divide your bread with the hungry, and bring the homeless poor into the house . . . ?" (Isaiah 58:6–7a)

NOVEMBER 11

SURVEY GLOBAL MINISTRIES AND NGOs

✳   My friend Emily is one of the most joyful women I know, yet she's
✳ ✳ daily aware of horrors women face . . . women she *knows*. How is it possible to be so joyful and painfully aware at the same time? It's because she

knows them entirely, not just their suffering but also their creativity, resilience, strength, and overcoming love. They are such a blessing to her.

They fill her with so much hope. She comes alongside them and brings others with her.

She was the Founder/President of an organization called Tirzah International. Tirzah encompasses over 150,000 women leaders worldwide who tackle these seven issues affecting women:

Poverty—70 percent of the world's poorest are women.

Education for Girls—90 million girls are excluded from school annually because of their gender.

HIV/AIDS—60 percent of HIV sufferers aged 15–24 are women.

Modern Day Slavery—80 percent of slaves are female.

Violence Against Women—One in three women are beaten or abused by an intimate partner.

Female Circumcision—At least three million girls are at risk each year for this procedure.

Forced Early Marriage—In the next decade, 100 million girls are expected to enter forced marriages.[94]

Frederick Buechner said, "The place God calls you to is the place where your deep gladness and the world's deep hunger meet." Emily's deep gladness meets the world's deep hunger. And Tirzah is a global ministry that's making a world-class difference.

DAILY SEED: Where does your joy in helping meet what moves you to tears? Survey *global* ministries and NGOs (non-governmental organizations) and find a fit.

"NGOs have contributed to the achievement of "the defeat of apartheid in South Africa; the end of the dictatorship in Chile; the political transformation of the Philippines; the overthrow of the Communist regimes in Central Europe; the creation of an international treaty prohibiting land mines; and the establishment of an international criminal court."[95]

NOVEMBER 12

CAMEO (by Emily Voorhies[96])

Not everyone has the courage to stand strong in the face of a military dictatorship. But my friend Dorothy does. When we first met, I was struck by her gentle spirit, sweet smile and peaceful demeanor. My immediate thought was, "How can she be so calm and brave?

I knew Dorothy lived in a country that was ruled by a ruthless military dictator. Her movements as a Christian and pastor were watched closely. She never knew when her work would be closed down, or whether she would be arrested and interrogated. On my first visit to her nation, we held our meetings in a van for safety and privacy.

But Dorothy is a risk-taker and she quietly continued with her ministry, including empowering AIDS widows and orphans through a medical outreach program. Working with other women leaders in her nation, she has been part of an outreach to families living in villages, educating them about the risk of human trafficking for their young, innocent daughters.

When asked about her fears, Dorothy shares numerous instances where God provided protection, encouragement and courage. One of her greatest joys is to see young people in her country understand God's love, and to mentor them in their faith and life. The stories of transformed young lives give great hope for the future of her nation.

Dorothy's life sows the seeds of faith, joy, courage and commitment. Our friendship has impacted my life in so many ways and I am grateful to call her my friend.

DAILY SEED: Pray for Dorothy and others who are threatened. Pray for "Dorothy Courage" within.

"Be strong and courageous, do not be afraid or tremble at them, for the Lord your God is the one who goes with you. He will not fail you or forsake you." (Deuteronomy 31:6)

"Take courage, son; your sins are forgiven." (Matthew 9:2)
"Take courage, your faith has made you well." (Matthew 9:22)
"Take courage; it is I, do not be afraid." (Mark 6:50)
"Take courage; I have overcome the world." (John 16:33)

NOVEMBER 13

SUPPORT LOCAL MINISTRIES AND NONPROFITS

* * * Recently, a friend dropped off some clothes at DenverWorks' professional clothing closet. She met a volunteer who had worked at the closet for eight years. The volunteer told my friend that her half day a week at Denver-Works was the highlight of her week. She got to help ladies (who had little going their way) look and feel beautiful.

Unbeknownst to the volunteer, my friend was the one who gave the seed money for the clothing closet in the first place. Both the volunteer and the donor are seed-planters.

There's an amazing network of ministries in Denver, each specializing in a "slice of the pie" and referring clients to each other's slices. No doubt your city has an amazing network too. Pray that God will show you your slice of the pie.

We all have a place.

DAILY SEED: Where does your joy in helping meet what moves you to tears? Survey *local* ministries and nonprofits and find a fit.

"The Amish question, 'What will this do to our community?' tends toward the right answer for the world." (Wendell Berry, "Out of Your Car, Off Your Horse," in *Sex, Economy, Freedom and Community: Eight Essays*)

NOVEMBER 14

TAKE CARE OF MISSIONARIES AND EXPATRIATES

I have an American friend who lives in India as a missionary. Here's her account of a wedding she recently attended.

"After the wedding, we went to the house where the return bus would pick us up. Hours dragged by waiting for the other guests to come. For entertainment, we watched fifteen ladies making bindis (cigarettes made from tree leaves). Finally all the other guests arrived. Bus wouldn't start.

We finally arrived back at the compound. The search began of where to place us for the night. When everyone got settled for the night, it looked like spoils from combat—bodies everywhere, scattered wherever there was available space; arms and legs draped over the next person—it was quite a sight. The neighbors gave us permission to sleep on their rooftop. It had a weather-worn tarp for us to use, which was laid between a haystack and pile of small trees used for construction scaffolding. On top of the tarp, our paper thin blanket was spread out for the mattress. The pillows we were given were as fluffy as bags of cement. Even though a street light was beaming in our eyes, it was much cooler and quieter than being inside.

Next morning came and everyone did their morning routines—brushing teeth, standing in line for the one toilet stall and one bath stall, washing faces and feet in the laundry area. Later in the morning, just after tea time, dinner arrived—a live goat. From where I was stationed, I couldn't see the complete killing, but could see it took longer than expected for its life to be finished. When I came out of the room, the head and front forelegs were placed nearby and the carcass was hanging from a tree at the laundry area. An uncle was butchering it."[97]

Well, I don't know about you, but I get impatient when my computer won't boot up quickly enough, much less having to deal with delays that take hours (or days) rather than a few seconds, searing heat, power outages, cement-like pillows, contaminated water, hole-in-the-floor toilets, bucket baths, carcasses hanging from trees, flies thick in the air.

My friend, Terri, who wrote the wedding narrative above, was happy to experience the highs and lows of India. She assisted community health workers and indigenous pastors with structure, reporting, etc. so they could do their work without encumbrances.

Some expatriates live in foreign countries to better enable them to do important work, sort of like missionaries. We can ask them what they need. (We might be surprised.) We can financially and prayerfully support them. We can host them when they come home. We can send them what they can't get in-country. In India, they ask for American brands of deodorant and children's cereal. Who knew?

DAILY SEED: Ask missionaries and expatriates what they need. Many are living sacrificial lives.

"Some wish to live within the sound of a chapel bell; I wish to run a rescue mission within a yard of hell." (C.T. Studd, British cricketer and missionary)

NOVEMBER 15

TAKE CARE OF YOUR OWN

Mother Teresa said, "Love begins by taking care of the closest ones—the ones at home."

What does "taking care of the ones at home" mean to you? Going to work to provide? Choosing *not* to work outside the home in order to take care of the kiddos? Caring for elderly parents?

Taking care of the ones at home can be the hardest work of all. And I fear that some *run* to "save the world" before they *stay* to take care of their own. We must have correct priorities.

DAILY SEED: Does anyone within your household need some extra care?

"But if anyone does not provide for his own, and especially for those of his household, he has denied the faith and is worse than an unbeliever." (1 Timothy 5:8)

NOVEMBER 16

TAKE NOTE OF WHAT GOD WANTS

In the movie *Wild*, the heroine was mad at God. Really mad. She hurled her hiking boot off a mountain and screamed obscenities. It would have been bad timing to say, "Now dear one, what do you think God wants of you?" She would hurl *me* off the mountain.

Maybe you're a little mad at God. Some days, I am too.

That being said, I'm not giving up. I trust his heart. And I want to do what he wants. It's the only formula that makes sense and gives me peace because he has the big picture and I don't.

This is what the Lord said through the prophet Isaiah:

"This is the kind of fast day I'm after: to break the chains of injustice, get rid of exploitation in the workplace, free the oppressed, cancel debts.

"What I'm interested in seeing you do is: sharing your food with the hungry, inviting the homeless poor into your homes, putting clothes on the shivering ill-clad, being available to your own families.

"Do this and the lights will turn on, and your lives will turn around at once. Your righteousness will pave your way. The God of glory will secure your passage. Then when you pray, God will answer. You'll call out for help and I'll say, 'Here I am.'

"If you get rid of unfair practices, quit blaming victims, quit gossiping about other people's sins, if you are generous with the hungry and start giving yourselves to the down-and-out, your lives will begin to glow in the darkness, your shadowed lives will be bathed in sunlight.

I will always show you where to go. I'll give you a full life in the emptiest of places—firm muscles, strong bones. You'll be like a well-watered garden, a gurgling spring that never runs dry. You'll use the old rubble of past lives to build anew, rebuild the foundations from out of your past. You'll be known as those who can fix anything, restore old ruins, rebuild and renovate, make the community livable again." (Isaiah 58:6–12, MSG)

DAILY SEED: What does God want you to do?

"O taste and see that the Lord is good; how blessed is the man who takes refuge in Him!" (Psalm 34:8)

NOVEMBER 17

TAKE PHOTOS

When you return from a trip or life-changing experience, most people you'll talk to will be polite.

And they'll have about a two-minute attention span. Your world has been turned upside down. Theirs has stayed about the same. Photos can draw them in.

Nanci's written a photo book called *To Love the Slumdog: My Journey Serving the "Untouchables"—The Dalit.* It's full of images that capture her experience and emotions. Each time she returns from a trip to India, she shares the story in pictures on her laptop. "This lady has leprosy and this beach was devastated by the tsunami and this is a church meeting under a banana tree."

Some images are haunting. Some are hauntingly beautiful. All are unforgettable.

DAILY SEED: Capture "seeds of change" in photos.

"When words become unclear, I shall focus with photographs. When images become inadequate, I shall be content with silence." (Ansel Adams, photographer and environmentalist)

NOVEMBER 18

TARGET THE U.N.'S MILLENNIUM DEVELOPMENT GOALS (MDGs)

* Previously (June 30) I wrote about the eight Millennium Development
* * Goals adopted by the United Nations General Assembly in September of 2000. They range from halving extreme poverty rates to halting the spread of HIV/AIDS, all by 2015. They form a blueprint agreed to by all the world's countries and leading development institutions to build a better world.

There are between 330,000 and 450,000 churches in America today. What if these churches decided to join hands with the United Nations in focusing on the current Millennium Development Goals? It would be world-changing. Here are the Cooperative Baptist Fellowship's innovative ideas for doing just that. Your church or denomination could borrow these ideas or come up with your own:

For MGD #1 regarding poverty, their suggested activity is a barn dance.

For MGD #2 regarding universal primary education, a Scrabble night.

For MDG #3 regarding gender equality, a sacred sewing circle.

For MDG #4 regarding child mortality, a baby bears project.

For MDG #5 regarding maternal health, a global baby shower.

For MDG #6 regarding HIV/AIDS and other diseases, volleying for nets.

For MDG #7 regarding environmental sustainability, an intergenerational garden club.

For MDG #8 regarding global partnerships for development, microenterprise investing.

By being wise, unified, and collaborative, the Church can create synergy that can change the world.

We can be more than the sum of our parts.

DAILY SEED: Check out www.un.org for the post-2015 MDGs. Check out www.thefellowship.info for more info on the Cooperative Baptist Fellowship's innovations on the MDGs.

"Between now and 2015, we must make sure that promises made become promises kept. The consequences of doing otherwise are profound: death, illness and despair, needless suffering, lost opportunities for millions upon millions of people."

"The MDGs were never meant to be a one-way street—something that rich countries do for poor ones. Quite the contrary: our long-standing work for development in general has always been based on global solidarity, on a shared interest, on a powerful sense of community and linked fates in an interconnected world." (U.N. Secretary-General Ban Ki-moon)

NOVEMBER 19

MDG #1—ERADICATE EXTREME POVERTY

In the mid-90s, my hand flew to my mouth when I saw the photograph of the starving child in the foreground with a waiting vulture in the background. I still have that reaction when I see it. I'm guessing you do too. Photographer Kevin Carter committed suicide three months after taking the photo and one week after winning the Pulitzer Prize for it.

One person can't bear the weight of eradicating extreme poverty alone. Kevin Carter and the little girl in the picture suffered the same fate. Together, however, as the Church, as a compassionate country, as a "first world" society, we must bear the weight together . . . and act.

DAILY SEED: How can your church or group team up to tackle MDG #1?

"As covetousness is the root of all evil, so poverty is the worst of all snares." (Daniel Defoe, author of *Robinson Crusoe)*

NOVEMBER 20

MDG #2—ACHIEVE UNIVERSAL PRIMARY EDUCATION

✳ ✳ ✳ Ankana was one of 150 women crowded into a room in India. We were all sitting on the floor, listening to a women's conference talk. I was taking notes. Ankana kept watching my hand, mesmerized. Long story short, through an interpreter, I learned that she didn't know how to read or write. She had never held a pen.

So I found out her name and wrote it for her, then gave her the pen and paper so she could do it for herself. She did . . . and glowed.

Achieving universal primary education so all can read and write will be world-changing. It may be the least complex of the eight MDGs. What a worthy fight for not only Ankana's children and grandchildren, but for Ankana herself.

DAILY SEED: How can your church or group team up to tackle MDG #2?

"Once you learn to read, you will be forever free." (Frederick Douglass, African-American social reformer)

NOVEMBER 21

MDG #3—PROMOTE GENDER EQUALITY
AND EMPOWER WOMEN

✳ ✳ ✳ In India, China, and many other parts of the world, girls are killed before or after birth (or abandoned) simply because they are girls.

In China, the reason was the One Child Policy. China's government boasts that it has prevented 400 million lives through its One Child policy. I wonder how many of those were girls' lives? Thankfully, the policy is undergoing change because of the overabundance of boys in China.

In India, girls create an economic kiss of death for millions of poor families due to cultural norms such as payment of dowries. Thankfully, many people are working to change these "norms" that promote gender inequality.

DAILY SEED: How can your church or group team up to tackle MDG #3?

"We must raise both the ceiling and the floor." (Sheryl Sandberg, *Lean In: Women, Work, and the Will to Lead*)

NOVEMBER 22

MDG #4—REDUCE CHILD MORTALITY

The 2013 infant mortality rate (deaths per 1000 live births) was 187.5 in Afghanistan, 42 in India, and 5.2 in the United States.[98] The disparity obviously isn't about genetics; it's about location.

I held a feverish three-pound newborn in a remote Indian village a few years ago. We were sitting on the dirt between two tiny concrete block homes. There were no hospitals nearby. The odds would have been iffy even if the baby had been born in the United States. In India, I just prayed and cried.

DAILY SEED: How can your church or group team up to tackle MDG #4?

"Where you live should not determine whether you live . . . or whether you die." (Bono, musician and social activist)

NOVEMBER 23

MDG #5—IMPROVE MATERNAL HEALTH

Christy Turlington Burns is a beautiful model who suffered childbirth complications. Had she been in a developing country at the time of the birth, the odds are great that she would have died. Being a world-class model couldn't have saved her. Long story short, she created the organization "Every Mother Counts"[99] with the vision of reducing the number of women who die due to complications during pregnancy and childbirth (98 percent of which are preventable).

DAILY SEED: How can your church or group team up to tackle MDG #5?

"Women are not dying of diseases we can't treat. . . . They are dying because societies have yet to make the decision that their lives are worth saving." (Mahmoud Fathalla, past president of the International Federation of Obstetricians and Gynecologists)

NOVEMBER 24

MDG #6—COMBAT HIV/AIDS, MALARIA, AND OTHER DISEASES

It's been said that malaria has killed half of the people who have ever lived. That's hard to verify, but suffice it to say that malaria took the lives of over a half million people in 2013 alone, according to the World Health Organization. And malaria is preventable and curable.

We can fight the good fight against infectious diseases.

DAILY SEED: How can your church or group team up to tackle MDG #6?

"Victory is always possible for the person who refuses to stop fighting." (Napoleon Hill, American author and impresario)

NOVEMBER 25

MDG #7—ENSURE ENVIRONMENTAL SUSTAINABILITY

* John Chapman (1774–1845) became known as Johnny Appleseed. He
* * was a nurseryman who introduced apple trees to parts of the eastern
United States. He was kind and generous and a leader in conservation, attributing symbolic importance to apples. He also cared deeply for animals. When he heard a horse was to be put down, he bought it plus some land so it could graze and recover. Then he gave the horse to someone needy, *if* they promised to treat the horse humanely.

In other words, he was an early environmentalist. Today's environmental sustainability issues are hugely complex, but we can all have a Johnny Appleseed spirit and take care of our land (with its flora and fauna). We can all plant seeds of change.

DAILY SEED: How can your church or group team up to tackle MDG #7?

"When one tugs at a single thing in nature, he finds it attached to the rest of the world." (John Muir, wilderness preservationist)

NOVEMBER 26

MDG #8—DEVELOP GLOBAL PARTNERSHIPS FOR DEVELOPMENT

* The International Red Cross and Red Crescent Movement is the world's
* * largest group of humanitarian non-governmental organizations. There
are societies in 189 countries, which is one in almost every nation of the world. This global partnership quietly meets needs and saves lives while nation-fighting dominates the news.

The Movement's logo has a cross next to a crescent, i.e., a global partnership for development with an "all hands on deck" approach.

DAILY SEED: How can your church or group team up to tackle MDG #8?

"I have found no greater satisfaction than achieving success through honest dealing and strict adherence to the view that, for you to gain, those you deal with should gain as well." (Alan Greenspan, former longtime chairman of the Federal Reserve)

NOVEMBER 27

TEACH CHILDREN

Children seem better than adults at embracing a lot of things, such as diversity. I think prejudice is a learned concept. In fact, I think the next generations will find the prejudice of past generations repugnant. So, maybe this entry should remind the children to teach the grown-ups.

That being said, however, we as adults can do our best.

A couple of years ago we held a Global Kidz Fair on the lawn of a church. We had food, music, and booths. The Stand4Kids booth invited kids to add their red paint handprint to a mural with an "anti-child-soldier recruitment" message. (The mural was later sent to the U.N.) The Women of Vision booth invited kids to break up bricks with sledgehammers, demonstrating child labor. The Love 146 booth was geared to the grown-ups, reminding them about the sex trade that preys on children.

It was a teaching day for the children *and* the grown-ups, as most teaching days are.

DAILY SEED: Teach a child something important today.

"If I could relive my life, I would devote my entire ministry to reaching children for God!" (Dwight L. Moody, evangelist)

THINK ABOUT "MUSTARD SEED" POWER

✳
✳ ✳ Americans have more power to bring about positive change in our little fingers (figuratively-speaking) than any people in history. Jesus spoke about little things with great power in His mustard seed parables.

We can do so much with so little sacrifice. We can plant small seeds. So let's do it. Think "small sacrifice actions with big results."

My go-to book in the 80s was *The Mustard Seed Conspiracy: You Can Make a Difference in Tomorrow's Troubled World* by Tom Sine. (He got the "tomorrow's troubled world" part right.)

He spoke of the "conspiracy of the insignificant," meaning . . . us. First Corinthians 1:27–29 says, *"but God has chosen the foolish things of the world to shame the wise, and God has chosen the weak things of the world to shame the things which are strong, and the base things of the world and the despised God has chosen, the things that are not, so that He may nullify the things that are, so that no man may boast before God."*

Again and again we see ordinary people doing extraordinary things. If you're an ordinary person, plant a seed.

DAILY SEED: Do something small with great love today.

"I have a mustard seed and I'm not afraid to use it!" (Joseph Ratzinger [Pope Benedict XVI])

THINK ABOUT SACRIFICE

✳
✳ ✳ In contrast to glancing at little mustard seeds for motivation, sacrifice is more like giving up a kidney to be transplanted into a friend's dying body.

Jesus gave His life for us and we're called to take up our cross and follow Him. For some, the call could mean death. But for some missionaries I know, they *want* to be doing what they're doing and the threat of danger or even death doesn't faze them, at least not enough to stop them. That's the interesting thing about sacrifice, when we're called to it, His yoke is easy and his burden is light.

DAILY SEED: Have you ever been called to sacrifice? Muse on that. Be open to future sacrifice. The yoke may be easy and the burden light once the sacrificial step is taken.

"Only the man who follows the command of Jesus single-mindedly and unresistingly lets his yoke rest upon him, finds his burden easy, and under its gentle pressure receives the power to persevere in the right way. The command of Jesus is hard, unutterably hard, for those who try to resist it. But for those who willingly submit, the yoke is easy, and the burden is light." (Dietrich Bonhoeffer, *The Cost of Discipleship*)

"Sometimes when you sacrifice something precious, you're not really losing it. You're just passing it on to someone else." (Mitch Albom, *The Five People You Meet in Heaven*)

NOVEMBER 30

THINK ABOUT THE POWER OF A FEW

✳ Twelve guys devoted themselves to Jesus and became his inner circle. ✳ ✳ A small group of disabled folks chained themselves to our local buses a few decades ago to petition for bus access.

We know that handful of disciples changed the world a couple thousand years ago. And guess what? Our local buses now have lifts for wheelchairs.

According to Judges 6–8, Gideon destroyed the town's altars to the foreign gods Baal and Asherah, per God's instruction. The Midianites and Amalekites were not pleased, so Gideon gathered together an army with the help of other tribes. However, God told Gideon that the men he had gathered were too many. With so many men, the Israelites could claim the victory instead of acknowledging that God had saved them.

So God told Gideon to send home those men who were afraid. 22,000 left and 10,000 remained. Yet there were still too many, according to God. Eventually, the number was reduced to 300, and those 300 defeated the enemy.

DAILY SEED: Who are "the few" with whom you can collaborate?

"Never doubt that a small group of thoughtful, committed citizens can change the world; indeed, it's the only thing that ever has." (Margaret Mead, cultural anthropologist)

DECEMBER

DECEMBER 1

THINK ABOUT THE POWER OF MANY

✳ ✳ ✳ The best example I can think of regarding "the power of many" is the Church. The Evangelical Council for Financial Accountability (ECFA) reported that charitable giving to its nearly 1800 churches and ministries reaches $20 billion in revenue annually. That's the power of a lot of donations.

There's a book called *Change the World for 10 Bucks: Small Actions x Lots of People = Big Change*. What if you could galvanize thousands of people to each contribute $10 to your cause? True, it's easier to seek a $20,000 grant than to seek 2000 people to give $10, but "the many" might renew annually or convert their gifts to monthly support. Net gain!

DAILY SEED: What would you ask a thousand people to do to change the world?

"The power of one, if fearless and focused, is formidable, but the power of many working together is better." (Gloria Macapagal-Arroyo, past president of the Philippines)

DECEMBER 2

THINK ABOUT THE POWER OF ONE

✳ ✳ ✳ Nancy Brinker. Agnes Bojaxhiu. Mordecai Ham.

Nancy Brinker's older sister was Susan G. Komen, who died of breast cancer in 1980. In her memory, Nancy created the Susan G. Komen Breast Cancer Foundation which has raised over $1 billion for research. I doubt that Nancy knew she would change the world.

Agnes Bojaxhiu became Mother Teresa. I doubt that Agnes knew she would change the world.

Mordecai Ham preached the revival where Billy Graham gave his life to Christ. I doubt that Mordecai knew he would change the world.

DAILY SEED: What can *you,* just you, do to change the world?

"Let there be peace on earth and let it begin with me." (Jill Jackson Miller and Sy Miller)

DECEMBER 3

THINK ABOUT "THE SOUL OF THE NEXT ECONOMY"

✳
✳ ✳ "Pam Wilhelms, an environmental engineer and business consultant, was rounding the corner on the 44th floor of a skyscraper along the San Francisco Bay when she stopped dead in her tracks. 'I turned to the left and saw pictures of the company's landholdings and factories—in the same Central American country I'd seen the night before,' said Pam. The previous night, she had attended a fundraiser for a nonprofit that digs wells in Central America. There she learned about a village whose water source had been destroyed by an American company upstream—one that looked awfully familiar.

"'I didn't realize how complicit I was. By day I was helping leaders and executives go after their economic bottom line, and by night I was on the board of not-for-profits trying to clean up the mess.'

"'We're never going to create a sustainable planet as long as we have a false dichotomy that says nonprofits do good and for-profits make money.'"

An example: "Chances are you have a smartphone lying within a few feet of you right now. Was the coltan for that smartphone mined from a conflict area in the Congo? Were the workers who put it together among those who threatened mass suicide in the Chinese Foxconn factory last year? Many of these questions . . . touch all of us—from the upstream of society all the way down to its most vulnerable members."[100]

Pam's initiative is called the Soul of the Next Economy. The companies involved seek a triple bottom line (economic, social, and environmental) rather than merely the profit bottom line. And the companies are noteworthy, like Nike. If you are interested in poverty reduction, economic empowerment, sustainable development, corporate/charity collaboration, or social responsibility, research this groundbreaking work and consider attending the next Soul of the Next Economy Forum.[101]

DAILY SEED: Support socially and environmentally responsible companies as much as possible.

"Commit your works to the Lord and your plans will be established." (Proverbs 16:3)

DECEMBER 4

THINK OF YOUR NEIGHBORHOOD AS EXTENDED FAMILY

One of my favorite songs is "You Are Not Alone" (Michael Jackson). It's come to my rescue on lonely days and gut-wrenchingly hard days. That song is part of shared life with my Fab friends. Occasionally, if I'm hurting, one of them will send me an e-mail with four little words—you are not alone. That's all I need.

What if we got more intentional with our neighbors in much the same way? What if we got together with them, discussed a shared vision for our little nook of the planet, shared resources, gardened together, formed babysitting co-ops, hung out on each other's porches, talked about important things . . . did life together? I'm guessing there would be less isolation and loneliness, because truly, one of your soul mates might live next door rather than across the country. The key is *intentional community*.

One of my best friends starts Bible studies with her neighbors. They're not stuffy and pedantic studies; they just flow out of her life. Organic, you might say. They're safe places where people can question and vent and cry and have "ah-ha!" moments. And knowing her, they laugh a lot too.

They are not alone.

DAILY SEED: What would an uptick of "intentional community" look like in your neighborhood?

"Do not forsake your own friend or your father's friend, and do not go to your brother's house in the day of your calamity; Better is a neighbor who is near than a brother far away." (Proverbs 27:10)

DECEMBER 5

THINK ROOTS

✳ The bubonic plague killed 30 to 60 percent of Europe's population in ✳ ✳ the fourteenth century. It was transmitted by a rat flea, but that was unknown at the time. The rat was the root cause. Once that was known, the plague could be dealt with.

I think we need to carefully think through our missions and social services efforts—to deal with the roots and rats rather than *just* treating symptoms.

For example, many in developing countries hadn't known how AIDS is spread until recently. Once they knew, they could deal with it.

DAILY SEED: What is the root cause of an issue that compels you? Roots are underground and it may take a lot of digging to find them, but knowing root causes can change everything.

"When solving problems, dig at the roots instead of just hacking at the leaves." (Anthony J. D'Angelo, founder of Collegiate EmPowerment)

THINK SYSTEMS CHANGE

Most Dalits are desperately poor. What is the root cause of their poverty? Little access to jobs? Lack of education? Caste oppression?

If the caste *system* were to be abolished, I completely believe that the Dalits, given a few generations, would rise as equals. Abolishing the caste system would be a systems change. Gandhi himself advocated ending untouchability but not abolishing the caste system. He planted some seeds, but so much more needs to be done.

Systems changes require social upheaval. Probably even death for some. It was true of our civil rights movement. It was true of the ending of apartheid. For many around the world, it's true of becoming a Christian. Without systems changes, however, we would be stuck in some very dark ages.

DAILY SEED: Ask the leader(s) of a cause important to you what systems changes they want to see.

"If there is no struggle, there is no progress." (Frederick Douglass)

"Change, instead of meaning disaster to him [the American], seems to give birth only to miracles all about him." (Alexis de Tocqueville, *Democracy in America*)

TITHE

Hebrews 13:5–6 ties together two concepts—money and security. It doesn't advocate a certain financial plan or savings formula. On the contrary, it speaks of *not tying our security to money*. It speaks of being *free* from the love of money. But where is security? It's in the fact that God has promised not to forsake all of us who trust in him.

"Make sure that your character is free from the love of money, being content with what you have; for He Himself has said, "I will never desert you, nor will I ever forsake you," so that we confidently say, "The Lord is my helper, I will not be afraid. What will man do to me?" Isn't freedom from the *supremacy* of money an attractive concept?

One of the ways we can get out hands pried loose from our dollars is to tithe. A tithe is usually considered a tenth of income, set apart as an offering to God. God said in Malachi 3:10, *"'Bring the whole tithe into the storehouse, so that there may be food in My house, and test Me now in this,' says the Lord of hosts, 'if I will not open for you the windows of heaven and pour out for you a blessing until it overflows.'"*

Give a percentage away, wisely, but away. And be free.

DAILY SEED: Consider taking the leap of faith (if you haven't already) . . . and tithe.

"[God] wants you to go home, look at your bucket of seed, and determine in your heart how much you'd like to sow. He wants you to consider thoughtfully your current circumstances, your life, your potential, and your finances. He wants you to involve your family. He wants you to pray about it. And then He wants you to come up with a plan." (Andy Stanley, *Fields of Gold*)

DECEMBER 8

TITHE ON YOUR BUSINESS

Jill has a pottery business called Twinkle Tree. Once a quarter, she tallies up her proceeds and sends a percentage to a ministry. Gay has a faith-based jewelry business called Gemerosity. Every $20-and-under purchase through Gemerosity provides up to $11 as a donation to a nonprofit, a perfect example of "spreading the word of faith through works of faith." Debi self-published a book, sold some copies at a nonprofit event, and gave 100 percent of the proceeds to the nonprofit.

DAILY SEED: If you are a business owner, consider tithing on your proceeds.

"Honor the Lord from your wealth and from the first of all your produce; so your barns will be filled with plenty and your vats will overflow with new wine." (Proverbs 3:9–10)

DECEMBER 9

TITHE ON YOUR MONEY

Mike Holmes wrote an article in the July 10, 2013 issue of *Relevant Magazine* entitled, "What Would Happen if the Church Tithed?—How Giving 10% Could Change the World." Here's an excerpt:

"The church of today is not great at giving. This isn't exactly news. But it is a statistical fact:

Tithers make up only 10–25% of a normal congregation.

Only 5% of the U.S. tithes, with 80% of Americans giving only 2% of their income.

Christians are only giving at 2.5% per capita, while during the Great Depression they gave at a 3.3% rate.

"Numbers like that can invoke a lot of guilt, which isn't really the point. The larger point is what would happen if believers were to increase their giving to a minimum of, let's say, 10%. There would be an additional $165 billion for churches to use and distribute. The global impact would be phenomenal. Here are just a few things the Church could do with that kind of money:

$25 billion could relieve global hunger, starvation and deaths from preventable diseases in five years.

$12 billion could eliminate illiteracy in five years. . . .

$1 billion could fully fund all overseas mission work."[102]

DAILY SEED: Talk to your church about these statistics. Encourage your fellow Christians to tithe.

"I never would have been able to tithe the first million dollars I ever made if I had not tithed my first salary, which was $1.50 per week." (John D. Rockefeller, Sr., industrialist and philanthropist)

DECEMBER 10

TITHE ON YOUR TALENT

For every ten piano students, teach one who can't afford to pay. For every ten pieces of art sold, donate one to an auction for a cause. For every ten counseling clients who pay, take on a referral from a woman's shelter.

DenverWorks held an annual fundraising event called "Live at the Lake." We found venues near lakes or water features (and sometimes we were *very* creative about that lake part) and provided live entertainment—a bluegrass band, a classical guitarist, salsa dancers, a jazz singer. And often, the entertainers gave us a reduced rate as their contribution to the cause. In a sense, they tithed on their talent.

DAILY SEED: What are your talents? How might you use them for the greater good?

"Use what talents you possess: the woods would be very silent if no birds sang there except those that sang best." (Henry Van Dyke, American author and educator)

DECEMBER 11

TITHE ON YOUR TIME

I never cared for the game "Monopoly" because it takes f-o-r-e-v-e-r to play, but of course, my kids loved playing it with me because they could get a l-o-t of Mom's attention (and time). Rick Warren said, "Time is your most precious gift because you only have a set amount of it. You can make more money, but you can't make more time. When you give someone your time, you are giving them a portion of your life that you'll never get back. Your time is your life. The best way to spell love is T-I-M-E."

I hate to admit this, but as a working mom, playing "Monopoly" was a sacrifice. (I actually considered laundry to be higher priority. What was I thinking?) Did I devote 10 percent of my time solely to my kids, eyeball-to-eyeball, without distractions? Did I tithe on my time and give them the "first fruits" of it? Oh, I hope I did, but most likely it was done imperfectly.

It's funny how "time" changes us because now when I get to take care of my grandkiddos, I probably spend 90+ percent of my time singly focused on them. The laundry can wait.

DAILY SEED: Schedule undistracted time for loved ones (or for some seed-planting) each week.

"But what minutes! Count them by sensation, and not by calendars, and each moment is a day." (Benjamin Disraeli)

DECEMBER 12

TOUCH LIVES

✱
✱ ✱ Jenn is a massage therapist (and operations director and hospitality director and youth director and counselor and . . .). She's multi-talented. However, what she wants to do most is trauma touch. She's being trained to combine counseling with therapeutic massage to help trauma victims, such as the abused or those suffering from PTSD.

Touch can communicate so much—acceptance, warmth, caring, safety. Massage can bring out tears or toxins and are *far* more valuable than mere relaxation (although that is important too). Hands can be hands of mercy.

These days we fear touch because of all the stories of "bad touch." But wouldn't it be tragic to lose "good touch?" The touch of hand on hand when a friend is hurting. The touch of a pat on the back. The touch of a hug.

DAILY SEED: Reach out and touch someone today.

"Your body needs to be held and to hold, to be touched and to touch. None of these needs is to be despised, denied, or repressed. But you have to keep searching for your body's deeper need, the need for genuine love." (Henri Nouwen, Dutch priest, professor, writer, and theologian)

DECEMBER 13

TRUST GOD'S HEART

When I'm struggling, I often turn to the song "Trust His Heart," written by Babbie Mason, sung by Cynthia Clawson and Wayne Watson. The lyrics address those perennial questions mankind has been asking since the beginning. Why do the innocent suffer? Why is evil so rampant? Why can't we just get along? Why doesn't God intervene more often? Why can't I always see it when He does?

Trusting God's heart helps. He has the heart of a parent. When I think of what lengths I would go to help my children, I understand his heart better. Sometimes, when they were young, I could see what my children couldn't see (danger ahead, for example). As little ones, they had to trust my heart.

God can see what we can't see. We can trust him.

DAILY SEED: Find a quiet place and listen to the song, "Trust His Heart."[103]

"Trust in the Lord with all your heart and do not lean on your own understanding. In all your ways acknowledge Him, and He will make your paths straight." (Proverbs 3:5–6)

DECEMBER 14

TRY MISSION TOURISM (OR NOT)

✱ If you sponsor a child in another country, you might wish to visit him/
✱ ✱ her and plan a vacation around that. There are a *lot* of options for mission trips. But please take heed to these words by Bob Lupton, author and founder of Focused Community Strategies Urban Ministries, from his blog on "Religious Tourism": "Naïve 'vacationaries' . . . spend millions of dollars traveling to various countries, perform work that locals could better do for themselves, and create a welfare economy that deprives a people of the pride of their own accomplishments—all in the name of Christian service."[104] He cites the Bahamas, where there is one short-term missionary for every fifteen residents.

The Welfare Reform Act of 1996 resulted in a return to dignity for millions of Americans. Although well-intentioned after the Great Depression, "welfare" became over-used between 1935 and 1996 (in my opinion). Helping harmed able-bodied Americans. Assisting those in true need is one of America's hallmarks of greatness, but we must be careful and thoughtful about what constitutes true need, both on our own soil and abroad. There are many ways to help without "doing for" when "doing for" causes damage.

It's essential to make sure mission trips are taken with the right motives, *not just to feel good about one's do-gooding.* It's key to figure out in advance whether or not the mission creates dependency and causes unintended harm. It's a tough call, because mission trips also change us for the better. Motive-checking should precede all of our seed-planting endeavors.

DAILY SEED: What motivates you to help others? Help in the most helpful ways.

"'Above all, do no harm.' It's the bottom line of the Hippocratic Oath that has guided the conduct of physicians for centuries. It is time for the Western church to apply the same principle." (Bob Lupton)

DECEMBER 15

TUTOR

✳
✳ ✳ Statistics show that 14 percent of adults in the United States are functionally illiterate, making it impossible for them to help their children with reading. Tutoring is important, yet hear these words by Ron Suskind, author of *A Hope in the Unseen: An American Odyssey from the Inner City to the Ivy League.* "Brown (University) offers plenty of counseling and tutoring to struggling students, but, as any academic dean will tell you, it's up to the students to seek it out, something that a drowning minority student will seek to avoid at all costs, fearing it will trumpet a second-class status."

If you can tutor, enroll with a tutoring organization that can connect you with students in a mutually respectful way. Seek out your student's strengths. What might he/she teach *you*?

DAILY SEED: Check out tutoring agencies in your area.

"An investment in knowledge pays the best interest." (Benjamin Franklin)

DECEMBER 16

UNITE WITH OTHERS

✳
✳ ✳ Unification took down the Berlin Wall. People started going to the border following protests. Police became overwhelmed and started letting people pass freely. Then the wall came down. People united. Things happened.

Jenifer gathered people around coffee at DenverWorks once a month. All had some interest in job development as job*seekers*, employers, trainers, funders. The gathering was called "Community Cup." People united. Things happened.

Sometimes there is a groundswell of awareness among regular people like us. We can unite with others on issues with which we agree. We can bring down walls. We can sign petitions. We can vote.

We can drink coffee.

DAILY SEED: Who can you unite with regarding your cause?

"I [Paul] planted the seed, Apollos watered it, but God has been making it grow." (1 Corinthians 3:6, NIV)

USE LESSON PLANS

✳ Compassion International has a Christian homeschool curriculum on-
✳ ✳ line. These lessons teach children about impoverished countries where Compassion works. They provide creative activities that lead to spiritual and academic growth. And we can download them for free, whether or not we use them for homeschooling. These online lessons are great for our kiddos and grand-kiddos, and we can peer over their shoulders as they learn.

DAILY SEED: Check out curriculums online.

"When one teaches, two learn." (Robert Heinlein, American science fiction writer)

USE THE WEB WISELY

✳ Stretch . . . if you're under-using the Web and missing out on informa-
✳ ✳ tion and world-changing ideas.

Shrink . . . if you're over-using it and missing out on *life*. Oh, and if we ever hang out together, let's put our devices aside for a while. I want to get to know *you*.

DAILY SEED: Watch/listen to something online today, like a TED Talk.[105]
"A journey of a thousand sites begins with a single click." (Unknown)

DECEMBER 19

USE YOUR "TAKEN FOR GRANTED" SKILLS

Sometimes we overlook our most valuable offerings, like being able to read and write. They come easily to us and are just part of our nature. They don't feel particularly noteworthy, but they are like gold to others.

J'anne has a seminary degree and speaks Spanish. She started teaching Sunday school in Spanish at her church, which opened the door to a whole Spanish-speaking ministry. Gold.

Cindy counsels people and weeps with them. Weeps. To her it's second nature. To them . . . Gold.

Carla "throws together" meals that could be served at the finest restaurants. Gold.

My son knows how to fix computers. He just has a brain for that stuff. I don't. Gold.

DAILY SEED: What skills do you have that you take for granted? Might those be used in service to others?

"No work is insignificant. All labor that uplifts humanity has dignity and importance and should be undertaken with painstaking excellence." (Martin Luther King, Jr.)

"Never forget that you are one of a kind. Never forget that if there weren't any need for you in all your uniqueness to be on this earth, you wouldn't be here in the first place. And never forget, no matter how overwhelming life's challenges and problems seem to be, that one person can make a difference in the world. In fact, it is always because of one person that all the changes that matter in the world come about. So be that one person." (Richard Buckminster Fuller, architect and visionary)

DECEMBER 20

VISIT OTHERS

* My daughter was a nurse in a long-term care facility. She was amazed at
* * how many residents *never* had visitors. Not even family.

My dad did visitation through our church for many years. He was a deacon, and that's what deacons did. He visited the sick, the hospitalized, and those in need of prayer or comfort. The word "deacon" comes from the Greek word, *diakonos*, meaning servant or minister.

Nowadays, we have Stephen Ministers, people "trained to provide one-to-one, Christ-centered care to hurting people."[106]

And there's this from the cover of a church bulletin:

Pastor: Rev. So-and-So

Ministers: All the People

We can all be visitors. Visit the elderly. Visit neighbors. Visit the sick. Visit prisoners. Visit the lonely. Visit the grieving.

DAILY SEED: Who needs a visit from you?

   "Rejoice with those who rejoice, and weep with those who weep." (Romans 12:15)

   "A tear is made of 1% water and 99% feelings." (Unknown)

DECEMBER 21

VOLUNTEER

* The estimated value of volunteer time for 2013 was $22.55 per hour,
* * according to the Independent Sector.[107] Sure, that averages envelope-stuffing with volunteer professional work (like legal or accounting), but I can speak from experience; nonprofits are dependent on volunteers. Volunteers are priceless. Events need to be chaired, mailings need to be sent, people need to be called, kids need to be tutored, clients need to be greeted with open arms.

And here's the kicker. Volunteers often cite their volunteer work as their *favorite* work.

DAILY SEED: If time and money weren't constraints, where would you like to volunteer?

"Here's to all volunteers, those dedicated people who believe in all work and no pay." (Robert Orben, American comedy and speechwriter)

"I can no other answer make, but, thanks, and thanks." (William Shakespeare)

DECEMBER 22

VOTE

* Native American activist Leonard Peltier said, "Each of us is the swing
* * vote . . . " That kind of makes you want to vote, doesn't it? Our votes matter. And we can also "vote" on issues (weigh in on them) in other ways too. That's what this book is about (i.e., using your influence, speaking up, fighting for change, letting your light shine).

James Chaney, Andrew Goodman and Michael Schwerner were murdered while registering black voters in Mississippi in 1964. *That's* how important voting is. Worth dying for.

DAILY SEED: Vote on Election Day but also speak up on issues Every Day.

"Don't vote? Don't complain." (Unknown)

WAGE PEACE

A few years ago, the Navajo Nation courts saw 28,000 criminal cases a year, but had jail space for only 220 people. So they went back to their roots and instituted a peacemaking rather than a punishment model. A peacemaker facilitated meetings between the accused and the victim. Family members of the accused were brought in to help him/her not re-offend. Symbols (like horses) were used to make amends. They waged peace.[108]

We, too, can wage peace. It's so easy to keep person-to-person wars going. That's what gossip does.

It's so easy to keep nation-to-nation wars going. That's what hatred does.

We can sow seeds of peace toward each other and toward our enemies.

DAILY SEED: What situation needs your touch of peacemaking?

"Blessed are the peacemakers, for they shall be called sons of God." (Matthew 5:9)

WASH PEOPLE'S FEET

Have you ever had your feet washed at an old-fashioned foot washing? I have. It made me cry.

There was something so vulnerable about it. I didn't deserve such tender care.

That's how we are to serve others, by washing their feet—their icky, smelly feet. We can take care of their vomiting baby while they take a break. We can scrub their sooty walls. We can invite their hyper kid over, even though nobody else will.

DAILY SEED: Who needs your tender care today?

"Then He [Jesus] poured water into the basin, and began to wash the disciples' feet and to wipe them with the towel with which He was girded." (John 13:5)

DECEMBER 25

WATCH GOD WORK

A few years ago I was agonizing over a particular situation. What did God whisper to my soul? "Watch me work."

That's it. Just . . . watch. And he *is* working in that situation. He's not yet finished, but he's *very* active. It's sort of like watching the garden grow. We can't see the seeds sprout (unless we sit there for hours and hours) and we certainly can't *make* the seeds sprout. Only God can impart life into a situation or a seed.

So pray . . . and watch God work. Plant seeds . . . and watch God work.

DAILY SEED: Today, watch God work.

"This is the confidence which we have before Him, that, if we ask anything according to His will, He hears us. And if we know that He hears us in whatever we ask, we know that we have the requests which we have asked from Him." (1 John 5:14–15)

"Yet those who wait for the Lord will gain new strength; they will mount up with wings like eagles, they will run and not get tired, they will walk and not become weary." (Isaiah 40:31)

DECEMBER 26

WELCOME QUESTIONS

*
* * I started learning the power of asking questions in grad school. Before that, I'd assumed that it was my job to be Answer Woman. And that's a heavy burden to bear.

We're supposed to be grounded in our beliefs so we can defend them, but sometimes asking the right questions can serve us well too. During my time in grad school, the abortion question was raging, particularly the viability-outside-the-womb issue. Most of my classmates were on the pro-choice side. The rest of us were on the pro-life side (i.e., all two of us). The "how viable are *you* without oxygen?" question served the two of us well.

Some situations are hard and beg difficult questions. We must search the questions and define our positions. I also believe God can handle it when we ask *him* questions.

And sometimes God might ask *us* questions. God called Adam and Eve out in Genesis 3 by asking them questions.

To summarize, I don't think we should fear questions. We should welcome them, as hard as that might be. They make us more shrewd and on-point. They make us stronger.

DAILY SEED: What questions surround the causes near to your heart?

"Jesus entered the temple courts, and, while he was teaching, the chief priests and the elders of the people came to him. 'By what authority are you doing these things?' they asked. 'And who gave you this authority?' Jesus replied, 'I will also ask you one question. If you answer me, I will tell you by what authority I am doing these things. John's baptism—where did it come from? Was it from heaven, or of human origin?' They discussed it among themselves and said, 'If we say, "From heaven," he will ask, "Then why didn't you believe him?" But if we say, "Of human origin"—we are afraid of the people, for they all hold that John was a prophet.' So they answered Jesus, 'We don't know.' Then he said, 'Neither will I tell you by what authority I am doing these things.'" (Matthew 21:23–27, NIV)

WHEN IT'S TIME TO END, END WELL

Years ago, we were in a small group at church. After a while, it was time to bring our group to a close. Nobody was moving away. Nobody was mad. We just all knew. We had had a great season together, but it was time to move on to other things.

There is an appointed time for everything. And there is a time for every event under heaven—
A time to give birth and a time to die;
A time to plant and a time to uproot what is planted.
A time to kill and a time to heal;
A time to tear down and a time to build up.
A time to weep and a time to laugh;
A time to mourn and a time to dance.
A time to throw stones and a time to gather stones;
A time to embrace and a time to shun embracing.
A time to search and a time to give up as lost;
A time to keep and a time to throw away.
A time to tear apart and a time to sew together;
A time to be silent and a time to speak.
A time to love and a time to hate;
A time for war and a time for peace. (Ecclesiastes 3:1–8)

Sometimes, we begin something with an end point in mind. Sometimes, along the way, life happens, so something must end. I think we fear endings too much. Sometimes they're necessary. We retire. We move aside so someone else can have a turn. We die.

When I die, I hope I'm finished, fully used-up, mission accomplished, whether my life is cut short or prolonged. I want to live well . . . and end well.

DAILY SEED: What would "mission accomplished" look like in your life?

"I have seen people change in remarkable ways even as they die. They do not become someone else, but somehow more themselves, often more accepting and forgiving of themselves, and more loving toward themselves and with others." (Dr. Ira Byock, Professor of Medicine at Dartmouth)

DECEMBER 28

WHY NOT YOU? WHY NOT NOW?

Russell Wilson, Seattle Seahawks quarterback, asked his teammates at the beginning of the 2013 season, "Hey, why not us?" And a few months later they won Super Bowl XLVIII.

He talked about his late father. "He used to always tell me 'Russ, why not you?' And what that meant was believe in yourself, believe in the talent God has given you even though you are 5-foot-11, and you can go a long ways. That's why I decided to play football, and I wanted to go against the odds a little bit."

So . . . the world needs you and me. Why not make your mark? Why not start today?

DAILY SEED: Why shouldn't you be the one to be fantastic?

"The gracious, eternal God permits the spirit to green and bloom and to bring forth the most marvelous fruit, surpassing anything a tongue can express and a heart conceive." (Johannes Tauler)

"Then I heard the voice of the Lord, saying, 'Whom shall I send, and who will go for Us?' Then I said, 'Here am I. Send me!'" (Isaiah 6:8)

DECEMBER 29

WRITE A BOOK

✳ I did. You can too.
✳ ✳ In other words, try your hand at something you've been longing to do. For me, it was writing.

What is that *something* for you?

Some of our longings may become successful; others may not. One of my longings is to ski moguls well, and I'm at about a C-minus on that one, alas. But all of us can be successful seed-planters. God brings the increase, but we sow the seeds.

As I write this, I'm asking God to show me what seeds He wants me to sow today. And my eyes fall on the plaque above my desk. "Speak kindly, care deeply, love generously, forgive freely, and *make a difference daily.*"

So today, I write. I live out my longing. And today, I sow. I live out my calling. And for all time, I seek to make a difference daily.

DAILY SEED: Live out your God-inspired longings. Live out your calling. Make a difference daily.

That's the seedy life. That's the abundant life.

"I came that they may have life, and have it abundantly." (John 10:10)

DECEMBER 30

YOUR TURN

✳ I knew there was one book I was supposed to write—this one. I've been
✳ ✳ collecting these ideas for years. I heard another great idea yesterday. And I'll keep listening for them, because our turns to plant seeds of change never cease.

As we draw near to the end of the year, I'd like to leave you with this excerpt from a note from F.B. Meyer (noted British Baptist pastor) to George Truett (noted American Baptist pastor) on September 6, 1929. "Our lives on earth may not meet as often as we'd like but this thought expresses my hope. . . . "The only thing to do is for us to make a tryst to meet, as soon as possible, if not before our arriving in Heaven, at the Middle Gate on the East Side of the New Jerusalem. There we will go off together, for a ramble by the River of Water of Life, and will doubtless find a nook, where we can have a quiet talk . . . and perhaps the Prince Himself will join us. There will be much to talk about."

DAILY SEED: It's your turn. What's your story to write? What's your purpose? What will your seeds look like as they grow?

"It's when the seed grows up that it is known as a tree. Nobody calls the seedling a tree and no seedling is ever useful if it doesn't produce fruit. You got to grow up." (Israelmore Ayivor)

DECEMBER 31

THE END . . . AND BEGINNING

In closing, I'm thinking about our perennial garden. Frankly, right now it's a bunch of gray-brown stalks sticking through the snow. It's dormant, but dormant doesn't mean dead. It means biding its time, waiting, probably chuckling about the crazy comments to come when people see it in full bloom. "I've never even *seen* that color before! Come look! This is the best garden *yet!*"

I believe God's into gardening, planting seeds of change into *us*. We, in turn, can plant seeds of change into the soil of the world. We don't have to sow everyone's seeds, just the ones God has chosen for us.

What's the Gardener saying to you? Maybe he's getting excited about the new life to come for you and through you.

I know one thing is true. Life awaits those who sow their pocketful of seeds.

DAILY SEED: Tomorrow's a new day, a new beginning. Consider these words to the exiles of Israel as today ends and tomorrow begins.

"'For I know the plans that I have for you,' declares the Lord, 'plans for welfare and not for calamity to give you a future and a hope. Then you will call upon Me and come and pray to Me, and I will listen to you. You will seek Me and find Me when you search for Me with all your heart. I will be found by you,' declares the Lord." (Jeremiah 29:11–14a)

What a promise for them . . . and for us.

Be blessed. Be a blessing.

Welcome to the garden.

Acknowledgments

* I am deeply grateful for the influences of so many on my life—my
* * mentors, both formal and informal, many of whom you get a glimpse
of in this book, my husband, who is patient and kind and encouraging, my
children, who spur me on and make me laugh when I get stressed out, my
sister Jill, who literally waters the garden when I need to write, my sister Nita,
who texts me jokes to keep me going, my dad and stepmom, who keep the fires
of our family history stoked, my extended family, who daily add elements of
love and growth, my friends, who make me feel like a gem (even though I'm
ordinary), my pastors and teachers, who point me in the right direction, my
colleagues, who are so passionate about empowering the poor I smile as I write
this, our DenverWorks clients, who courageously step into better lives against
all odds, the Dalits, who are the heroes of our generation, the many people I'm
privileged to know who inspire and elevate those around them, the people I
quote (but have never known), who planted seeds that have changed my life,
the people who have given me ideas (seeds) over the years that turned into this
book, but mostly, God, because he can bring life out of dirt.

Specifically, I thank Steve and Bonita Seelig for reading an early draft.
Their encouragement (the next day!) moved the book from a lingering document on my computer to, well, this. I thank Kit and Andy at Deep River
Books for their professionalism and efficiency from day one. And I can't wait
to meet you, Kathy Deering (my editor). I feel like you *know* me and I want
to get to know you. Thank you, Irnie, for teaching me so much about *how* to
garden; Leah McEachern, for your photography that captures the garden; the
Fabs for helping me process this book journey at our gatherings even *before* we
practiced our "Thriller" choreography; and my family and friends, for everything you are. I am indeed blessed.

About the Author

* Debbie Johnson has a passion for changing lives. In 1995, she founded DenverWorks to equip the unemployed in her community. She led the organization for ten years before she left to serve first as the VP of Programs at Dalit Freedom Network, then as the Executive Director of India Transformed. She finally visited the Taj Mahal after seven trips to India's slums. In 2015, she returned to DenverWorks.

Debbie grew up in Little Rock, Arkansas. She obtained a master's in music education from Ouachita Baptist University, which has little to do with her social work, except that Beethoven and jazz ensembles are good for the soul. She and her husband live on a farm by the Rocky Mountains. Debbie loves picking vegetables from their garden and fixing good ol' Southern meals for her family and friends.

Notes

1 www.businessasmission.com

2 www.ahaprocess.com

3 www.sojo.net

4 www.cidi.org

5 http://beingcaballero.blogspot.com/

6 From her book, *You Learn by Living: Eleven Keys for a More Fulfilling Life*

7 Mark Brewer has been a mega-church pastor in Colorado and California.

8 Mother Teresa, *A Simple Path* (New York: Ballantine/Random House, 1995), 79.

9 Jack Weatherford, *Genghis Khan and the Making of the Modern World* (New York: Random House, 2004).

10 www.isionline.org

11 Jeffrey W. Pryor & Alexandra Mitchell, *Compassionate Careers: Making a Living by Making a Difference* (Pompton Plains, NJ: New Page Books, 2015).

12 www.smartplanet.com

13 www.gsa.gov

14 www.one.laptop.org, www.kiva.org

15 Global Ideas Bank, *500 Ways to Change the World* (New York: Harper, 2006).

16 www.encore.org

17 www.milehighmin.org

18 www.cityyear.org

19 www.usaid.gov

20 www.ccda.org

21 www.ccda.org/about/ccd-philosophy/relocation

22 www.ccda.org/about/ccd-philosophy/reconciliation

23 www.ccda.org/about/ccd-philosophy/redistribution

24 Nicholas D. Kristof, Sheryl WuDunn, *Half the Sky* (New York: Random House, 2009), xvi.

25 www.thecell.org

26 www.doctorswithoutborders.org

27 www.givingpledge.org

28 www.amnesty.org

29 www.enterprisecommunity.com

30 "Report Finds 400 Million Children Living in Extreme Poverty," October 10, 2013 (www.worldbank.org).

31 www.backtothebible.org

32 Elisa Morgan, *She Did What She Could (SDWSC): Five Words of Jesus That Will Change Your Life* (Carol Stream, Ill., Tyndale, 2009). Elisa was named by *Christianity Today* as one of the top fifty women influencing today's church and culture. She has authored over twenty-five books on mothering, spiritual formation, and evangelism. She currently serves as co-host of the nationally syndicated daily radio program, *Discover the Word* (www.discovertheword.org). For twenty years, Elisa Morgan served as CEO of MOPS International. She received her MDiv from Denver Seminary.

33 *500 Ways to Change the World.*

34 Barb is Director of Caring Ministry at Cherry Creek Presbyterian Church in Englewood, Colorado. (Website www.barbroberts.com) She has written a book entitled *Helping Those Who Hurt: A Handbook for Caring and Crisis* (NavPress) which is used widely across the United States. An upcoming book about her deceased niece, to be published by CrossBooks, has the working title of *With Her Last Breath: A Tale of Suicide and the Hope of Heaven.*

35 www.30hourfamine.org

36 www.oxfamamerica.org

37 www.wateraid.org

38 www.waterforpeople.org

39 www.end.org

40 www.malaria.com

41 www.indiatransformed.org

42 www.compassion.com

4 3 www.kiva.org

44 Note: Muhammad Yunus was awarded the Nobel Peace Prize for founding the Grameen Bank and pioneering the concepts of microcredit and microfinance.

45 www.theidaleeproject.org

46 www.heifer.org

47 According to The National Coffee Association and The Specialty Coffee Association of America

48 www.extremecommunitymakeover.org

49 www.habitat.org

50 www.heartsandminds.org

51 www.govtrack.us

52 www.cidi.org

53 www.waterstone.org

54 www.nationalchristian.com

55 Angela Epstein, October 13, 2009, "Believe it or not, your lungs are six weeks old and your taste buds just ten days! So how old is the rest of your body?" at www.dailymail.co.uk

56 http://disabilitycompendium.org

57 www.bpnews.net/35104

58 www.wma.net

59 http://www.undp.org/content/undp/en/home/sdgoverview/mdg_goals.html

60 https://www.cbf.net

61 Find them at http://www.undp.org/content/undp/en/home/sdgoverview/post-2015-development-agenda.html

62 www.unece.org/mdg/publications.html

63 Robert K. Greenleaf, *Servant Leadership: A Journey Into the Nature of Legitimate Power and Greatness* (New York: Paulist Press, 1977), 15.

64 www.elisamorgan.com

65 www.ziglar.com

66 Emily Strickfaden is a young world-changer. She is majoring in biology at California Polytechnic State University. She spends her free time traveling abroad with family, mentoring teen girls and more.

67 Dr. Farmer is an American anthropologist, physician, and professor at Harvard University.

68 www.strengthsfinder.com

69 Cavell, T., DuBois, D., Karcher, M., Keller, T., & Rhodes, J. (2009). *Strengthening mentoring opportunities for at-risk youth.* Retrieved from http://www.mentoring.org/downloads/mentoring_1233.pdf. See more at: http://youth.gov.

70 http://danwhitejr.blogspot.com/2014/03/missional-minimalism.html

71 Dave Beckwith, with Cristina Lopez, "Community Organizing: People Power from the Grassroots" (https://comm-org.wisc.edu/papers97/beckwith.htm)

72 www.gatesfoundation.org

73 www.wikihow.com / How to Host a Mystery Dinner

74 www.fundraising-ideas.org/DIY/cakewalk.htm

75 www.auctions.nettop20.com

76 www.howtoadvice.com/PaintingCurbs

77 www.pennies.org

78 Sasha Dichter is Chief Innovation Officer at Acumen Fund, a nonprofit venture fund that is creating a world beyond poverty by investing in social enterprises, emerging leaders, and breakthrough ideas.

79 www.ccda.org

80 www.caedmonscall.com. Album: "Share the Well," 2004

81 www.mtmonline.org

82 Gregg Bettis served as Director of the Campus Life division of Youth for Christ USA and later as president of Kids Across America, a camping and education ministry equipping urban youth to become Christian leaders. He graduated from Biola University with a degree in Camping and Recreation Administration.

83 *500 Ways to Change the World* (The Institute for Social Inventions, p. 302).

84 www.wateraid.org/uk/donate/adanech

85 Inter-agency Group for Child Mortality Estimate (IGME) 2014, led by UNICEF and WHO

86 www.usaid.gov/div

87 www.coloradocommunity.org

88 www.fpa.org

89 Sarah A. Lanier, *Foreign to Familiar: A Guide to Understanding Hot- and Cold-Climate Cultures* (Hagerstown, MD: McDougal Publishing, 2000), 10.

90 www.ccda.org

91 http://morningstarnews.org/2014/02/

92 www.opendoorsusa.org

93 www.soallmayeat.org

94 www.law.harvard.edu/current/careers/opia/public-interest-law/public-international/nongovernmental-organizations.html

95 www.law.harvard.edu

96 Emily Voorhies is the Founder/past President of Tirzah International, a global network of grassroots movements partnering with women leaders in their own nations to combat poverty, exclusion from education, modern-day slavery, HIV/AIDS, and violence against women and girls (www.tirzah.org). She is now COO at Voorhies International Consulting.

97 From the e-diary of Terri Ryder, missionary with Operation Mobilization/India—used by permission.

98 2011 revision of the United Nations World Population Prospects report by five year averages and the CIA World Factbook

99 www.everymothercounts.org

100 Roxanne Stone, "Stewards of Wealth Streams," *Christianity Today,* May 1, 2013 (http://www.christianitytoday.com/ct/2013/may/stewards-of-wealth-streams.html).

101 www.facebook.com/NextEconomyForum

102 Read more at http://www.relevantmagazine.com/god/church/what-would-happen-if-church-tithed#rG2xuDomJ9qWjLYo.99.

103 http://grooveshark.com/#!/search?q=trust+his+heart

104 www.fcsministries.org/fcs-ministries/urban-perspectives/religious-tourism?rq=Religious%20Tourism

105 www.ted.com/talks

106 www.stephenministries.org

107 www.independentsector.org and www.volunteeringinamerica.gov

108 *500 Ways to Change the World*